Leon Trotsky on Britain

Leon Trotsky on Britain

INTRODUCTION BY GEORGE NOVACK

PATHFINDER

New York   London   Montreal   Sydney

ISBN 978-0-87348-850-1
Library of Congress Catalog Card Number 72-92147
Manufactured in Canada

First edition, 1973
Fourth printing, 2012

Cover photo: A 1926 meeting of miners.

Pathfinder gratefully acknowledges the permission of the following
institutions to use in this book materials in their possession:
MacGibbon and Kee (London), and Humanities Press, Inc. (New York), for
their English translation of "The Future of the British Communist Party,"
published under the title "Verbatim Report of the Political Bureau of the
Russian Communist Party," as an appendix in J.T. MacFarlane's *The British
Communist Party*. The Harvard College Library, for the Russian text of
"Resolution of the General Strike in Britain, Submitted to the July 1926
Plenum by the Opposition."

Pathfinder
www.pathfinderpress.com
E-mail: pathfinder@pathfinderpress.com

Contents

Introduction

Trotsky's writings on British history and politics from 1925 to 1928 are gathered in this volume. The first part reprints the 1925 book *Where Is Britain Going?*, which was printed in the United States under the title *Whither England?* The second part is the first translation in the United States of the collection published in the Soviet Union in 1926 under the title *Where Is Britain Going? Part Two*. The third part, here given the title "After the General Strike," consists of articles and statements between 1926 and 1928, which were banned in the Soviet Union.

Trotsky had long been acquainted with Great Britain and its rulers. After escaping from Siberia, the young revolutionist had visited England in 1902 to discuss his future activities in the Russian Social Democratic movement with the exiled Lenin. Trotsky did not remain in England long, but for the rest of his life he followed developments in that center of world capitalism from a distance.

Trotsky's first direct clash with the British government came in March–April 1917, when he was on his way from the United States to Russia after the outbreak of the February revolution. British officers boarded the Norwegian ship on its stop in Halifax, Nova Scotia, arrested Trotsky and his family, and interned them for a month in a concentration

---

George Novack, a noted Marxist scholar, is the author of many books, including Democracy and Revolution, Origins of Materialism, *and* Understanding History.

camp with German prisoners of war.

The British Embassy in Petrograd issued an official statement that he was traveling "under a subsidy from the German embassy, to overthrow the Provisional Russian government." The Soviets rejected this crude frame-up. Lenin's *Pravda* wrote on April 16: "Can one even for a moment believe the trustworthiness of the statement that Trotsky, chairman of the Soviet of Workers' Delegates in St. Petersburg in 1905—a revolutionary who has sacrificed years to a disinterested service of revolution—that this man had anything to do with a scheme subsidized by the German government? This is a patent, unheard-of, and malicious slander of a revolutionary." Such protests forced the British jailers to let him go.

After the victory of the October insurrection, which he led, Trotsky, as the first Soviet Commissar of Foreign Affairs, the head of the Red Army, and a co-leader with Lenin of the Third International, had complicated diplomatic, military, and political encounters with the British agents and armed forces. Their culmination came in the final spasm of the civil war, when Lord Curzon threatened the Soviets with war if the Red Army did not halt its advance on Poland.

This belligerence met with solid resistance from the British labor movement. On August 9, 1920, the Labour Party and union chiefs, assembled in the House of Commons, unanimously decided to warn the government that "the whole industrial power of the organized workers will be used to defeat this war," and instructed their members and the central and local councils of action that had sprung up in every important center to get ready for a general strike. The imperialists had to call off their adventure.

Trotsky undertook this study of English affairs when the next showdown in class relations was brewing there. The most significant internal upheavals in the 1920s took place in Germany, China, and England. After the default of Communist policy during the Ruhr crisis of 1923, Trotsky and other Comintern leaders turned their attention to England as a likely theater of revolutionary developments.

The first Labour government had come into office in January 1924 under Ramsay MacDonald. It was defeated in the general elections that October by a combination of Liberal and Conservative parties, which conducted a "red scare" campaign around a forged "letter from Zinoviev" purporting to show that the Comintern was interfering in British affairs.

This onset of reaction stimulated discussions for united action between the British, West European, and Russian trade union movements. Such a liaison acquired urgency in the eyes of the Soviet leaders, who feared another imperialist assault. The willingness of the British union officials to promote better relations was interpreted as a sign of the deteriorating international situation of British capitalism and the radicalization of its working class.

Trotsky was one of the first to detect the immense shift in the balance of forces in the capitalist world produced by the rise of the United States to the status of great power, and to explain its impact upon England. In a speech, "Europe and America," he pointed out that the ascension of the United States would be primarily at the expense of England, which, along with the rest of Europe, would suffer a relative decline in military, naval, diplomatic, and economic might. European capitalism would more and more become dependent upon American support: the United States would "put Europe on American rations."

American expansion was a factor of increasing instability that would enhance revolutionary prospects on both the European continent and in the British Isles, as its accumulated effects were felt. The displacement of British imperialism by American predominance would for the first time in many decades give reality to the specter of proletarian revolution in that formerly impregnable stronghold of the capitalist system.

Trotsky wrote *Where Is Britain Going?* in the winter and spring of 1925. The Left Opposition he had organized in 1923 had suffered defeat in its initial efforts to stem the growing bureaucratization and conservatization of the leadership of the Soviet Communist Party and the Communist International. His book was to play a part in the resumption of that fateful struggle.

The work was written with a double objective in mind. On its face and in substance it presented a deep-probing analysis of the worsening situation of postwar British capitalism, which was intensifying collisions between the possessing and laboring classes. This was coupled with a devastating polemic against the views of the official labor leadership.

Its arguments were also indirectly aimed at the line of Stalin, Bukharin, Zinoviev, and others in command of the Comintern, who tended to substitute a shaky alliance with the trade union bureaucrats for a consistent class struggle policy.

In 1924, the newly elected heads of the trade unions were disposed to move closer to their Soviet counterparts for protection against the bosses and as a concession to their restive ranks. In November 1924, a delegation led by A.A. Purcell, chairman of the British Trades Union Congress, had visited Moscow and issued a favorable report on Soviet achievements upon its return.

The Soviet leaders grabbed hold of this overture in order to overcome their isolation and put a stumbling block in the path of the imperialist war-planners. In May 1925, just as Trotsky completed this book, Tomsky, the head of the Russian trade unions, reciprocated Purcell's visit and led a Soviet delegation to the annual congress of the British unions. The Anglo-Russian Trade Union Unity Committee, officially launched on May 14, 1925, was the product of their discussions. The leaders of both movements agreed to promote international trade union unity and to struggle against capitalist reaction and the danger of new wars.

The Anglo-Russian Committee soon became a focus of contention. While Trotsky approved the entente between the trade union movements of the two countries, he feared—correctly, as it turned out—that the agreement might raise exaggerated expectations about its value in furthering the workers' struggles in England and curbing the warmakers. He was especially alarmed by the illusions nourished and spread by Stalin-Bukharin in regard to the British right-wing and centrist leaders, who in the last resort would be more faithful to the British ruling class than to the workers they represented. Embellishment of the pact with them could disorient the British workers and cripple the growth and influence of the weak, inexperienced Communist Party of Great Britain.

In fact, in 1925, while the British Tories under Baldwin and Chamberlain had broken off relations with Moscow and jailed Communists, the Labour Party at its annual conference in Liverpool had excluded the Communists from membership.

Trotsky did not trust either the British trade union leaders or Stalin-Bukharin's attitude toward them. "The book," he later wrote, "was aimed essentially at the official conception of the Politbureau, with its hope of an evolution to the left by the British General Council, and of a gradual and painless penetration of communism into the ranks of the British Labour Party and trades-unions" (*My Life*, p. 685) [2010 printing].

The chain of argumentation he set forth was forged of the following links: the decline of the empire, American superiority, and deteriorating economic conditions were inexorably pushing Britain toward a grave social crisis and violent class battles. The officialdom of the workers' industrial and political organizations were incapable of foreseeing these developments and unwilling to prepare the workers to meet them. Their objective function was to hamstring the workers in the face of the coming capitalist attacks.

These leaders not only were cowardly and incompetent, but also held hopelessly antiquated ideas. As an antidote to their religious-mindedness, Fabian gradualism, and adaptation to petty-bourgeois prejudices, Trotsky recalled the two main authentic revolutionary traditions of the English people: the Cromwellian warriors of the mid-seventeenth century bourgeois revolution, and the Chartists of the mid-nineteenth century, pioneers of the proletarian revolution.

He concluded that just as the shock of great events had enabled the Labour Party to displace the Liberals, conditions were ripening that could give the Communists a chance, as the crisis of British capitalism deepened, to come to the fore as the organizers of the aroused masses, replace the reformists and centrists, and go forward to victory.

When the book appeared in England, Trotsky's views were greeted with derision and dismissed by skeptics as the ravings of a foreigner ignorant of British conditions and traditions. Trotsky, the doctrinaire Bolshevik, falsely expected to see the October Revolution duplicated on British soil. Trotsky reprinted some of the more pungent comments of this sort as appendices to *Where Is Britain Going? Part Two.*

Yet a few months later, the strike of the coal miners detonated the general strike, the most momentous event of British history between the two world wars. On May 1, 1926, the resolution for a general strike was carried by 3,653,529 votes to 49,911 in the General Council of the Trades Union Congress. It began on May 4 and lasted for nine days, bringing all Britain to a standstill. This magnificent display of labor solidarity and strength was supported by most of the population. The majestic British government could not get a single linotype operator to set up its official newspaper.

Trade unions the world over engaged in solidarity actions and collected funds for the British strikes. Most enthusiastic were the Russian workers, who subscribed millions of pounds for their British comrades. "The British workers," declared the chairman of the Leningrad Trade Union Council, "prevented in 1920 the intervention of the British bourgeoisie against Soviet Russia. We will pay back our debt a hundredfold." However, when the Soviets sent the first installment, their strike support was rejected by the General Council, one member of which described it as "damned Russian gold."

This test of strength between the capitalist regime and the organized workers was an acute expression of class warfare that directly posed the problem of power. Frightened by the revolutionary implications of the nationwide mobilization of the industrial workers, which threatened to unsettle the existing social and political order, the union leaders called off the strike at the peak of its effectiveness.

Aneurin Bevan, the Welsh miners' MP and future Labour minister, explained the basic reason for the capitulation of the trade union officials in a book published in 1952. He told about an interview between the leaders of the Triple Alliance of miners, transport workers, and railwaymen with canny Prime Minister David Lloyd George at a similar juncture in 1919, related to him by the miners' leader Robert Smillie.

> "He said to us: 'Gentlemen, you have fashioned, in the Triple Alliance of the unions represented by you, a most powerful instrument. I feel bound to tell you that in our opinion we are at your mercy. The Army is disaffected and cannot be relied upon. Trouble has occurred already in a number of camps. We have just emerged from a great war and the people are eager for the reward of their sacrifices, and we are in no position to satisfy them. In these circumstances, if you carry out your threat and strike, then you will defeat us.

"'But if you do so,' went on Mr. Lloyd George, 'have you weighed the consequences? The strike will be in defiance of the Government of the country and by its very success will precipitate a constitutional crisis of the first importance. For, if a force arises in the State which is stronger than the State itself, then it must be ready to take on the functions of the State, or withdraw and accept the authority of the State.

"'Gentlemen,' asked the Prime Minister quietly, 'have you considered, and if you have, are you ready?'

"From that moment on," said Robert Smillie, "we were beaten and we knew we were."

Bevan goes on to comment: "After this the General Strike of 1926 was really an anticlimax. The essential argument had been deployed in 1919. But the leaders in 1926 were in no better theoretical position to face it. They had never worked out the revolutionary implications of direct action on such a scale. Nor were they anxious to do so" (*In Place of Fear*, pp. 20–21).

What Bevan explained long after the fact, Trotsky had warned against a year before it happened: "If the general strike proved the rightness of the Marxist forecast against the home-made estimates of the British reformists, the behavior of the General Council during the general strike signified the collapse of Stalin's hopes of Purcell" (*My Life*, p. 686).

Trotsky, who had been undergoing treatment for an enigmatic illness in a Berlin clinic, returned to Moscow and demanded an immediate breakup of the bloc with the British General Council because of its betrayal. He won Zinoviev to his side. The Russian trade unions did issue a sharp criticism of the General Council's conduct, which the Council refused to acknowledge. But the Stalin-Bukharin team stubbornly refused to withdraw from the Anglo-Russian Committee.

The dispute between the Russian party officialdom and the Leninist Left Opposition over relations with the committee thereupon became one of the central issues in the struggle of the contending factions. Before the general strike, Stalin's man Uglanov had stated that the Anglo-Russian Committee "will become the organizing center of the international forces of the proletariat in the struggle against all attempts of the international bourgeoisie to start up a new war." Recalling this endorsement, Trotsky wrote:

> The members of the General Council are liberal labor politicians of diverse shades. As is always the case with liberals, they have been plunged to the left by the first and still formless revolutionary wave. The general strike swept them to the right. They can have no independent policy. Swept to the right, they become transformed into the active agency of the bourgeoisie. Their role will be counterrevolutionary. Since they have betrayed the general strike of their own workers, and the strike of their own coalminers, only a pathetic philistine can pin any hope on the possibility that these people would protect the Chinese revolution or the Soviet Union from the blows of British imperialism. Quite the contrary. In the critical moment they will come to the aid of imperialism against the revolution. ["What We Gave and What We Got"]

For more than a year after the general strike the Stalin-Bukharin faction rejected the criticisms of the Opposition. At the July 1926 plenum of the CPSU, Stalin reaffirmed support to the Anglo-Russian Committee and justified his position in the following terms: "The aim of this bloc consists in organizing a wide working class movement against new imperialist wars in general, and against intervention into our country on the part of the most powerful of the imperialist powers of Europe—on the part of England in particular." He characterized the Opposition's doubts about Purcell as the guardian angel of the workers' state as a deviation from "Leninism to Trotskyism."

(The developments of this debate were summed up in two important documents by Trotsky: "What We Gave and What We Got," and "The Struggle for Peace and the Anglo-Russian Committee," reprinted here in Part Three.)

By the end of 1926, the second Chinese revolution was approaching its bloody denouement. The General Council supported British imperialism's repression of the Chinese struggle. The Opposition urged the Russians to denounce the complicity of the General Council in the bombardment of Nanking. Instead, clinging to the reformists to the bitter end, the delegation of the Central Committee of the Russian unions met for a third time with the representatives of the British unions in April 1927 in Berlin, and renewed its mandate of faith in the Anglo-Russian Committee.

A few weeks later, Chamberlain raided the Soviet trade buildings in London. Four months afterwards, under the stress of the imperialist offensive against the second Chinese revolution, the British unionists broke up the Anglo-Russian Committee. "The British trades-unionists waited until their acute inner crisis was at an end, and then uncivilly kicked their generous but muddle-headed ally away," was Trotsky's caustic comment (*My Life*, p. 686).

Trotsky believed that the British general strike and the Anglo-Russian Committee experience contained instructive lessons for revolutionaries. His evaluation of the issues subsequently formed an essential part of the platform of the Russian Left Opposition. A clear recognition of their political significance in the struggle against Stalinism became mandatory for the original international cadres of Trotskyism.

The events confirmed, it seemed to him, the growing

instability of European capitalism under U.S. pressure; the ever-present potential of the eruption of class confrontations that could raise the question of power; the folly of putting faith in the capacity of the reformists to lead the workers' struggles or of making unbreakable blocs with them for that purpose; the inevitable vacillations of the centrist elements whose temporary leftward swings enabled them all the better to leave the workers in the lurch at the next turn; the categorical requirement that Communists maintain their political independence and freedom of action through all tactical maneuvers; and the priority to be accorded to constructing the revolutionary Marxist party as the indispensable instrument of anticapitalist organization.

The controversy over the Anglo-Russian Committee clearly counterposed an opportunistic to a revolutionary line. The debacle flowed from a false understanding and false application of the united front policy. This tactic had been put forward by the Comintern after 1920 as a means of defending the interests of the workers and promoting their struggles under conditions where the Communists were a minority and the Social Democrats a majority in the ranks of labor. The policy was intended to extend the influence of Communism and weaken the reformists' hold upon the masses.

The experiment with the Anglo-Russian Committee produced the opposite results. The alliance proved to be useless at the moments of greatest need. It did nothing during the general strike or the miners' strike; it did nothing in the Nanking bombardment or the Arcos raid. That showed what rotten materials it was made of, said Trotsky.

Clinging to the bloc for salvation misled and miseducated both the British and the Russian workers, and served to shield the union leaders from the justified criticisms and wrath of the ranks after their miserable showing in the general strike. It strengthened British capitalism and weakened the international position of the Soviet Union.

Most serious was the harm Stalin's policy did to the young Communist Party of Great Britain. The year 1926 should have converted the small CP into a major political factor. This opportunity was missed.

Trotsky viewed all political situations through the eyes of a revolutionary organizer and party activist. He regarded the building of the revolutionary party as "the question of questions." Stalin and Bukharin thought they could bypass this prolonged and onerous task by trying to transform a temporary and legitimate agreement into a permanent institution. "The point of departure for the erroneous line in the question of the Anglo-Russian Committee was the straining to *supplant* the growth of the influence of the Communist party by skilled diplomacy in relation to the leaders of the trade unions," Trotsky emphasized.

Stalin's course staked everything on the British trade union leaders just as it depended on Chiang Kai-shek in China. Both ended in disaster. These were the first fruits of the tendency to substitute coalitions with petty-bourgeois and even bourgeois elements and forces in place of mobilizing the independent actions of the working masses in defense of their own class interests and the Soviet Union. They presaged still more treacherous and catastrophic practices of class collaboration by the Kremlin in the decades ahead.

George Bernard Shaw called Trotsky the "prince of pamphleteers." *Where Is Britain Going?* is one of the wittiest of his polemics. He slashes without mercy at the teachings of gradualism, pacifism, and Fabianism. It is one of the most forceful and persuasive indictments of these political currents in the whole of Marxist literature.

Isaac Deutscher wrote: "Despite its errors of prognostication *Where Is Britain Going?* is the most, or rather the only effective statement of the case for proletarian revolution and communism in Britain that has ever been made"

(*The Prophet Unarmed,* p. 218). As such, this book retains its validity and value for the Marxist movement in Great Britain today, when the decay of the empire and the infirmities of aged British capitalism are far more advanced and conspicuous than they were when Trotsky's work was written almost five decades ago.

George Novack
JULY 1, 1972

Part 1

Where is Britain going?

Editorial note

Trotsky's book *Kuda idet Angliya? (Where is Britain Going?)* was first issued in Russian, by the State Publishing House, Moscow-Leningrad, in 1925. The preface is dated May 24, 1925. The American edition, by International Publishers, followed later the same year. Its title was *Whither England?*

The first British edition, *Where Is Britain Going?,* appeared in February 1926 under the imprint of George Allen and Unwin Ltd., with an introduction by H.N. Brailsford; it was reprinted in October 1926, the same month that the Communist Party of Great Britain published its own edition of the book, retaining the same translation and title, but dropping Brailsford's introduction and substituting Trotsky's May 6, 1926, preface to the second German edition.

The American and British translations were different. Part 1 of the present volume consists of the American translation, except for minor stylistic changes and corrections made after comparison with the Russian and British versions.

Preface to the American edition

The present work is devoted to a consideration of the ultimate destinies of England, a subject that may be of interest to the American reader for two reasons: first, because England occupies a very prominent position in the world; second, because the United States and Great Britain may be regarded as twin stars, one of which grows dim the more rapidly as the brilliancy of the other increases.

The inference to which I am led by my study is that England is heading rapidly toward an era of great revolutionary upheavals. Of course, the English secret service men and their American disciples will declare that I am engaging in propaganda for a proletarian revolution, as if it were possible for an outsider, by means of pamphlets, to alter the course of evolution of a great nation! As a matter of fact, I am simply attempting, by analyzing the most important factors in the historical development of England, to explain the historical path by which that country will be made to encounter obstacles—internal as well as external—to its continued existence. To accuse me of revolutionary meddling in the affairs of foreign countries, on the basis of such statements, would be almost equivalent to accusing the astronomer of bringing about a solar eclipse because he has predicted its occurrence.

But do not understand me as saying that astronomical phenomena are parallel to the phenomena of society. The former are accomplished outside of us, the latter through our agency. Which does not mean, however, that historical events may be achieved by our mere wish or directed with the assistance of pamphlets. Far more books and newspapers have come out and are still coming out with the avowed purpose of defending and maintaining capitalism—including British capitalism—than have ever been published to attack it. Ideas of any kind may be effective only when they are based on the material conditions of social evolution. England is headed for revolution because she has already entered the stage of capitalist disintegration. If the guilty must be found, if we must ask what accelerates England's progress on the path of revolution, the answer is not Moscow but New York.

This answer may appear paradoxical, yet it is the simple truth. The powerful and constantly growing influence of the United States on world affairs is rendering more and more impossible and hopeless the situation of British industry, British trade, British finances, and British diplomacy.

The United States cannot but tend to expand in the world market, failing which its own industry will be threatened with apoplexy because of the richness of its blood. The United States can only expand at the expense of the other exporting countries, which means, particularly, England. In view of the patented Dawes method of harnessing the economic life of an entire mighty nation in the traces of American supervision,[1] it almost provokes a smile to hear people speak of the revolutionary significance of one "Moscow" pamphlet or another. Under the cover of what is called the pacification and rehabilitation of Europe, immense revolutionary and military conflicts are being prepared for the morrow. Mr. Julius Barnes,[2] who enjoys the confidence of the Department of Commerce at Washington, suggests that the European debtors of the United States be assigned to exploit such portions of the world market as will not bring the impoverished and indebted European cousins of the United States into competition with the expansion of their creditor across the seas. In aiding to restore the European monetary system, the United States is simply exploding one inflated illusion after the other, by giving the Europeans an opportunity to express their poverty and dependence in the language of a firm currency. By exerting pressure on its debtors, or giving them an extension, by granting or refusing credit to European countries, the United States is placing them in a gradually tightening economic dependence, in the last analysis an ineluctable situation, which is the necessary condition for inevitable social and revolutionary disturbances. The Communist International,[3] viewed in the light of this knowledge, may be considered an almost conservative institution as compared with Wall Street. Morgan,[4] Dawes, Julius Barnes—these are among the artificers of the approaching European revolution.

In its work in Europe and elsewhere, the United States is generally acting in cooperation with England, through the agency of England. But this collaboration means for England an increasing loss of independence. England is leading the United States to hegemony, as it were. Relinquishing their world rule, the diplomats and magnates of England are recommending their former clients to deal with the new master of the world. The common action of the United States and England is the cloak for a profound worldwide antagonism between these two powers, by which the threatening conflicts of the perhaps not remote future are being prepared.

This brief preface is not the place in which to speak of the fate of America itself. There is no doubt that capital today nowhere feels itself so strong as in America. American capitalism grew marvelously, chiefly at the expense of the European belligerents at first, now by reason of their "return to peace," their "rehabilitation." But in spite of all its huge power, American capitalism is not a self-contained factor, but a part of world economy. Furthermore, the more powerful the industry of the United States becomes, the more intimate and profound becomes its dependence on the world market.

Driving the European countries farther and farther down their blind alley, American capitalism is laying the foundation for wars and revolutionary upheavals, which in their frightful rebound will not fail to strike the economic system of the United States also. Such is the prospect for America. In revolutionary development, America does not stand in the front rank; the American bourgeoisie will still enjoy the privilege of witnessing the destruction of its older European sister.[5] But the inevitable hour will strike for American capitalism also: the American oil and steel magnates, trust and export leaders, the multimillionaires of New York, Chicago, and San Francisco, are performing—though unconsciously—their predestined revolutionary function. And the American proletariat will ultimately discharge theirs.

L. Trotsky

MOSCOW, MAY 24, 1925

Foreword

England at present faces a crisis, a greater crisis, perhaps, than is faced by any other capitalist country, and England's crisis—to a very great extent—means a crisis for four continents and at least the beginning of a crisis for the fifth, at present the most powerful continent, America. But the political development of England presents remarkable peculiarities, the result of all its past history, which now lie directly in the way of its future growth. Without burdening our exposition with figures and details which the reader may easily find in works of reference and in special studies of the economic policy of England, we have undertaken to isolate and describe those historical factors and circumstances which must determine the history of England in the present epoch. We speak of England only, not of the British Empire; of the mother country, not of the colonies and dominions. The latter have their own paths of development, diverging more and more from those of the home country.

Our exposition, for the most part, will be critical and polemical in character. History is made by men; the evaluation of the living forces producing the history of the present cannot be otherwise than active. In order to learn what are the classes, parties, and party leaders engaged in the struggle, and what the morrow will bring for them, we must work our way through a mass of political complications, lies, hypocrisies, and an all-pervading parliamentary "cant."* Under

---

* Cant: a specific form of conventional lie, tacitly acknowledged by all through considerations of social hypocrisy. According to Carlyle, cant

these circumstances, the polemical method is the necessary method of political analysis. The question we ask ourselves, and to which we attempt to give an answer, is quite objective: "Whither England?"

---

is the art "whereby a man speaks openly what he does not mean." In parliamentary-Protestant Britain this art has been carried to extraordinary heights—or depths.—L.T.

England's decline

Capitalist England was launched by the political revolution in the seventeenth century and the so-called industrial revolution at the end of the eighteenth century. England emerged from the epoch of the civil war and Cromwell's dictatorship[6] a little nation, with hardly 1,500,000 families; it entered the imperialist war in 1914 an empire, embracing within its boundaries one-fifth of all mankind.

The English Revolution of the seventeenth century, of the Puritan school,[7] the hard school of Cromwell, prepared the English people, particularly its middle classes, for their approaching world function. After the middle of the eighteenth century, the universal might of England is indisputable. England rules on the seas and on the world market which is its creation.

In 1826, an English conservative publicist depicted the era of industry as follows:

> The age which now discloses itself to our view promises to be the age of industry. . . . By industry alliances shall

be dictated and national friendships shall be formed. . . .
The prospects which are now opening to England almost
exceed the boundaries of thought, and can be measured
by no standard found in history. . . . The manufactur-
ing industry of England may be fairly computed as four
times greater than that of all the other continents taken
collectively, and sixteen such continents as Europe could
not manufacture so much cotton as England does. . . .
[Quoted by Max Beer, *History of British Socialism*.
Vol. I, p. 283]

The tremendous industrial preponderance of England over
the rest of Europe and over the rest of the world was the
basis of its wealth and of its unprecedented world position.
The industrial century was simultaneously the century of
Great Britain's world hegemony.

From 1850 to 1880, England was the industrial school for
Europe and America. But this very fact undermined its special monopolistic position. With the 1880s, England begins
perceptibly to weaken. New nations, particularly Germany,
enter the world arena. Simultaneously, the capitalist primacy
of England begins for the first time to reveal its unfavorable
and conservative aspects. Powerful blows are delivered by
German competition to the doctrine of free trade.

The crowding out of England from its position of world
ruler thus begins to appear clearly as early as the last quarter
of the nineteenth century, giving rise, at the beginning of
the present century, to a condition of internal uncertainty
and ferment in the upper classes, and profound molecular
processes, basically of revolutionary character, in the working
class. Mighty conflicts of labor and capital played the chief
part in these processes. Not only the aristocratic position of
English industry in the world was shaken, but also the privileged position of the labor aristocracy in England.

The years 1911–13 were a period of unparalleled class battles waged by mine workers, railroad workers, and the transport workers in general. In August 1911, there developed the general strike on the railroads. In those days the vague specter of revolution hovered over England. The leaders exerted all their strength to paralyze the movement, under the slogan of "patriotism"; this was at the time of the Agadir incident,[8] menacing war with Germany. The prime minister, as we know now, summoned the labor leaders to a secret conference and called upon them to save the fatherland. And the leaders did all they could to strengthen the bourgeoisie and in this way prepare the imperialist war.

The war of 1914–18 interrupted this revolutionary process and stopped the growth of the strike wave. Ending in the destruction of Germany, it seemed to restore to England the role of world hegemony. But it soon became apparent that instead of retarding the decline of England, the war had actually accelerated this decline.

In the years 1917–20, the English labor movement entered into an extremely stormy phase. Strikes assumed immense proportions. MacDonald was signing manifestoes from which he now recoils with shudders.[9] Only after 1920 did this phase terminate with Black Friday, when the leaders of the Triple Alliance of coal miners, railroad and transport workers betrayed the general strike.[10] The energy of the masses, frustrated in the economic field, turned to the political sphere. The Labour Party seemed to spring up overnight.[11]

What is the cause of this shift in the external and internal situation of Great Britain?

During the war, the enormous economic preponderance of the United States was developed and revealed in its full proportions. The emergence of that country from the stage of an overseas provincialism suddenly forced Great Britain into second place.

The "cooperation" of America and Great Britain is the expression, for the moment peaceful, of the increasingly pronounced outdistancing of England by America. This "co-operation" may at any specific moment be directed against a third party: nonetheless, the fundamental world antagonism is that between England and America, and all other antagonisms, perhaps more bitter at the present moment, and more immediately threatening, may be understood and evaluated only on the basis of the Anglo-American antagonism. The Anglo-American "cooperation" thus prepares war, as an epoch of reforms prepares the epoch of revolution. The very fact that England has entered the path of "reforms," i.e., concessions forced from her by America, will clarify the situation and shift it from the stage of cooperation to that of opposition.

The productive forces of England, particularly its living productive force, the proletariat, no longer correspond to the position of England on the world market. Thus the chronic state of unemployment.

The commercial, industrial, and naval hegemony of England has in the past almost automatically assured the bonds between the various portions of the empire. The New Zealand minister, Reeves, wrote before 1900: "Two things maintain the present relation of the colonies with England: first, their faith in the generally peaceful intentions of England's policy; second, their faith in England's rule of the seas." Of course, the decisive factor is the second. The loss of hegemony on the seas proceeds parallel with the development of the centrifugal forces within the empire. The preservation of the unity of the empire is more and more threatened by the diverging interests of the dominions and the struggles of the colonies.

The advances in military technology seem to militate particularly against Great Britain's security. The growth of aviation and of the instruments of chemical warfare have completely annihilated the immense historical advantage of England's insular position. America, that great island, bounded by oceans on either hand, remains inaccessible. But the most important living centers of England, particularly London, may be reduced in the course of a few hours of murderous bombardment from the air, at the hands of a continental power.

Having lost the advantages of an inaccessible isolation, the English government has been obliged to engage more and more directly in purely European matters, and in European military agreements. The overseas possessions of England, its dominions, are not at all interested in this policy. They are concerned with the Pacific Ocean, the Indian Ocean, in part with the Atlantic, but by no means with the Channel. This divergence of interests will expand, at the first clash, into a yawning abyss in which the bonds of empire will be swallowed up. Foreseeing this condition, the British policy is paralyzed by internal friction, leading to an essentially passive attitude, and consequently to an aggravation of the empire's world problems.

Military expenditures, at the same time, must consume a greater and greater part of the diminished national income of England.

One of the conditions of "cooperation" between England and America is the repayment of the gigantic British debt to America, while there is no hope of England's ever obtaining a repayment of the debts incurred by the continental states. The economic alignment of forces is thus further shifted in favor of America.

On March 5, 1925, the Bank of England raised its discount rate from four to five percent following the action of the New York Federal Reserve Bank, which had raised its rate from three to three and one-half percent. In the City [London's banking district] this served as a harsh reminder of its financial dependence on its transatlantic cousin. But what else could they do? The American gold supply amounts to about $4,500,000,000, while the English does not exceed

$750,000,000, i.e., about one-sixth as much. America has a gold currency, while England is merely making desperate efforts to reestablish one. It is therefore natural to find that when America raises its discount rate from 3 to 3½ percent, England is obliged to fall in with a rise of from 4 to 5 percent. This measure reacts to the disadvantage of English trade and industry by rendering more costly its necessary supplies. In this way, America is showing England her place at every step: on the one hand, by the methods of diplomatic pressure; on the other, by measures of a banking nature, always and everywhere a pressure of America's gigantic economic preponderance.*

---

* Since these lines were written, the English cabinet has resorted to a number of measures of a legislative and financial character to assure the transition to a gold basis, which is represented as a "great victory" for English capitalism. As a matter of fact, nothing could express the decline of England more sharply than this financial achievement. England has been obliged to accomplish this costly operation under the pressure of the sound American dollar and the financial policy of its own dominions, which were more and more basing their transactions on the dollar, thus ignoring the pound. England could not accomplish the leap to a gold basis without immense financial "assistance" from the United States, and this means that the destiny of the pound falls into a state of direct dependence on New York. The United States is thus supplied with an instrument of powerful financial reprisals. England must pay a high rate of interest for this dependence, a rate which must be imposed on her already suffering industries. In order to prevent her gold from being exported, England is obliged to decrease her exports in goods. She cannot at present refuse to shift to a gold basis without hastening her own decline on the financial world market. This ruinous combination of circumstances produces feelings of acute discomfort among the ruling circles of England, and is expressed in bitter but impotent wailings in the Conservative press. The *Daily Mail* writes: "In passing to a gold basis, the English Government is enabling the Federal Bank (practically under the influence of the United States Government) *to bring about a money crisis in England at any moment.* . . . The English Government is subordinating the entire financial policy of the country to another nation. . . . The British Empire is becoming

At the same time, the English press uneasily observes a "gigantic progress" in various branches of German industry, particularly in the German shipbuilding industry. The London *Times* writes on March 10 [1925]:

> It is probable that one of the factors which makes for the ability of German yards to compete is the complete "trustification" of material, from the mine to the fitted plate, from the financing bank to the sale of tickets. This system is not without its effect on wages and the cost of living. When all these forces are turned into the same direction, the margin for a lowering of costs becomes very considerable.

In other words, the *Times* here notes that the organic advantages of the more modern German industry are again being revealed in all their strength, as soon as the industry of Germany obtains an opportunity to give an outward sign of life.

Of course, there is reason to believe that the orders for ships were given to Hamburg shipyards with the special ob-

---

mortgaged to the United States." "Thanks to Churchill," writes the conservative *Daily Express,* "England falls under the heel of American bankers." The *Daily Chronicle* puts the matter still more strongly: "England is actually brought down to the level of a forty-ninth state of the United States." It would be impossible to put the thing more clearly! All these harsh revelations, which show that there is no hope and no future, are answered by Churchill, Chancellor of the Exchequer, with the statement that England has no other recourse than to bring her financial system into agreement "with reality." Churchill's words mean: We have become immeasurably poorer, the United States immeasurably richer; we must either fight America or submit to her; in making the destinies of the pound depend on the American banks, we are only expressing our general economic debacle in terms of the gold basis; water will not rise higher than its level; we must be "in accord with reality."—L.T.

ject of frightening the trade unions and thus preparing the ground for exerting pressure upon them for the purpose of lowering wages and increasing the length of the working day. It is hardly necessary to point out that such a maneuver is more than plausible, but this by no means weakens our general observations on the inefficient organization of English industry and the large overhead expenditures resulting therefrom.

For fully four years the number of unemployed officially registered in England has not been less than 1,135,000; this number usually fluctuates between 1,250,000 and 1,500,000. Chronic unemployment is the most crying expression of an unsatisfactory system; also, it is its Achilles' heel. The unemployment insurance, begun in 1920, was considered at the time a purely temporary measure. Yet, unemployment has been constant; the insurance has ceased to be insurance merely; the doles given to the unemployed are by no means covered by the sums paid in for the purpose. Unemployment in England is no longer the "normal" reserve army, decreasing and increasing by turns, constantly changing its membership; it is now a permanent social stratum, born of industry in its prosperity and left without ground to stand on in its decline. It is a gouty induration in the social organism, owing to poor metabolism.

The chairman of the Federation of British Industries, Colonel Willey, declared early in April that the earnings of industrial capital in the past two years had been so low as not to encourage industrialists to develop their industries. The plants do not yield greater dividends than securities with fixed interest (national loans, etc.). "Our national problem is not a production problem, but a sales problem." Now how is a sales problem to be solved? Of course, by producing more cheaply than others. But this requires either a radical reorganization of industry, or a reduction of taxes, or a reduction of wages, or a combination of all three. A lowering of wages, which would hardly result in a great decrease of production costs, would meet with stubborn resistance, for the workers are already fighting for higher pay. It is impossible to lower taxes, for the debts must be paid, the gold currency restored, the apparatus of empire maintained, and besides, 1,500,000 unemployed must be supported. All this goes into the price of the product. As for reorganizing industry, that is possible only by introducing fresh capital. But low profits are forcing free capital into government and other loans.

Stanley Machin, chairman of the Association of British Chambers of Commerce, recently declared that the solution of the unemployment problem could be found in emigration. The amiable fatherland calls upon a million or more of its toilers, who together with their families, count several millions of citizens, to submit to being bundled into boats and borne off to other countries. The complete bankruptcy of the capitalist system is here admitted without circumlocution.

We must consider the internal life of England, in connection with the above-described prospect of a sharp and ever-increasing decline in Great Britain's world role, for, while that country still retains intact its possessions, its apparatus and traditions of world rule, the nation is in fact being steadily driven into a secondary position.

The destruction of the Liberal Party crowns the century-long development of capitalist economy and bourgeois society.[12] England's loss of world hegemony has led entire branches of English industry into a blind alley, and has dealt a mortal blow to independent industries and small trading capital, which are the basis of liberalism. Free trade has been driven into an impasse.

In the meantime, the internal stability of the capitalist system was to a great extent determined by the division of labor and responsibility between Conservatives and Liberals. The breakdown of liberalism also expresses all the other contradictions of bourgeois England's world situation, and likewise, the source of the system's internal instability. The Labour Party, in its upper ranks, is politically very close to the Liberals, but it is incapable of restoring to English parliamentarism its former stability, for the party itself, in its present form, is merely a provisional stage in the revolutionary development of the working class. MacDonald's leadership is not more secure than Lloyd George's.[13]

Karl Marx counted at the beginning of the 1850s on an early elimination of the Conservative Party,[14] and on the fact that the further course of political evolution would take the form of a struggle between liberalism and socialism. This prediction was based on the assumption of a swift growth of the revolutionary movement in Europe and in England. Just as in Russia, for example, when the Constitutional Democratic Party,[15] under the pressure of the revolution, became the sole party of the landowners and the bourgeoisie, English liberalism would have absorbed the Conservative Party, thus becoming the sole party of property, if the revolutionary advance of the proletariat had grown in the second half of the nineteenth century. But Marx's prediction was made on the very eve of a new period of immense capitalist development (1851–73). Chartism completely disappeared.[16] The labor movement assumed the form of trade unionism. The ruling classes were enabled to express their contradictions in the form of a struggle between the Liberal and Conservative parties. In the parliamentary pendulum, swinging from right to left and from left to right, the bourgeoisie had a means of enabling the opposition tendencies of the working masses to express themselves.

German competition was the first serious warning to British world hegemony, and inflicted the first serious injuries. Free trade encountered the superior German technique and organization. English liberalism was only the political generalization of free trade. The Manchester School had occupied a dominant position since the time of the bourgeois election reforms of 1832, and the abolition of the Corn Laws in 1846.[17] For half a century after this time, free trade was an unalterable platform. Accordingly, the leading role fell to the Liberals, the workers trailing behind them. With the middle of the 1870s, poor business sets in; free trade is discredited; the protectionist movement begins; the bourgeoisie is conquered more and more by imperialist tendencies.

Symptoms of decay in the Liberal Party already became apparent under Gladstone, when the group of liberals and radicals with Chamberlain at the head raised the banner of protectionism and joined with the Conservatives.[18] Beginning with 1895, business improved, retarding the political transformation of England, and at the beginning of the twentieth century, liberalism, being the party of the middle bourgeoisie, was already broken. Lord Rosebery, its leader, came out openly for imperialism.[19] However, the Liberal Party, before its final elimination, was still destined for another period of power. Under the influence of the manifest decline in the hegemony of British capital, on the one hand, and of the powerful revolutionary movement in Russia, on the other hand, the working class in England became politically invigorated, and in its insistence on the creation of a Parliamentary Labour Party, brought grist to the mill of the Liberal position just when it was needed. Liberalism again came into power in 1906. But in the very nature of the case, its success could not be of long duration. The political action of the proletariat leads to a further growth of the Labour Party. Up to 1906 the number of Labour Party representatives had increased more or less uniformly with the increase of the Liberal representation. After 1906, the Labour Party began to grow obviously at the expense of the Liberals.

Formally, it was the Liberal Party which declared the war, through Lloyd George. But actually, the imperialist war, from which England was not able to rescue the time-honored system of free trade, was destined inevitably to strengthen the

Conservatives, who were the most consistent party of imperialism. This finally prepared the conditions that brought the Labour Party to the fore.

The organ of the Labour Party, the *Daily Herald,* ceaselessly ruminating on the question of unemployment, draws from the capitalist admissions quoted by us in the previous paragraphs the general inference that since English capitalists prefer making loans of money to foreign governments instead of expanding their own industries, the English workers have nothing left for them but to produce without the capitalists. This inference, speaking in general, is correct; but it is not offered as a means of arousing the workers to drive out the capitalists, but only in order to spur the capitalists to "progressive efforts." We shall observe that this is the basis of the entire Labour Party policy. With this purpose the Webbs write their books,[20] MacDonald delivers his speeches, the *Daily Herald* editors print their daily articles. And yet, if these terrible warnings have any effect on the capitalists, it is precisely in the opposite direction. Every sensible English bourgeois knows that behind these mock-heroic threats by the leaders of the Labour Party lies the real danger from the side of the profoundly discontented proletarian masses, and for this reason our wise bourgeois infers that he must not tie up any more resources in industry.

The bourgeoisie's fear of revolution is not always and under all circumstances a "progressive" factor. Thus, there can be no doubt that the English economic system would obtain immense advantages from a cooperation of England and Russia. But this would presuppose a broadly conceived plan, large credits, the adaptation of a very large portion of British industry to the needs of Russia. The obstacle to this consummation is the bourgeoisie's fear of revolution, the capitalists' uncertainty as to the morrow.

The fear of revolution has hitherto driven English capitalists along the path of concessions and readjustments, for the material resources of English capitalism have always been unlimited or have at least seemed so. The impact of European revolutions has always been clearly expressed in the social development of England. They have always led to reforms, so long as the English bourgeoisie, owing to its world leadership, still had in its hands great resources for its maneuvers. It was in a position to legalize the trade unions, to abolish the Corn Laws, to raise wages, to extend the suffrage, to introduce social reforms, etc., etc. But now, in view of the present radically weakened world situation of England, the threat of revolution is no longer capable of driving the bourgeoisie forward; on the contrary, it paralyzes the last remnant of industrial initiative. The thing now needed is no longer a menace of revolution, but revolution itself.

The factors and circumstances enumerated above are by no means accidental or temporary in character. They all move in the same direction, that of systematically aggravating the international and internal situation of Great Britain, imposing upon that situation the character of having, historically, no way out. The contradictions undermining the social structure of England will necessarily be aggravated as time goes on. We are not prepared to predict the precise rate of this process, but it will be measured in any case in terms of a few years, at most in half-decades, certainly not in decades. The general outlook is such as to oblige us first of all to put the question: Will it be possible to organize a Communist Party in England, which shall be strong enough and which shall have sufficiently large masses behind it, to enable it, at the psychological moment, to carry out the necessary practical conclusions of this ever-sharpening crisis? This question involves the entire destiny of England

Mr. Baldwin and 'gradualness'

On March 12, 1925, Mr. Baldwin, the prime minister of England and leader of the Conservative Party,[21] delivered a long speech on the destinies of England before a Conservative audience at Leeds. This speech, like many other expressions on the part of Mr. Baldwin, was filled with nervous apprehension. We consider this apprehension to be well-founded from the point of view of Mr. Baldwin's party, while we ourselves approach these questions from a somewhat different angle. Mr. Baldwin is afraid of socialism, and in his proofs of the dangers and difficulties attending the path to socialism, he makes a somewhat unexpected attempt to invoke the authority of the author of these lines. This gives us, we hope, a right to answer Mr. Baldwin without the risk of being accused of interference in the internal affairs of Great Britain.

Baldwin considers—and not without reason—that the greatest danger to the system supported by him is the growth of the Labour Party. It appears that Mr. Baldwin hopes for victory, for "our [Conservative] principles are in closer accord with the character and traditions of our people than any traditions or any principles of violent change." Nevertheless, the Conservative leader reminds his listeners that the verdict of the last election was by no means a final one.

Baldwin, of course, is certain that socialism cannot be carried out. But since he is in a state of nervous confusion, and since, furthermore, he is speaking to an audience already convinced of the impossibility of socialism, Mr. Baldwin's proofs in this connection are not characterized by great originality. He reminds the Conservative audience that people are not born free or equal or brothers. Appealing to each mother who is present, he asks: Were her children born equal? His answer is a modest and contented laughter from his audience. To be sure, the masses of the English people had already heard such reasoning from Mr. Baldwin's great-grandparents in answer to their demand for the right to enjoy freedom of religion and to construct churches of their own. The same evidence was advanced later against the demand of equality before the law; still later, not so long ago, against the right of universal suffrage.

People are not born equal, Mr. Baldwin; then why should they answer before the same courts and be judged by the same laws? We might also point out to Mr. Baldwin that though people are not born absolutely alike, mothers nevertheless usually feed their unlike children at the same table and make every effort in their power to see to it that each of them is provided with a pair of shoes. Of course, a wicked stepmother might act differently.

We might also explain to Mr. Baldwin that socialism is not at all proposing for itself the task of creating complete anatomical, physiological, and mental equality, but merely to assure all human beings of uniform material conditions of existence. We shall not, however, burden our readers by expounding any further these rudimentary notions. Mr.

Baldwin himself, if he is interested, may turn to the proper sources and, since he is—by reason of his general view of life—more inclined to old and purely British authors, we may recommend to him Robert Owen, who, though having absolutely no idea of the class dynamics of capitalist society, nevertheless provides extremely valuable general information as to the advantages of socialism.[22]

But the socialist goal, however objectionable it may be, does not frighten Mr. Baldwin so much as the use of violence in order to attain that goal. Mr. Baldwin discerns two tendencies in the Labour Party. One of these, according to his words, is represented by Mr. Sidney Webb, who has recognized the "inevitability of gradualness." But there also exists another type of leader, like Cook or Wheatley, particularly after the latter left his post in the ministry, who believes in violence.[23] In general, Mr. Baldwin says, the responsibilities of government have always exerted a redeeming influence over the leaders of the Labour Party and have induced them, like the Webbs, to recognize the undesirability of revolutionary methods and the advantage of gradual changes. At this point, Mr. Baldwin made a number of mental incursions into Russian affairs in order to reinforce his rather meager arsenal of evidence against British socialism.

We shall now quote literally from the *Times* report of his speech.

> The prime minister quoted Trotsky, who, he said, had discovered in the last few years and written that "the more easily the Russian proletariat pass through the revolutionary crisis, the harder becomes now its constructive work." Trotsky had also said what no leader of the extremists had yet said in England: "We must learn to work more efficiently." "I should like to know," said Mr. Baldwin, "how many votes would be given for revolution in England if people were told that the only [!?] result

would be that they would have to work more efficiently. [*Laughter and cheers.*] Trotsky said in his book, 'In Russia before and after the Revolution, there existed and still exists unchanged Russian human nature [?!].' Trotsky, the man of action, studied realities. He had slowly and reluctantly discovered what Mr. Webb discovered two years ago, "the inevitability of gradualness." [*Laughter and applause.*]

It is indeed very flattering to be recommended to the Conservative audience at Leeds: mortal man could not ask for more. It is almost equally flattering to be mentioned in the same breath with Mr. Sidney Webb, the prophet of gradualness. Yet, before accepting this distinction, we should not be averse to receiving from Mr. Baldwin a number of authoritative explanations.

It has never occurred, either to my teachers or to myself, even before the experience "of the last few years," to deny the fact of "gradualness" in nature or in human society, in its economy, politics, or morals. But we should wish to have greater clearness as to the nature of these gradual changes. Thus, to take an example which lies close to Mr. Baldwin, as a protectionist, we are perfectly ready to admit that Germany, gradually entering into the field of world competition during the last quarter of the nineteenth century, was becoming England's most dangerous rival. As is well known, this was the path that led to war. Does Mr. Baldwin consider war to be an expression of gradual, evolutionary methods? During the war, the Conservative Party demanded the "destruction of the Huns" and the overthrow of the German kaiser with the force of the British sword. Those who advocate the theory of gradual changes should—I suppose—have rather depended on a general softening of the German nature and a gradual improvement of the mutual relations between Germany and England. Yet Mr. Baldwin, in the years 1914–18, as far as we remember, categorically rejected the application of the method of gradual changes to Anglo-German relations, and made every effort to solve the question with the aid of the greatest possible quantity of explosive materials. We submit that dynamite and lignite may hardly be considered instruments of a conservative-evolutionary mode of action.

Prewar Germany, in turn, had not emerged one fine morning in shining armor from the sea-foam. Germany had developed gradually out of its former economic insignificance. This gradual process had not been without its interruptions: thus, we have the wars waged by Prussia against Denmark in 1864, against Austria in 1866, against France in 1870, which played a tremendous role in enhancing its power, and afforded it the possibility of successful competition with England on a worldwide scale.

Wealth, the result of human labor, is doubtless accumulated with a certain gradualness. But perhaps Mr. Baldwin will join us in admitting that the growth of the wealth of the United States in the years of the war presents immense leaps and bounds. The gradual nature of the accumulation was sharply interrupted by the catastrophe of war, which reduced Europe to poverty and led to a mad expansion of wealth in America.

Mr. Baldwin himself has told, in a parliamentary speech devoted to the trade unions, of the leaps and bounds in his own private life. When a young man, Mr. Baldwin managed a factory, which was handed down from generation to generation, in which workers were born and died, and which therefore is a perfect example of the rule of the principle of a patriarchal gradualness. But there came a coal miners' strike, the factory could not work because of the lack of coal, and Mr. Baldwin was obliged to shut it down and to turn out on the street a thousand of "his" workers. To be sure, Baldwin will blame this on the ill will of the miners, who obliged him to abandon this time-honored conservative principle. The miners will probably blame the ill will of their employers, who obliged them to undertake a great strike, which constituted an interruption in the monotonous process of exploitation.

Yet, in the last analysis, subjective motives are not very important in a given case: it is sufficient for us to note that gradual changes in various domains of life proceed side by side with catastrophic changes, explosions, sudden leaps, upward or downward. The long process of jealousy between two governments *gradually* prepares war; the discontent of the exploited workers *gradually* prepares a strike; the poor management of a bank *gradually* prepares bankruptcy.

The honored Conservative leader may, to be sure, reply that such interruptions of the gradual process as war and bankruptcy, the impoverishment of Europe and the enrichment of America at Europe's expense, are very tragic and that we should make every effort to fight such sudden changes, generally speaking. We can reply to this only by pointing out the fact that the history of nations is in large measure the history of wars and that the history of economic growth is embellished with bankruptcy statistics. Mr. Baldwin would probably answer that such are the properties of human nature. This we should admit. But it is equivalent to saying that human "nature" evidently includes gradual evolution and catastrophic changes.

However, the history of humanity is not only the history of wars, but also the history of revolutions. Feudal rights, which prevailed for centuries and under which the economic advancement was held up for further centuries, were wiped out in France by the single blow of August 4, 1789. The German revolution, on November 9, 1918, destroyed German absolutism, which had been undermined by the struggle of the proletariat and demoralized by the military successes of the Allies. We have already pointed out that one of the war slogans of the British government, of which Mr. Baldwin was then a member, was: "War to the complete destruction of German militarism!" Doesn't Mr. Baldwin think that the military catastrophe, brought about by Mr. Baldwin's aid, prepared a revolutionary catastrophe in Germany, and that both these events were somewhat of a disturbance in the process of gradual historical changes? One might raise the objection that German militarism is to be blamed for all these, with the evil ambitions of the kaiser to boot. We are ready to believe that if Mr. Baldwin were creating the world he would people it with the most benevolent kaisers and the most good-natured militarisms. But that was not the condition facing the English prime minister; furthermore, we have heard him say that people—including the kaiser—are not born equal, or good, or brothers. We must take the world as it is. Furthermore, if the destruction of German militarism is a good thing, we must admit that the German revolution was a good thing, for it crowned the accomplishment of the military defeat; therefore the catastrophe, which suddenly overthrew the thing which had been formed by a gradual process, was a good catastrophe.

Mr. Baldwin may indeed answer that all this has no direct bearing on England, and that only in this chosen country has the principle of gradual change found its complete expression. But if such were the case, Mr. Baldwin had no reason to refer to my words, which dealt with Russia, and thereby assign to this principle of gradual changes a general, universal, absolute character. My political experience does not support this observation. I recall three revolutions in Russia: that of 1905, that of February 1917, and that of October 1917.[24] As for the February revolution, Mr. Baldwin's not undistinguished ambassador, Buchanan, afforded a certain modest assistance to that revolution, for he apparently considered, and not without the knowledge of his government, that at the moment a little revolutionary catastrophe in Petrograd would be more useful to the affairs of Great

Britain than Rasputin's gradual methods.[25]

But is it entirely true that the "character and history of the English people" are so decisively and unconditionally filled with the Conservative traditions of gradual change? Is it true that the English people are so hostile to "changes by force"? As a whole, the history of England is a history of violent changes, introduced by the British ruling class into the lives—of other nations. For example, it would be interesting to know whether the conquest of India or of Egypt was advanced with the aid of the principle of gradualness. The policy of the possessing class in Great Britain with regard to India was expressed most frankly in the words of Lord Salisbury, "India must be bled!"[26] It may be appropriate here to recall that Salisbury was the leader of the same party that is now led by Mr. Baldwin. Parenthetically, we might also add that by reason of an excellently organized conspiracy of the bourgeois press, the English people actually know nothing of what is going on in India (and this is called a democracy). Perhaps it might be well to point out the history of unhappy Ireland, which is particularly rich in manifestations of the *peaceful actions of the British ruling classes.* As far as we know, the subjugation of southern Africa did not meet with any protest on the part of Mr. Baldwin, and yet the troops of General Roberts, when they broke through the defensive front of the Boer farmers, were hardly considered by the latter as a very convincing evidence of gradualness.[27]

To be sure, all these examples are taken from the *external* history of England. But it is nevertheless strange that the principle of evolutionary and gradual change recommended to us as a general principle should not apply outside of England's boundaries, for instance, within the boundaries of China, when it is necessary to resort to war to make the Chinese buy opium; or in Turkey, when Mosul must be taken away from her; or in Persia or Afghanistan, when they must be made to debase themselves before England.

May we not conclude from these examples that England has succeeded the better in realizing "gradualness" within its own boundaries, the more it has resorted to the use of force on other peoples? Such is precisely the case; for three centuries England has waged an unbroken chain of wars, aiming at an expansion, by the methods of piracy and force against other nations, of its theater of exploitation, seizing the wealth of others, killing foreign commercial competition, destroying foreign naval forces, and thus enriching the British ruling classes. A serious study of the facts and of their internal relations will lead inevitably to the conclusion that the English ruling classes have succeeded all the better in escaping revolutionary upheavals within their country, by reason of their greater success in increasing their material powers by means of wars and all kinds of disturbances in other countries, thus enabling them, by mean and sordid temporary concessions, to restrain the revolutionary ardor of the masses. But this conclusion, irrefutable as it is, shows precisely the opposite condition from that which Mr. Baldwin tries to prove, for all the history of England as a matter of fact bears witness that this "peaceful development" can only be assured with the aid of a series of wars, colonial oppression, and bloody upheavals. This does not look much like gradualness.

Gibbins, in his outline of modern English history, writes: "In general—though, of course, *there are exceptions to this rule*—the guiding principle of English foreign policy has been the support of political freedom and constitutional government." This is truly a noteworthy sentence: it is a profoundly semiofficial, "national," traditional view which is here expressed; it leaves no room for the hypocritical doctrine of noninterference in the affairs of other nations; it likewise bears witness to the fact that England has supported the constitutional movement in other countries only insofar as this has been of advantage to her own trading and other interests; where such support has not been to her advantage, the words of the inimitable Gibbins apply: "There are exceptions to this rule." For the information of her own people, the entire past history of England, in spite of the doctrine of noninterference, is represented as a holy war of the British government for freedom all over the world. Each new act of treachery and violence—the war with China on the opium question, the enslavement of Egypt, the Boer War, the intervention in support of czarist generals—is interpreted as a mere accidental exception to the rule. In general, we thus find that there are remarkable breaks and gaps in the process of "gradualness," both on the side of "freedom" and on the side of despotism.

It is possible to go so far as to say that violence in international relations is admissible and even inevitable, while in the relations between classes it is quite reprehensible. But then why speak of the natural law of gradualness, which is represented as dominating in the development not only of nature but also of society? Why not simply say: the oppressed class must support the oppressing class of its nation, when the latter is applying force in pursuit of its objective; but the oppressed class has not the right to make use of force in order to secure for itself a better situation in a society based on oppression. This would not be a "law of nature," but a law in the bourgeois criminal code.

However, even in the internal history of Great Britain, the principle of peaceful and gradual evolution is by no means so prevalent as is stated by some Conservative philosophers. In the last analysis, all of modern England grew up out of the revolution in the seventeenth century. The great civil war of that period gave birth to Tories and Whigs, who have alternately imposed their stamp on the history of England for nearly three centuries. When Mr. Baldwin appeals to the conservative traditions of English history, we must take the liberty to remind him that the tradition of the Conservative

Party itself is based on this revolution in the middle of the seventeenth century. Likewise, this reference to the "character of the English people" makes us recall that this character was forged by the hammer of the civil war between Roundheads and Cavaliers.[28] The character of the Independents, who were petty-bourgeois merchants, artisans, free farmers, owners of small feudal estates—busy, honorable, respectable, frugal, hardworking, enterprising—came into sharp conflict with the character of the idle, dissipated, arrogant ruling classes of old England, the courtiers, the titled officialdom, and the higher clergy.

Yet all these men were Englishmen! With the heavy hammer of military force, Oliver Cromwell forged, on the anvil of civil war, this same national character, which in the course of two and a half centuries has secured the gigantic advantages of the English bourgeoisie in the struggle for world supremacy, in order later, at the end of the nineteenth century, to reveal itself as too conservative even from the point of view of capitalist development. Of course, the struggle of the Long Parliament with the autocracy of Charles I,[29] and Cromwell's severe dictatorship, were prepared by the previous history of England. But this simply means that revolutions cannot be made when you want them, but are an organic product of the conditions of social evolution, being stages in the development of the relations between the classes of the same nation which are as inevitable as are wars in the relations between organized nations. Does Mr. Baldwin find, perhaps, some theoretical solace in the gradual nature of these preparations?

Old conservative ladies—such as Mrs. Snowden, who recently disclosed that the royal family is the most hardworking class of society—must of course wake up in terror at night when they recall the execution of Charles I.[30] Yet even Macaulay, a fairly reactionary writer, had a pretty good understanding of this situation.

Those who had him in their grip [says Macaulay] were not midnight stabbers. What they did they did in order that it might be a spectacle to heaven and earth, and that it might be held in everlasting remembrance. They enjoyed keenly the very scandal which they gave. That the ancient constitution and the public opinion of England were directly opposed to regicide made regicide seem strangely fascinating to a party bent on effecting a complete political and social revolution. In order to accomplish their purpose, it was necessary that they should first break in pieces every part of the machinery of the government; and this necessity was rather agreeable than painful to them. . . . A revolutionary tribunal was created. That tribunal pronounced Charles a tyrant, a traitor, a murderer, and a public enemy; and his head was severed from his shoulders before thousands of spectators in front of the banqueting hall of his own palace. [Macaulay, *History of England*]

From the point of view of the Puritan effort to smash all the parts of the old government machine, it was quite a secondary matter that Charles Stuart was a harebrained, lying, cowardly cad. The Puritans dealt the death blow not only to Charles I but to royal absolutism as such, and the preachers of parliamentary and gradual changes are enjoying the fruits of their act to this day.

The role of revolution in the political—and in general, the social—development of England is not exhausted by the seventeenth century. In fact, it may be said—though this may sound paradoxical—that *the entire recent evolution of England has taken place on the shoulders of European revolutions.* We shall give here only an outline of the most important factors, which may be of advantage not only to Mr. Baldwin.

The great French Revolution imparted a powerful stimulus to the growth of democratic tendencies in England, and particularly to the labor movement, which had been driven underground by the repressive laws of 1799. The war against revolutionary France was popular only among the ruling classes of England; the masses of the people sympathized with the French Revolution and were indignant with Pitt's government.[31] The creation of the English trade unions was to a considerable extent the result of the influences of the French Revolution on the working masses of England. The victory of reaction on the Continent strengthened the position of the landlords and led in 1815 to the restoration of the Bourbons in France and to the introduction of the Corn Laws in England.

The July Revolution of 1830 in France[32] was the moving force behind the first election reform bill, in England, in 1831; the bourgeois revolution on the Continent brought forth a bourgeois reform in the island kingdom.

The radical reorganization of the administration of Canada, involving much wider autonomy for the latter, was carried out after the uprisings of 1837–38 in Canada.[33]

The revolutionary movement of Chartism led in 1844–47 to the introduction of the ten-hour working day, and in 1846 to the abolition of the Corn Laws. The downfall of the revolutionary movement of 1848 on the Continent not only meant the downfall of the Chartist movement, but also retarded for a long time the democratization of England's Parliament.

The election reform of 1868 was preceded by the Civil War in the United States. When the war between the North and the South broke out in 1861, the English workers gave voice to their sympathy with the Northern states, while the sympathies of the ruling classes were entirely on the side of the slaveholders. Naturally, the Liberal Palmerston, the so-called firebrand lord, and many of his colleagues, including the illustrious Gladstone, sympathized with the South and hastened to recognize the Southern states not as mutineers but as a belligerent party.[34] English shipyards built warships for the southerners. Yet, the North came out victorious, and this revolutionary victory on American territory *gave the right of suffrage to a portion of the English working class* (Law of 1867). In England itself, the election reform was accompanied literally by a stormy movement leading to the "July Days" of 1868, when serious disorders lasted for two days and nights.

The defeat of the revolution of 1848 weakened the English workers; the Russian revolution of 1905 suddenly strengthened them. As a result of the general elections of 1906, the Labour Party for the first time constituted an important fraction of Parliament, having forty-two members; this was unquestionably due to the Russian revolution of 1905.

In 1918, even before the end of the war, a new election reform was carried out in England, which considerably increased the number of workers entitled to the suffrage and for the first time admitted women to the polls. Surely Mr. Baldwin will not deny that the Russian Revolution of 1917 was the chief incentive for the introduction of this reform. The English bourgeoisie considered that it would thus be possible to escape revolution. Consequently, the principle of gradualness is not sufficient of itself to bring about reform measures; a real threat of revolution is needed.

If we regard the history of England during the last century and a half from the point of view of European and world development, it will appear that England has utilized other countries not only economically but also politically, in order to lessen its own "expenditures" at the expense of the civil wars of the peoples of Europe and America.

What is the meaning of the two questions quoted by Mr. Baldwin from my book, and alleged by him to be in opposition to the policy of the revolutionary representatives of the English proletariat? It is not hard to show that the clear and obvious sense of my words was precisely the opposite of what Mr. Baldwin needed. The easier it was for the Russian proletariat to seize power, the greater are the obstacles encountered by it in the path of its socialist construction. I did say that; I repeat it now.

Our old ruling classes were economically and politically insignificant. We had practically no parliamentary or democratic traditions. This made it easier for us to free the masses from the influence of the bourgeoisie and to overthrow the latter's rule. But for the very reason that our bourgeoisie had come into the field late and had accomplished little, our inheritance was a poor one. We are now obliged to build roads, construct bridges and schools, teach adults to read and write, etc., i.e., to carry out most of the economic and cultural tasks which had already been carried out by the bourgeois system in the older capitalist countries. That is what I meant by saying that the more easily we disposed of our bourgeoisie, the more difficult was it for us to accomplish our socialist construction.

But this plain political theorem implies also its converse: the more wealthy and civilized a country is, the older its parliamentary-democratic traditions, the more difficult will it be for the Communist Party to seize power; but also, *the more swift and successful will be the progress of the work of socialist construction after the seizure of power.* To put the thing more concretely: to overthrow the rule of the English bourgeoisie is not an easy task; it requires an inevitable "gradual" process, i.e., serious preparatory activity; but, after having seized the power, the land, the industrial, commercial, and banking mechanism, the English proletariat will be able to put through its reorganization of the capitalist economy into a socialist economy with much smaller sacrifices, with much more success, and with much greater speed. This, the converse of my theorem, which it never for a moment occurred to me to expound or explain, is directly connected with the question that interests Mr. Baldwin.

However, that is not all. When I spoke of the difficulties of the work of socialist construction, I had in mind not only the backwardness of our country, but also the enormous opposition from the outside. Mr. Baldwin surely knows that the British government of which he was a member expended about one hundred million pounds on military intervention and on the blockade against Soviet Russia. The aim of these expensive operations—we might point out—was the overthrow of the Soviet power; the English Conservatives and also the Liberals—at least at that period—decisively rejected the principle of "gradualness" with regard to the workers' and peasants' republic, and made every effort to solve this question of history by the catastrophic method. A mere reminder of this situation should be sufficient to show that the entire philosophy of gradual change was at that moment very much like the morality of the monks in Heine's poem, who advise their flocks to drink water, but drink wine themselves.*

However that may be, the Russian worker, since he was the first to seize power, had against him at first Germany, later all the Allied countries led by England and France. The English proletariat, after it has seized power, will find itself opposed by neither the Russian czar nor the Russian bourgeoisie. On the contrary, it can depend on the immense material and human resources of our Soviet Union, for— we do not conceal this fact from Mr. Baldwin—the cause

---

* As we do not wish to transcend the bounds of modesty, we do not ask, for example, whether forged documents ascribed to a foreign government and exploited for election purposes may be considered an instrument of "gradualness" in the evolution of the so-called Christian morality of civilized society. But while we do not wish to touch upon this delicate question, we can nevertheless not refrain from recalling that Napoleon long ago declared that forged diplomatic documents were nowhere used so extensively as by English diplomacy. No doubt technical methods have been much improved since then!—L.T.

of the English proletariat is at least as much our own as the cause of the Russian bourgeoisie was and still is that of the English Conservatives.

My words concerning the difficulties of our work of socialist construction are interpreted by the British prime minister as equivalent to my saying that the game was not worth the candle. Yet my thought was precisely the opposite: our difficulties arise from an international situation that is unfavorable to us because we are the pioneers of socialism; in conquering these difficulties, we are altering this circumstance to the advantage of the proletariat of other countries; thus, in the international balance of power, not a single one of our revolutionary efforts has been wasted or is being wasted.

There is no doubt that we are aiming—as Mr. Baldwin points out—at a higher productivity of labor. In no other way is it possible to increase the prosperity and culture of our people, and of course this constitutes the fundamental task of communism. But the Russian worker is now working for himself. Having taken possession of the country's economic life, which had been disorganized first by the imperialist war, then by the civil war, then by the intervention and the blockade, the Russian workers have nevertheless been able to bring their industries—which almost perished in 1920–21—to a productivity amounting to 60 percent of the prewar figure.

This accomplishment, modest though it be when measured by our ultimate aims, is an unquestionable and important advance. If the one hundred million pounds thrown away by England on attempts to bring about catastrophic seizures of power had been invested in Soviet industry in the form of loans, or of capital in concessions, in order *gradually* to build up our industry, we should doubtless by this time have exceeded our prewar level, paid a high percentage on the English capital advanced, and most important, would already constitute a wide and ever-increasing market for England. It is not our fault that Mr. Baldwin violated the principle of gradualness precisely where it should not have been done. But even at the present—still very low—level of our industry, the position of the workers has been much improved as compared with a few years ago. When we reach our prewar level—a matter of the next two or three years—the position of our workers will be incomparably superior to what it was before the war.

It is for this reason, and only for this reason, that we feel we have a right to call upon the proletariat of Russia to increase the productivity of labor. It is one thing to work in machine-shops, factories, shipyards, mines, that belong to capitalists; it is quite another thing to work in one's own factories, mines, etc. That is a great distinction, Mr. Baldwin! And when the English workers have taken control of the mighty instruments of production created by them and their predecessors, they will make every effort to increase the productivity of labor.

English industry is greatly in need of such an increase, for, in spite of its great accomplishments, it is too much obstructed by the meshes of its own past. Baldwin knows this very well; at least he says in the speech mentioned above: "We owe our position and our place in the world largely to the fact that we were the first nation to endure the pangs which brought the industrial age into the world; but we are also paying the price for this privileged priority, and the price in part is our badly planned and congested towns, our back-to-back houses, our ugly factories, and our smoke-laden atmosphere." Add to this the fact that English industry is scattered, that it is technically conservative, that its organization lacks elasticity—this is why English industry is now receding before German and American industry.

English industry needs, to redeem it, a broad and bold reorganization. The soil and subsoil of England must be re-

garded as the basis of a single economic system; only this
attitude will make it possible to reconstruct the coal mining
industry on a healthy basis. The electrical industry of England is distinguished by its extremely scattered and backward nature; all efforts to render it more rational encounter
the opposition of private interests at every step. Not only
were the English cities, by reason of their historical origin,
planned very badly, but the entire English industry, "gradually" accumulating its resources, is without system or plan.
It will be possible to infuse fresh blood into it only if it is
approached as a single unit.

But such an attitude is inconceivable if private property
in the means of production be retained. The chief aim of
socialism is to raise the economic power of the people; only
thus is it possible to create a more civilized, more harmo-
nious, more happy human society. If Mr. Baldwin, with
all his sympathies for the old English industry, is forced
to recognize that the new capitalist form—the trusts and
combines—represent a forward step, it is our opinion that
the socialist combination of industry in turn constitutes a
gigantic step forward as compared with the capitalist trusts.
But this program cannot be carried out without handing
over all the instruments of production to the working class,
i.e., without expropriating the bourgeoisie. Baldwin himself
recalls the "titanic powers liberated by the industrial revolution of the eighteenth century, which changed the face of
the country and all the earmarks of its national life."

Why does Baldwin in this case speak of revolution, and
not of a gradual development? Because, at the end of the
eighteenth century, a radical alteration took place in a short
period of time, leading particularly to the expropriation of
small-scale industrial enterprises. Anyone who is seeking
an explanation of the internal logic of the historical process
certainly must understand that the industrial revolution
of the eighteenth century, which re-created Great Britain

from top to bottom, would have been impossible without the political revolution in the seventeenth century. Without the revolution for bourgeois rights and bourgeois enterprise—against aristocratic privileges and court idlers—the great spirit of technical inventions would never have been awakened, and no one would have been able to apply them for economic purposes. The political revolution of the seventeenth century, which grew up on the basis of the entire previous development, prepared the industrial revolution of the eighteenth century.

Now England, like all the other capitalist countries, needs an economic revolution, far exceeding in its historical significance the industrial revolution of the eighteenth century. But this new economic revolution, a reconstruction of the entire economy according to a single socialist plan—cannot be put through without a preceding political revolution. Private property in the means of production is now a much greater obstacle in the path of economic progress than were the guild privileges in their day, also a form of petty-bourgeois property. As the bourgeoisie will under no circumstances relinquish its property rights, it will be necessary to set in motion the use of an outright revolutionary force. History has not yet devised any other method. England will be no exception.

As for the second quotation, which Mr. Baldwin says he takes from me, I must admit I am completely at sea. I absolutely deny that I ever, anywhere, could have said that there exists a certain unalterable character of the Russian in the presence of which the revolution is powerless. Where is this quotation taken from? Long experience has taught me that not all persons, not even prime ministers, quote correctly. Quite accidentally, I have come upon a passage in my book, *Problems of Cultural Work*, which is wholly and completely concerned with the question we are now discussing, and which I shall therefore quote in full.

Just what are the reasons for our hopes of victory?

The first reason is that the popular masses have been roused to activity and to critical thought. Through the revolution, our people opened a window onto Europe for themselves—by "Europe" we mean culture—just as, over two hundred years ago, the Russia of Peter the Great opened not a window, but a peephole onto Europe for the elite of the aristocratic-bureaucratic system. Those passive qualities of meekness and humility, which were proclaimed by government-paid or intentionally idiotic ideologues as the peculiar, unchanging, and sacred qualities of the Russian people, but which were in fact only the expression of the people's slavelike subjugation and cultural alienation—these wretched, shameful qualities received a death blow in October 1917. This does not mean, of course, that we no longer bear within us the heritage of the past. We do, and will continue to for a long time. But a great transformation, not only material but also psychological, has been accomplished. No longer does anyone dare recommend to the Russian people that they base their destiny on meekness, humility, and long suffering. No; from now on, the virtues which are penetrating ever deeper into the people's consciousness are critical thought, activism, and collective creativity. And our hope for the success of our work is based above all else on this very great achievement of the national character. [From "Science in the Task of Socialist Construction," in Trotsky's *Problems of Everyday Life: Creating the Foundations for a New Society in Revolutionary Russia* (Pathfinder Press, New York)]

Of course, we at once see how little this resembles the statement ascribed to me by Mr. Baldwin. In justification of Mr. Baldwin, I must say that the British constitution does not impose upon the prime minister the duty of precision in his quotations. As far as precedents go—and precedents go very far in British life—I might say there is no lack of them: the example of William Pitt alone is worth a whole lot in the matter of false quotations.

It may be objected: What is the sense of discussing revolution with a Tory leader? Of what importance is the historical philosophy of a Conservative prime minister to the working class? The fact of the matter is this: the philosophy of MacDonald, Snowden,[35] Webb, and the other leaders of the Labour Party is merely a repetition of Baldwin's historical theory, as we shall show later, with all the necessary . . . gradualness.

Some peculiarities of
English labor leaders

On the death of Lord Curzon,[36] party leaders and others delivered eulogistic addresses; the socialist MacDonald closed his speech in the House of Commons with the words: "He was a great public servant, a man who was a fine colleague, a man who had a very noble ideal of public duty which may well be emulated by his successors." This about Curzon! When the workers protested against this speech, the *Daily Herald*, the Labour Party's organ, printed these protests under the modest heading, "Another Point of View." The wise editorial board apparently wished to indicate in these words that in addition to the courtier, Byzantine, bootlicking, lackey's point of view, there is also the point of view of the workers.

The well-known labor leader, Thomas,[37] secretary of the Railroad Workers' Union, formerly secretary for the colonies, attended at the beginning of April a dinner given by the board of directors of the Great Western Railway, at which Prime Minister Baldwin was also present. Baldwin had been

a director of this company, and Thomas had worked under
him as a fireman. Mr. Baldwin spoke with splendid friendli-
ness of his "friend" Jimmy Thomas, and Thomas proposed a
toast to the directors of the Great Western and their chairman, Lord Churchill.[38] Thomas spoke with great humility
of Mr. Baldwin who—just think of it!—had lived his entire
life as a worthy follower of his honored father. Thomas, the
peerless lackey, said he would of course be criticized for this
banquet and for his association with Baldwin, as a traitor
to his class, but he, Thomas, was not a member of any class,
for the truth does not belong to any class.

On the occasion of the debates by the "left" Labour delegates on the subject of appropriating money for the foreign
travels of the Prince of Wales, the *Daily Herald* delivered
itself of an editorial discussion of principles on the subject
of the royal power. Anyone who would conclude from these
debates that the Labour Party desires to abolish the royal
power, says this newspaper, would be greatly mistaken. Yet, on
the other hand, we must not overlook the fact that the royal
family is not improving its position in the public opinion of
intelligent persons: there is too much pomp and ceremony,
inspired perhaps by "unwise advisers"; too much attention
to the fluctuations of the inevitable totalizer; besides, the
Duke and Duchess of York have been hunting rhinoceroses,
and other game worthy of a better fate, in Eastern Africa.
Of course, the newspaper reflects, it would not be proper to
accuse a single royal family; tradition connects the family
too strongly with the manners and customs of a single class
only. But effort should be made to separate the family from
this tradition. This, in our opinion, is not only desirable but
absolutely necessary. We must find an occupation for the
successor to the throne, which will make him a part of the
government machine, etc., etc., in the same incomparably
vile, incomparably stupid and lackeyish tone. So in our own
country in the past, for example in 1905 or 1906, might the

organ of the Samaran peaceful regenerators have written.

The inevitable Mrs. Snowden of course also came out on the subject of the royal family, and in a short letter declared that only loudmouthed street orators could fail to recognize and understand that the royal family belongs to one of the hardest working elements in Europe. And since the Bible itself declares, "thou shalt not muzzle the mouth of the ox that treadeth out the corn," Mrs. Snowden is of course in favor of appropriating money for the travels of the Prince of Wales.

"I am a socialist, a democrat, and a Christian," this same lady once wrote, as an explanation of her opposition to Bolshevism. Of course, this does not exhaust the qualities of Mrs. Snowden, but courtesy impels me to refrain from further enumeration.

The honorable Mr. Shiels, Labour member for East Edinburgh, declared in the press that the voyage of the Prince of Wales was useful for trade, and consequently also for the working class; he, therefore, was for the appropriation.

Let us now take one of the "left" or semi-left Labour members. The question of certain property rights of the Scottish Church is being discussed in Parliament. The Scottish Labour member Johnston, taking his stand on the Act of Union of 1707,[39] denies the right of the British Parliament to interfere with the solemnly accorded privileges of the Scottish Church. The Speaker declines to table the question. Then another Scottish member, MacLean, declares that if the bill is passed, he and his friends will return to Scotland and insist that the Treaty of Union between England and Scotland has been violated and that the Scottish Parliament must be reestablished [*laughter from Conservatives and applause from Scottish Labour members*].

This is very instructive. The Scottish group, which is at the extreme left of the Parliamentary Labour fraction, protests against this ecclesiastical legislation, not because it favors a division of church and state, or for other considerations of real value, but because it wishes to defend the time-honored rights of the Scottish Church, guaranteed to the latter by treaty more than two centuries ago. In retaliation for the abrogation of the rights of the Scottish Church, these same Labour members threaten to demand the reestablishment of the Scottish Parliament, which would of course be of no use to them whatever.

George Lansbury, a left pacifist, in an editorial article in the daily organ of the Labour Party, declares that at one of the meetings in Monmouthshire, the men and women workers sang a religious hymn with the greatest enthusiasm, and that this hymn "helped" him, Lansbury.[40] Some persons may renounce religion, says Lansbury, but the labor movement, as a movement, cannot consent to this; our task requires enthusiasm, piety, and faith, and this cannot be attained by appealing only to personal interest. Therefore, if our movement is in need of enthusiasm, it must find this enthusiasm not in its own strength, according to Lansbury, but must borrow some from the priests.

John Wheatley, formerly minister of health in the Mac-Donald cabinet, is looked upon as almost of the extreme left. But Wheatley is not only a socialist but also a Catholic, or rather, he is in the first place a Catholic and then a socialist. Since the Pope of Rome has called for a battle against communism and socialism, the editors of the *Daily Herald*, who do not mention the Holy Father for reasons of courtesy, ask Wheatley kindly to explain the question of the mutual relations between Catholicism and socialism. It should be noted, however, that the newspaper does not ask whether a socialist may be a Catholic or a believer of any type; no, the question asked is whether a Catholic may be a socialist. No doubt is expressed as to a man's obligation to be a believer of some kind; the only matter in dispute is the right of the believer to be a socialist and still remain a good Catholic.

The "left" Wheatley assumes the same stand in his reply. He considers that Catholicism, which does not mingle directly in politics, determines "only" the moral rules of conduct and obliges the socialist to apply his political principles "with the greatest consideration for the moral rights of others." Wheatley is merely laying down the general rule of the British party on this question, for the party distinguishes itself from continental socialism in that it has never assumed an "anti-Christian" tendency. For this "left," the socialist politics are guided by private morality, and private morality by religion. This is in no way different from the philosophy of Lloyd George, who considers the Church as the central source of energy of all the parties. It is here that the policy of harmony obtains its religious illumination.

A socialist, writing in the *Daily Herald* about member Kirkwood,[41] who ran amuck with regard to the traveling expenses of the Prince of Wales, says that Kirkwood has in his veins a drop of the old Cromwell blood, meaning apparently the quality of revolutionary resoluteness. As to this, we cannot say, but there is no doubt that Kirkwood has inherited much of Cromwell's piety. In his speech in Parliament, Kirkwood declared that he has no private grudge against the prince and does not envy him. "The prince cannot give me anything. I am in excellent health, I am an independent man, and there is only one to whom I am answerable for my actions, my Creator." We are thus informed in his speech not only of the excellent health of the Scottish member, but also of the fact that this health is due not to biological or physiological laws, but to the thoughtfulness of a creator with whom Mr. Kirkwood entertains very definite relations, based on personal favors on the one hand and on a feeling of grateful obligation on the other.

We might add indefinitely to the number of such examples, or more correctly, almost all the political activity of the upper circles of the Labour Party may be resolved into such episodes, which constitute at the first glance only ridiculous and insignificant curiosities, but which in fact embody the peculiarities of the entire history of the past, just as stones in the bladder are a record of complicated processes in the organism. And it might not be out of place to point out that the "organic" character of the origin of any such peculiarities does not preclude the necessity of surgical intervention for their elimination.

The doctrine of the leaders of the English Labour Party is a sort of amalgam of conservatism and liberalism, at times adapted to the requirements of the trade unions, or more properly, their upper strata. All are imbued with the religion of "gradual changes." In addition, they also profess the religion of the Old and New Testaments. All consider themselves extremely civilized persons, and yet they believe that the heavenly father created mankind in order, in his loving kindness, to curse them and thereupon to make effort to right this wretched business somewhat through the crucifixion of his son. Such national institutions as the trade union bureaucracy, the first MacDonald ministry, and Mrs. Snowden have thus grown up from the spirit of Christianity.

The religion of national arrogance is closely related to that of gradual changes and to the Calvinist belief in predestination.[42] MacDonald is convinced that as his bourgeoisie was once the first bourgeoisie in the world, it would be improper for him, MacDonald, to learn anything from the barbarians and semibarbarians of the European continent. In this respect, as in all others, Macdonald is merely aping bourgeois leaders of the Canning type[43] who declared—but with much greater justification—that parliamentary England should not be expected to learn politics from the peoples of Europe.

Ceaselessly invoking the conservative tradition of England's political evolution, Baldwin doubtless appeals to the powerful prop of bourgeois rule in the past. The bourgeoisie has succeeded in imbuing the Labour Party aristocracy with conservatism. It is not an accident that the most resolute fighters for Chartism came from the ranks of artisans who had been proletarianized in one or two short generations by the onslaught of capitalism.

It is equally interesting to note that the most radical elements in the present-day English labor movement usually come from Ireland or Scotland (which rule must not be made to apply, however, to the Scotsman MacDonald). The combination of social oppression and nationalism in Ireland, together with the sharp antagonism between agricultural Ireland and industrial England, is bringing about sharp changes in men's minds. Scotland entered the path of capitalism later than England. The greater abruptness of the break in the lives of the masses of the people is producing a more abrupt political reaction. If our friends "the British socialists" were capable of studying their own history, particularly the role of Ireland and Scotland, they might perhaps be enabled to grasp why and how backward Russia with its sudden transition to capitalism brought forth the most resolute revolutionary party and was the first country to take the path of a socialist upheaval.

However, the buttress of conservatism in English life is being undermined irrevocably. For decades the "leaders" of the British working class imagined that an independent labor party was a sad privilege of continental Europe. Not a trace is now left of this naive and ignorant self-complacency. The proletariat has forced the trade unions to create an independent party. Nor is that all. The liberal and semi-liberal leaders of the Labour Party continue to believe that the social revolution is a sad privilege of the European continent. Here again, the event will show the backwardness of this view. It will take much less time to transform the Labour Party into a revolutionary party than was required for its creation.

The most important element in the conservatism of the political development has been—and to a certain extent still is—the Protestant religiosity of the English people. Puritanism was a school of severe training, a social discipline of the middle classes. The masses of the people, however, were always opposed to it. The proletarian does not feel that he is "chosen"; the Calvinistic predestination obviously does not favor him. English liberalism grew up on the basis of the Independents, and its chief mission was to train the mass of the workers, i.e., subordinate them to the bourgeoisie. Within certain limits and at certain times, liberalism succeeded in accomplishing this mission, but in the last analysis, it had as little success as did Puritanism in remolding the working class.

After the Liberals came the Labour Party, with the same traditions—Puritan and liberal traditions. If we consider the Labour Party only in its MacDonald-Henderson cross-section,[44] we might say that they have succeeded in accomplishing the impossible task of completely enslaving the working class to bourgeois society. But, in actual fact, another process is at work among the masses, opposing this desire; it will definitely dispose of the Puritan-liberal traditions, disposing of MacDonald at the same time.

For the English middle classes, Catholicism as well as Anglicanism was a tradition ready at hand, connected with the privileges of the court and the clergy. The young English bourgeoisie created Protestantism, as opposed to Catholicism and Anglicanism, as its form of belief and as a justification of its place in society.

Calvinism, with its cast-iron doctrine of predestination, was a mystical form of approach to the causal nature of the historical process. The rising bourgeoisie felt that the laws of history were on its side, and this consciousness took the form of the doctrine of predestination. The Calvinist rejection of freedom of the will by no means paralyzed the revolutionary energy of the Independents; on the contrary, it constituted their powerful support. The Independents felt themselves called to accomplish a great historical task. We may with perfect right draw an analogy between the doctrine of predestination in the Puritan revolution and the role of Marxism in the proletarian revolution. In both cases, the great efforts put forth are not based on subjective caprice, but on a cast-iron causal law, mystically distorted in the one case, scientifically founded in the other.

The English proletariat accepted Protestantism as a ready-made tradition, in other words, just as the bourgeoisie before the seventeenth century had accepted Catholicism and Anglicanism. And as the awakened bourgeoisie had opposed its Protestantism to Catholicism, so the revolutionary proletariat will oppose Protestantism with materialism and atheism. While Calvinism for Cromwell and his associates was a spiritual weapon for the revolutionary transformation of society, it inspires MacDonald only with a genuflectory attitude toward anything that has been created in a "gradual" manner. MacDonald inherits from Puritanism not its revolutionary ardor, but its religious prejudices. From the Owenites he inherits not their communist enthusiasm, but their utopian and reactionary hostility to the class struggle. From the past history of England, the Fabians have borrowed only the spiritual dependence of the proletariat on the bourgeoisie.[45] History turned her back to these gentlemen, and the chronicles they read in history became their program.

Their insular position, their wealth, their success in world policy, all these things, cemented by Puritanism, the "religion of the chosen people," was transformed into an arrogant contempt for everything continental or non-English in general. The middle classes of Great Britain for a long time were convinced that the language, science, technology, and civilization of other nations were not worth learning. And this quality has passed intact to the philistines now heading the Labour Party.

Even Hyndman issued a pamphlet, *England For All,* while

Marx was still alive, which is based entirely on Marx's *Capital*, but which does not mention either that work or its author, a strange omission due to the fact that Hyndman did not wish to shock the English reader by making it appear possible for an Englishman actually to learn something from a German.[46]

The historical dialectic process in this connection has played a sorry trick on England, in transferring the advantages of her early development into the causes for her present backwardness. We have already seen this in the field of industry, in science, in the government system, in the political ideology. England grew up without any precedents. She could not seek and find any pattern for her future among more advanced countries. She advanced by groping, empirically, looking ahead and generalizing as to her path only when absolutely necessary. The traditional cast of mind of the Englishman, particularly of the English bourgeois, is impressed with the seal of empiricism, and this same tradition was passed on to the upper layers of the working class. Empiricism became a tradition and a banner; it was combined with a contemptuous attitude for the "abstract" thought of the Continent.

Germany had long been philosophizing on the true nature of the state, while the British bourgeoisie actually constructed the form of state best adapted for the requirements of its rule. But it appeared in the course of time that the German bourgeoisie, backward in practical respects and therefore inclined to theoretical speculation, was turning its backwardness into an advantage and creating an industry far more scientifically organized and adapted for the struggle on the world market. The English socialist philistines took over from their bourgeoisie its contemptuous attitude toward the Continent at a moment when the former advantages of England were turning into their precise opposite.

MacDonald, in explaining the "innate" qualities of British socialism, declares that in seeking its ideological roots, "we must go back to Godwin, passing by Marx." Godwin was in his day a prominent figure. But a return to Godwin means for an Englishman what it would mean for a German to go back to Weitling, or for a Russian to go back to Chernyshevsky.[47] We do not at all mean to say that English imperialism and the English labor movement have not their "peculiarities." Even the Marxian school always devoted considerable attention to the peculiarities of the course of events in England. But we explain these peculiarities on the basis of the objective conditions, of the structure of society and its changes. Thanks to this circumstance, we Marxists understand far better the growth of the British labor movement and are in a far better position to predict its actions on the morrow than are the present-day "theoreticians" of the Labour Party. The old philosophic maxim "know thyself" was not uttered for them. They consider that they are called upon by destiny to rebuild from the bottom up the old social system, and yet they are completely prostrated on encountering the most insignificant details. How can they dare threaten bourgeois property, when they do not even dare refuse the Prince of Wales pocket money?

The royal power, they declare, "does not interfere" with the country's progress, and is cheaper than a president, if we count all the expenses of elections, etc., etc. These speeches of the labor leaders are characteristic of a phase of their "peculiar" nature which cannot be called by any other name than conservative stupidity. The royal power is weak because the instrument of bourgeois rule is the bourgeois Parliament and because the bourgeoisie does not need any special activities outside of Parliament. But in case of need, the bourgeoisie will make use of the royal power with great success as a concentration of all nonparliamentary, i.e., *real* forces aimed against the working class. The English bourgeoisie has always well understood the dangers even of the most fictitious monarch in certain situations. Thus, in 1837, the English government abolished the designation of "Great Mogul" in India and removed the bearer of the name from the holy city of Delhi, in spite of the fact that this name had already begun to lose its prestige. The English bourgeoisie knew that under favorable circumstances the Great Mogul might concentrate in himself the forces of the independent upper classes directed against English rule.

To proclaim a socialist platform and at the same time to declare that the royal power does not "interfere" and is actually cheaper, is equivalent, for instance, to a recognition of materialistic science combined with the use of magic incantations for toothache—since the latter are cheaper. Such little "insignificant" traits fully characterize a man by showing the complete emptiness of his recognition of material science and the complete fallaciousness of his system of ideas. The socialist cannot consider the question of monarchy from the point of view of present-day bookkeeping, especially with doctored books. The matter at stake is a complete transformation of society, a purification from all elements of serfdom. This task, both politically and psychologically, excludes any possibility of conciliation with the monarchy.

Messrs. MacDonald, Thomas, and others are indignant with those workers who protested when their ministers dressed up in clownish court dress. Of course, this is not MacDonald's chief offense, but it excellently symbolizes all the rest of his makeup. When the young bourgeoisie was fighting the nobility, it renounced side curls and silk doublets. The bourgeois revolutionists wore the black raiment of the Puritans. As opposed to the Cavaliers, the Puritans enjoyed the nickname of Roundheads. Each new content always seeks its new form. Of course, the form of dress is only a detail, but the masses simply will not understand—and they are right—why the representatives of the working class should submit to the complicated pomp of monarchic masquerade. And the masses are gradually beginning to learn that those who make mistakes in little things will also be undependable in big things.

The characteristics of conservatism, religiosity, national conceit, will be found in varying degree in all the present-day official leaders, from the extreme right Thomas, to the left Kirkwood. It would be entirely wrong to underestimate the stubbornness and permanence of these conservative peculiarities of the heads of the English working class. We do not mean to say that ecclesiastical and conservative-national tendencies are entirely absent from the masses. But while in the case of the leaders and disciples of the Liberal Party, these bourgeois-nationalist traits have entered into their very blood, they are incomparably less firmly rooted in the case of the working masses. We have already learned that Puritanism, the religion of the rising middle class, never succeeded in penetrating very far into the consciousness of the working masses. The same is true of liberalism. The workers voted for the Liberals, but remained, in the mass, workers—the Liberals being obliged to be constantly on their guard. Even the displacement of the Liberal Party by the Labour Party was the result of the pressure of the proletarian masses.

Under different conditions, i.e., if England should grow and become economically strong, a labor party of the present type might be able to continue and intensify the "educational" task of Protestantism and liberalism, thereby powerfully cementing the consciousness of great layers of the working class with the conservative-national traditions and the discipline of the bourgeois order.

But in the present state of England's obvious economic decline, with the present absence of hope, we must expect a turn precisely in the opposite direction. The war has already dealt a heavy blow to the traditional religiosity of the English masses. Mr. Wells has every reason to occupy himself with the concoction of a new religion, thus preparing himself for the career of a Fabian Calvin somewhere on the road between Earth and Mars. We must say we are doubtful of his success. The mole of revolution is working too fast! The working masses will swiftly free themselves from the national-conservative discipline, and will work out a discipline of their own for revolutionary action.

The leaders of the Labour Party will pale before these shocks from below. Of course, we do not mean that MacDonald will bleach into a revolutionist; no, he will be cast aside. But those who in all probability will bring about the first change, men of the type of Lansbury, Wheatley, and Kirkwood, will soon give evidence that they are only a leftist variation of the same Fabian type. Their radicalism is bounded by democracy and religion, and poisoned with a national conceit that completely subjects them to the British bourgeoisie. The working class will very probably be obliged to replace its leadership a number of times before a party will be born which truly corresponds to the historical situation and tasks of the British proletariat.

The Fabian 'theory' of socialism

Let us overcome our natural aversion and read through the article in which Ramsay MacDonald expounded his views a short time before leaving office.[48] We warn the reader in advance that we shall have to enter a mental junk shop in which the suffocating odor of camphor is not sufficient to retard the effective work of the moths.

"In the field of feeling and conscience," begins MacDonald, "in the spiritual field, socialism is the religion of service to the people." These words at once reveal the benevolent bourgeois, the left Liberal, who "serves" the people, approaching them from one side or—more properly—from above. This mode of approach is entirely rooted in the distant past, in the time when the radical intellectuals established settlements in the workers' sections of London with the object of engaging in educational and cultural work. These words are a remarkable anachronism when applied to the present Labour Party, which is built up directly on the trade unions!

The word "religion" must here be understood not only in

the rhetorical sense. MacDonald means Christianity, particularly its Anglo-Saxon interpretation. "Socialism is based on the gospels," preaches MacDonald, "it is an excellently conceived [sic] and resolute effort to Christianize government and society." Of course, some difficulties will be encountered, in our opinion, on this path. In the first place, the peoples enumerated in the statistics as Christian amount to approximately thirty-seven percent of the whole population of mankind. How about the non-Christian world?

In the second place, atheism is making considerable progress among Christian nations, particularly among the proletariat. In the Anglo-Saxon countries this is not yet very noticeable. But humanity, even Christian humanity, does not consist entirely of Anglo-Saxons. In the Soviet Union, which counts 130 million persons, atheism is an officially promulgated state doctrine.

In the third place, England has had control of India for several centuries; the European nations, headed by England, have long had free access to China; and yet the number of atheists is increasing more quickly than the number of Christians in India and China. Why? Because Christianity appears to the Chinese and Indians as the religion of their oppressors, misrulers, slaveholders, of powerful highwaymen who break into other people's houses by force. The Chinese know that Christian missionaries are sent to them in order to pave the way for cruisers. This is the real, historical, true Christianity! And this Christianity is to be taken as the basis for socialism? Say for China and for India?

In the fourth place, according to official records, Christianity is in its 1925th year, but before becoming the religion of MacDonald, it was the religion of the Roman slaves, of nomadic barbarians scattered all over Europe, of crowned and uncrowned despots, of feudal lords, of the Inquisition, of Charles Stuart, and in somewhat altered form, it was also the religion of Cromwell, who cut off Charles Stuart's head.

Finally, it is now the religion of Lloyd George, Churchill, the *Times*, and, we might add, of that respectable Christian who forged the "Zinoviev letter" in the interest of the Conservative elections of the most Christian of all democracies.[49] How could this Christianity which for two thousand years has been pounded into the brains of the European peoples with the aid of exhortations, compulsory religious instruction, threats of punishment in the next world, hellfire, and the sword of the police, thus becoming their official religion— how did this religion, in the twentieth century of its existence, lead to the most bloody and wicked of all wars, after the previous nineteen centuries of its history had already been filled with cruelty and crime? And what particularly good reasons have we for hoping that the "divine teaching" in the twentieth, twenty-first, or twenty-fifth century of its history will bring about equality and brotherhood where it has sanctified violence and enslavement?

We shall in vain expect an answer from MacDonald to this simple, schoolboy question. Our sage is an evolutionist, i.e., he believes that all changes take place "gradually" and, with the aid of God, for the better. MacDonald is an evolutionist; he does not believe in miracles; he does not believe in sudden changes, except the single sudden change which took place 1925 years ago, when a wedge was inserted into organic evolution in the person of none other than the Son of God, thus giving rise to a number of heavenly truths from which the clergy have since been deriving a rather respectable earthly income.

The Christian foundation of socialism is expressed in two decisive sentences in MacDonald's article: "Who can deny that poverty is evil, not only for the individual, but for society? *Who does not feel sympathy with poverty?*" We here find presented as a theory of socialism the philosophy of the socially minded, philanthropic bourgeois who feels "sympathy" with the poor and because of this sympathy makes

"religion his conscience," not permitting it, however, to interfere very much with his business habits.

Who does not feel sympathy with the poor? The entire
history of England is, as we know, a history of the sympathy of its possessing classes with the poverty of the toiling
masses. Not going back too far into history, it will be sufficient to trace this process, let us say, only from the sixteenth century, from the time of the enclosures of peasant
lands, i.e., the transformation of the peasants into homeless
tramps, when the sympathy with poverty was expressed in
the workhouse, the gallows, in the cutting off of ears, and
in other measures of Christian compassion. The Countess of
Sutherland carried out this "clearing" in the north of Scotland
at the beginning of the nineteenth century, and the moving
tale of this execution was written by Marx in deathless lines,
where to be sure we do not meet with drooling "compassion,"
but with the fire of revolutionary rage [Karl Marx, *Capital*
(Chicago, 1915), Vol. I, pp. 801, 802].

Who does not feel sympathy with the poor? Read through
the history of the industrial development of England, particularly the exploitation of child labor; the sympathy of the
rich for poverty never preserved the poor from humiliation
and need. In England, as well as elsewhere, poverty never
has succeeded in getting anything from wealth except when
it took the latter by the throat. Is there any need to point
this out in a country with a century-long history of class
struggles, a history, furthermore, of miserable concessions
and merciless legal judgments?

"Socialism does not believe in force," MacDonald goes on.
"Socialism is health and not mental disease . . . and therefore
in its very nature it must renounce violence with horror. . . .
It fights only with intelligent and honorable weapons." All
this is very fine, although not entirely new; you will find
the same thoughts expressed in the Sermon on the Mount,
in a somewhat superior style. And we know what all that

amounted to. We cannot see why the uninspired MacDonald paraphrase of the Sermon on the Mount should give any better result. Tolstoy, who was able to marshal much more powerful instruments to convince his readers, did not succeed in converting even the members of his own landowning family to the evangelical doctrine. MacDonald also must have learned something about the inadmissibility of force when he was in power. We recall that the police were not dismissed at that time, the courts were not abolished, jails were not torn down, warships were not sunk—in fact new ones were built. And insofar as we have any ability to judge this matter, the police, courts, jails, armies, and navies are instruments of force. The recognition of the truth that "socialism is health and not mental disease" by no means prevented MacDonald from following—in India and Egypt—in the sacred footprints of that great Christian, Lord Curzon. As a Christian, MacDonald recoils from the use of force "with horror"; as a prime minister, he brings to bear all the methods of capitalist oppression and hands over these instruments of force intact to his Conservative successor in office.

What does the renunciation of violence mean in point of actual fact? It simply means in practice that the oppressed must not use force against the capitalist state: the workers against the bourgeoisie, the farmers against the landlords, the Hindus against the British administration. The state, created by means of the force exerted by the monarchy over the people, by the bourgeoisie over the workers, by the landlords over the farmers, by officers over the soldiers, by Anglo-Saxon slaveholders over colonial peoples, by "Christian" over heathen, this bloody apparatus of centuries of violence inspires MacDonald to pious genuflections. "With horror" applies only to his attitude to force when used for liberation. Such is the holy content of his "religion of serving the people."

"In socialism there is a new school and also an old one," says MacDonald, "we belong to the new school." The ideal of Mac-Donald—for he has an "ideal"—is still the old-school ideal, but the new school has a "better plan" for realizing this ideal. What is this plan? MacDonald does not fail to give an answer: "We have no class consciousness. Our opponents— they are the people with a class consciousness. . . . Instead of a class consciousness, we wish to advance the conscious-ness of social solidarity." Continuing to thresh this empty straw, MacDonald concludes: "The class war is not the work of our hands. It was created by capitalism and always will remain the fruit of capitalism, as thistles will always be the fruit of thistles."

The fact that MacDonald has no class consciousness, while the leaders of the bourgeoisie have a class consciousness, is beyond dispute and merely goes to show—at bottom—that the English Labour Party has thus far been living without a head on its shoulders, while the party of the English bour-geoisie has a head—a head with a high and mighty brow, supported by a robust and powerful neck. And if MacDonald should content himself with an admission of the fact that "consciousness" is the point on which his head is weak, there would be no reason for quarreling with him. But MacDonald, from a head that is poor in "consciousness," wishes to con-struct a program, which is inadmissible.

"The class war," says MacDonald, "was created by capital-ism." This is of course not true. The class war existed before capitalism, but it is true that the *present* class war between the proletariat and the bourgeoisie is the creation of capital-ism. It is also true that it "always has been its fruit," i.e., that it will continue to exist as long as capitalism exists. But in a war there are manifestly two belligerent sides. One of these is the side of our enemies, who, according to MacDonald, "stand for the privileged class and wish to preserve it." It would appear, therefore, if we stand for the abolition of the privileged class, which does not wish to be eliminated, that we here have the fundamental content of a class struggle. But no, MacDonald "wishes to advance" the consciousness of social solidarity. Solidarity with whom? The solidarity of the working class is the expression of its internal union in its struggle with the bourgeoisie. The social solidarity preached by MacDonald is the solidarity of the exploited with the exploiters, i.e., a support given to exploitation. MacDonald boasts, furthermore, that his ideas are different from the ideas of our grandfathers: he means Karl Marx. As a matter of fact, MacDonald differs from "our grandfathers" in the sense that he resembles more our great-grandfathers, for the hodgepodge of ideas which MacDonald preaches as a new school signifies—on an entire new historical basis—a return to the petty-bourgeois sentimental socialism to which Marx devoted his annihilating criticisms in 1847 and earlier.

In opposition to the class struggle, MacDonald sets up the idea of a solidarity of all those virtuous citizens who are aiming to reconstruct society by the path of democratic re-forms. In his understanding, the class struggle yields place to a "constructive" activity of a political party, built up not on a class basis but on the basis of social solidarity. These excellent ideas of our great-grandfathers—Robert Owen, Weitling, and others—ultimately castrated and adapted for parliamentary reforms, sound very funny in present-day England, with its numerically powerful Labour Party based on the trade unions. There is no other country in the world in which the class character of socialism has been so objectively, obviously, unquestionably, empirically revealed by history as in England. For in this country, the Labour Party grew out of the parliamentary representation of the trade unions, i.e., the purely class organizations of wage labor. When the Conservatives, and the Liberals too, attempt to forbid the trade unions from collecting political contributions, they are thus not unsuccessfully setting up the idealistic MacDonald understanding of the party in opposition to the empirical class character which this party has actually assumed in England. It is true that the upper ranks of the Labour Party include a certain number of Fabian intellectuals and despairing Liberals; but in the first place, it is greatly to be hoped that the workers will soon sweep out this riffraff; and in the second place, already now the 4,500,000 votes given for the Labour Party are, with insignificant exceptions, the votes of the English workers. By no means all the workers yet vote for their party. But hardly any votes but those of workers are cast for the Labour Party.

We do not at all mean that the Fabians, Independents, and deserters from liberalism have no influence on the policy of the working class. On the contrary, their influence is very great, but it is not independent in character. Reformists who resist the proletarian class consciousness are, in the last analysis, a weapon in the hands of the ruling class. Throughout the history of the English labor movement we find a pressure exerted on the proletariat by the bourgeoisie through the radicals, intellectuals, parlor and church socialists, Owenites, who deny the class struggle and advance the principle of social solidarity, advocating collaboration with the bourgeoisie, confusing, weakening, and politically debasing the proletariat.

In full accord with this "tradition," the program of the Independent Labour Party shows that the party aims "at a union of the organized workers together with all persons of all classes who believe in socialism."[50] This consciously confused formulation has the object of obscuring the class character of socialism. No one, of course, demands that the doors be completely closed to experienced deserters from the other classes. But the number of such persons even now is quite insignificant unless we consider only the upper circles of the party, if we take the party as a whole; and in the future, when the party has entered the revolutionary path, this number will decrease still more. But the Independents need their phrase about "persons of all classes" for the purpose of deceiving the workers themselves with regard to the actual class source of their power, substituting for it the fiction of a solidarity with other classes.

We have mentioned that many workers still vote for the bourgeois candidates. MacDonald cudgels his brains to interpret even this fact in accordance with the political interests of the bourgeoisie. "We must look upon the worker not as a worker, but as a man," he inculcates, adding: "Even Toryism has to a certain extent learned . . . to approach men as men. That is why the majority of the workers voted for the Tories." In other words, when the Conservatives, frightened by the advance of the workers, begin to learn to adapt themselves to the more backward workers, to undermine their unity, to hoodwink them, to play upon their most reactionary superstitions, and to frighten them with false documents, this only goes to show that the Tories know how to approach men as men!

The English labor organizations that are most unalloyed in their class composition, namely the trade unions, built up the Labour Party directly on their own shoulders. This was equivalent to an expression of profound change in the situation of England: its weakening in the world market, the alteration of its economic structure, the elimination of the middle classes, the downfall of liberalism. The proletariat needs a class party, is making every effort to create such a party, exerts pressure on the trade unions, pays political contributions. But this increasing pressure from below, from the shops and factories, the docks and mines, is opposed by a pressure from above, from the domain of official English policy, with its national traditions of "love of freedom," of world leadership, of primacy in civilization of democratic and Protestant responsibility. If you prepare a political mixture of all these ingredients (for the purpose of weakening the class consciousness of the English proletariat), you will have the Fabian platform.

If MacDonald attempts to define the Labour Party, which is openly based on the trade unions, as a classless organization, the "democratic" government of English capital is for him even more classless in character. To be sure, the present state, governed by the landowners, bankers, shipbuilders, and coal magnates, is not a "perfect democracy." It still has certain defects: "Democracy and, let us say (!!), a system of industry not conducted by the people are two incompatible conceptions." In other words, democracy still has some minor defects: the wealth created by the nation does not belong to the nation but to an insignificant minority in the nation.

Perhaps this is an accident? No, bourgeois democracy is that system of institutions and measures with the aid of which the needs and demands of the working masses as they advance upward, are neutralized, distorted, rendered harmless, or in plain words, reduced to nothing. Anyone who would say that in England, France, the United States, and other democratic countries, private property is supported by the will of the people would be a liar. No one ever asked the consent of the people. The toilers are born and receive their training under conditions not of their creation. The national schools, the national church, imbue them with conceptions exclusively calculated for the maintenance of the existing order. Parliamentary democracy is merely a recapitulation of this condition. MacDonald's party is a necessary component part of this system.

When the course of events—usually catastrophic in nature, like the great economic upheavals, crises, wars—makes this social system intolerable for the working masses, the latter have neither the opportunity nor the inclination to express their revolutionary indignation through the channels of capitalist democracy. In other words, when the masses learn how long they have been deceived, they revolt. A successful revolution gives them power, and the fact that they hold power permits them to construct a state apparatus corresponding to their needs.

But MacDonald does not grasp even this. "The revolution in Russia," he says, "has given us a great lesson. It has shown that revolution means destruction and poverty and nothing else." Here the reactionary Fabian reveals himself before us in all his repulsive nakedness. Revolution leads only to poverty! But the English democracy led to the imperialist war; and not only in the sense of the general responsibility of all the capitalist states for the war. No, in the sense of a direct and immediate responsibility of English diplomacy, which consciously and deliberately pushed Europe into war. If the English "democracy" had declared that it would enter the war on the side of the Entente,[51] Germany and Austria-Hungary would probably have kept out. If England had declared that it would remain neutral, France and Russia would probably have kept out.

But the British government proceeded differently; it secretly promised the Entente its support and consciously deceived Germany with the possibility of England's remaining neutral. Thus, the English "democracy" deliberately worked for the war, with the devastations of which the poverty due to the revolution cannot of course begin to be compared. But, in addition, what sort of ears and brains have people who are able to declare in the face of a revolution that overturned czarism, the nobility, the bourgeoisie, inflicted a staggering blow on the church, awoke to new life 150 million people, a whole family of nations, that revolution means poverty and *nothing else?* MacDonald is here merely repeating Baldwin's words. He not only does not know and understand the Russian Revolution, but he knows nothing of English history.

We are obliged to bring to his attention what we have already brought to the attention of the Conservative prime minister. While in the economic field the initiative remained

with England up to the last quarter of the nineteenth century, in the political field, on the other hand, England for the
past century and a half has been developing chiefly on the
shoulders of European and American revolutions. The great
French Revolution, the July revolution in 1830, the revolution
of 1848, the Civil War in the United States in 1861–65, and
the Russian revolutions of 1905 and 1917 imparted impulses
to the social revolution of England and dotted the course of
its history with the milestones of the great legislative reforms. Without the Russian Revolution of 1917, MacDonald
would never have been prime minister in 1924; we hasten
to add that we do not consider the MacDonald cabinet to be
the highest achievement of the November revolution, but it
was at any rate a byproduct of the revolution.

We are taught even in children's primers that if you wish
to gather acorns, you must not uproot the oak tree. Besides,
how monstrous is this Fabian conceit: since the Russian Revolution has given "us" (whom?) a lesson, "we" (who?) will
get along without a revolution. But why didn't the lessons
of all the preceding wars enable "you" to get along without
the great imperialist war? Just as the bourgeoisie calls each
new war the last of all wars, so MacDonald calls the Russian
Revolution the last of all revolutions. Then why—really—
should the English bourgeoisie make any concessions to the
English proletariat and hand over their property peacefully
without a struggle, if they have received MacDonald's solemn assurance in advance that owing to the experience of the
Russian Revolution, English socialists will never proceed to
the use of force? When and where has any ruling class given
up its power and property by the method of peaceful elections, especially a class which, like the English bourgeoisie,
has behind it a century of global banditry?

MacDonald is opposed to revolution, but he is in favor of
organic evolution: he applies to society a few badly digested
biological conceptions. Revolution for him, as a sum of cu-

mulative partial changes, is similar to the evolution of living organisms, such as that which transforms the larva into a butterfly; and furthermore, in this latter process, he overlooks precisely the decisively critical moment when the new animal breaks through the old envelope by the method of revolution. It may be observed, by the way, that MacDonald is "in favor of a revolution like that which went on in the bowels of feudalism, when the industrial revolution was maturing." In his boundless ignorance MacDonald apparently imagines that the industrial revolution proceeded as a molecular process, without upheavals, without devastation. He simply does not know the history of England, not to speak of the history of other countries. And he above all does not understand that the industrial revolution, which had been maturing in the womb of feudalism in the form of the accumulation of commercial capital, led to the Reformation,[52] brought the Stuarts into conflict with Parliament, gave birth to the Great Rebellion, laid England waste and bare—in order later to enrich the country.

It would be too boring to dwell here on an interpretation of the process of the transformation from the larva into the butterfly, with the object of obtaining the necessary social analogies. It is perhaps simpler and more speedy to recommend to MacDonald to ponder on the time-honored comparison of revolution with the process of birth. Should we not learn a "lesson" from birth, as from the Russian Revolution? In birth also, there is "nothing" but agony and travail (of course, the baby does not count!). Should we not recommend the populace of the future to multiply by painless Fabian methods, by resorting to the talents of Mrs. Snowden as a midwife?

Of course, we are aware that the matter is not altogether a simple one. Even the chicken which is growing in the egg must apply force in order to break its calcareous prison; if any Fabian chicken should refrain—for Christian or other considerations—from this application of force, it would be suffocated by its hard shell of lime. English pigeon-fanciers, by a method of artificial selection, have succeeded in producing a variety by a progressive shortening of the beak. They have even gone so far as to attain a form in which the beak of the new stock is so short that the poor creature is incapable of breaking through the shell of the egg in which it is born. The unhappy pigeon perishes, a victim of its compulsory abstention from the use of force, and the further progress of the variety of short-billed pigeons is thus terminated. If our memory does not deceive us, MacDonald may read up on this matter in his Darwin.

Having been induced to enter the path of analogy with the organic world, which is such a hobby with MacDonald, we may say that the political skill of the English bourgeoisie consists in shortening the revolutionary beak of the proletariat and thus preventing it from breaking through the shell of the capitalist state. The beak of the proletariat is its party. A single glance at MacDonald, Thomas, Mr. and Mrs. Snowden is sufficient to convince us that the work of the bourgeoisie in the selection of short-billed and soft-billed specimens has been crowned with immense success, for these ladies and gentlemen are not only not fit for breaking through the shell of the capitalist system, but are good for nothing whatsoever.

But here the analogy ends, and reveals the disadvantage of basing one's argument on scattered facts obtained from textbooks of biology rather than on the scientific conditions and stages of historical development. Human society, although growing out of the conditions of the organic and inorganic world, is nevertheless so complicated and concentrated a combination of these conditions as to demand independent study. The social organism differs from the biological organism, for instance, in its much greater elasticity, adaptability of the elements for regrouping, for (to a certain extent) a conscious selection of their tools and methods, for (within certain limits) a conscious utilization of the experience of the past, etc. The little pigeon in its egg cannot change its short beak for a longer one, and therefore perishes. But the working class, when faced with the question "to be or not to be," will discard MacDonald and Mrs. Snowden and equip itself with the beak of a revolutionary party for the overthrow of the capitalist system.

It is particularly interesting to observe in MacDonald a combination of a crassly biological theory of society with an idealistic Christian hatred of materialism. "You speak of revolution, of catastrophic changes, but look at nature; how wise is the action of the caterpillar when it envelops itself in the cocoon; look at the worthy tortoise, and you will find in its movements the natural rhythm for the transformation of society. Learn from nature!" In the same spirit MacDonald brands materialism as a "vulgar, senseless claim, without any spiritual or mental delicacy. . . ." MacDonald and delicacy! Is it not an astonishing "delicacy" which seeks inspiration in the caterpillar for the collective social activity of man and simultaneously demands for its own private use an immortal soul and all the comforts of life in the hereafter?

"Socialists are accused of being poets. That is true," MacDonald explains; "we are poets. There are no good politics without poetry. In fact, without poetry there is nothing good." And so forth, all in the same style, until, at the conclusion: "Above all, the world needs a political and social Shakespeare." This prattle about poetry may be politically not quite so silly as the remarks on the inadmissibility of force. But the full lack of inspiration in MacDonald is here expressed even more strongly, if that were possible. The dull and timid miser in whom there is as much poetry as in a square inch of felt, tries to impress the world with his Shakespearian antics. Here you will really find the "monkey pranks" which MacDonald would like to ascribe to the

Bolsheviks. MacDonald, the "poet" of Fabianism! The policy of Sidney Webb, an artistic creation! The Thomas ministry, colonial poetry! And finally, Mr. Snowden's budget, a triumphant love song of the City of London!

While babbling about his social Shakespeare, MacDonald overlooks Lenin.[53] It is an excellent thing for MacDonald—though not for Shakespeare—that the great English poet produced his creations more than three centuries ago; MacDonald has had sufficient time to appreciate Shakespeare as Shakespeare. He would never have recognized him had Shakespeare been one of his contemporaries. So MacDonald ignores—completely and definitely ignores—Lenin. The blindness of the philistine finds its dual expression in pointless sighs for Shakespeare and in a failure to appreciate his most powerful contemporary.

"Socialism is interested in art and in the classics." It is surprising how this "poet" can corrupt by his mere touch thoughts that have nothing inherently vile about them. To convince himself of this, the reader need only read the inference: "Even where there exists great poverty and great unemployment, as is unfortunately the case in our country, citizens(?) should not deny themselves the purchase of paintings or of anything, in general, that may call forth joy and improve the minds of young and old." This excellent advice does not make it entirely clear, however, whether the purchase of paintings is recommended to the unemployed themselves, with the implication that the necessary supplementary appropriations will be made for this need, or whether MacDonald is advising well-born gentlemen and ladies to purchase paintings "in spite of unemployment" and thus to "improve their minds." We may assume that the second explanation is the correct one. But then, we are constrained to behold in MacDonald a priest of the parlor-Liberal Protestant school, who first speaks with powerful words of poverty and the "religion of conscience" and then advises his worldly flock not to surrender too much to despair and to continue their former mode of living. Let him who will—after this—believe that materialism is vulgarity and that MacDonald is a social poet, languishing with longing for a Shakespeare. As for us, we believe that if there is in the physical world an absolute zero, corresponding to the greatest attainable cold, there is also in the mental world a degree of absolute vulgarity, corresponding to the mental temperature of MacDonald.

Sidney and Beatrice Webb represent a different variety of Fabianism. They are accustomed to patient and laborious literary labor, know the value of facts and figures, and this circumstance imposes certain limitations on their diffuse thought. They are not less boring than MacDonald, but they may be more instructive when they do not attempt to transcend the bounds of investigations of fact. In the domain of generalization they are hardly superior to MacDonald. At the 1923 congress of the Labour Party, Sidney Webb declared that the founder of British socialism was not Karl Marx but Robert Owen, who did not preach the class struggle but the time-honored doctrine of the brotherhood of all mankind. Sidney Webb still considers John Mill a classic of political economy,[54] and accordingly teaches that the struggle should be carried on not between capital and labor but between the overwhelming majority of the nation and the expropriators of rents. This should be sufficient to indicate the theoretical level of the principal economist of the Labour Party!

The historical process, as we all know, does not proceed according to Webb's desires, even in England. The trade unions are an organization of wage labor against capital. On the basis of the trade unions we have the growth of the Labour Party, which even made Sidney Webb a cabinet minister. Webb carried out his platform only in the sense that he waged no war against the expropriators of surplus value. But he waged no war either against the expropriators of rents.

In 1923, the Webbs issued a book, *The Decay of Capitalist Civilization*, which has as its basis a partly outgrown, partly refurbished paraphrase of Kautsky's old commentaries on the Erfurt Program.[55] But the political tendency of Fabianism is again revealed in *The Decay of Capitalist Civilization* in all its hopelessness, this time half-knowingly. There is no doubt (for whom?), say the Webbs, that the capitalist system will change. The whole question simply is how it is to be transformed. "It may by considerate adaptation be made to pass gradually and peacefully into a new form" (*The Decay of Capitalist Civilization*, p. 1). But this requires a certain element: good will on both sides. "Unfortunately," the respected authors relate, "many who assent to this proposition of inevitable change fail to realize what the social institutions are to which this law of change applies. To them the basis of all possible civilization is private property in a sense in which it is so bound up with human nature, that whilst men remain men, it is no more capable of decay or supersession than the rotation of the earth on its axis. But they misunderstand the position" (pp. 1, 2). How unhappily have circumstances conspired to frustrate us! The whole business could be arranged to the general satisfaction by applying a method of "planful adaptation," if the workers and capitalists could only agree on the method of this consummation.

But since no such agreement has "hitherto" been attained, the capitalists vote for the Conservatives. What should be our conclusion? Here our poor Fabians fail us completely, and here *The Decay of Capitalist Civilization* assumes the form of a lamentable decay of Fabianism: "Before the Great War there seemed to be a substantial measure of consent," the book relates, "that the social order had to be gradually changed, in the direction of a greater equality, etc." (p. 177). By whom was this recognized? These people think their little Fabian molehill is the universe.

We thought, perhaps wrongly (!), that this characteristic British (?) acquiescence on the part of a limited governing class in the rising claims of those who had found
themselves excluded from both enjoyment and control,
would continue and be extended, willingly or reluctantly,
still further from the political into the industrial sphere;
and that whilst progress might be slow, there would at
least be no reaction. But after the War everything fell
into desuetude: the conditions of the lives of the workers
became worse, we are threatened with the reestablishment of the *veto* power of the House of Lords, with the
particular object of resisting further "concessions to the
worker." [p. 176]

What is the conclusion to be drawn from all this? It was
in their hopeless search for such a conclusion that the Webbs
wrote their little book. Its final sentence reads as follows: "In
an attempt, *possibly vain*, to make the parties understand
their problems and each other better—in the hope that it is
not always inevitable that Nature should harden the hearts
of those whom she intends to destroy—we offer this little
book" (p. 177).

Isn't this nice: a "little book" is offered as a means of
conciliating the proletariat with the bourgeoisie. Let us
recapitulate: before the war, "it seemed" to be generally
recognized that the present system must be altered for the
better; however, there was no general agreement as to the
character of this change: the capitalists stood for private
property, the workers against private property; after the
war, the objective situation became worse, and the political
divergence became further aggravated; *therefore*, the Webbs
write a little book in order to make both sides more inclined
toward conciliation; but this hope is admitted to be "possibly vain." Yes, possibly, quite possibly. The worthy Webbs,
who are so strongly imbued with a faith in the powers of

intellectual conviction, ought—it appears to us—in the interests of "gradual changes," to apply themselves at least at the beginning to a simpler task, namely, that of persuading a few high-placed Christian scoundrels to renounce their monopoly in the opium trade and their poisoning of millions of people in the Orient.

Oh, how poor, base, weak-minded, how vile in its intellectual cowardice is this Fabianism!

It is entirely impossible to attempt to enumerate all the philosophical varieties of Fabianism, for among this class "liberty of opinion" prevails in the sense that each of its leaders has his own personal philosophy, which consists, in the last analysis, of the same reactionary elements of conservatism, liberalism, and Protestantism as in any other such combination.

Not long ago, we were very much surprised to learn that so ingenious—we had thought—and so critical a writer as George Bernard Shaw[56] had advised us that Marx had been far surpassed by Wells's great work on history.* These revelations, an entire surprise to all of mankind, may be explained by the fact that the Fabians constitute, from the standpoint of theory, an absolutely closed microcosm of profoundly provincial nature, in spite of the fact that they live in Lon-

---

* I regret to say that before I read Shaw's letter, I had not even known of the existence of Wells's *Outline of History*. I later became acquainted with it; conscience prevents me from saying that I read it through, for an acquaintance with two or three chapters was quite sufficient to induce me to desist from a further waste of time. Imagine an absolute absence of method, of historical perspective, of understanding of the mutual dependence of the various phases of social life; in general, of any kind of scientific discipline; and then imagine the "historian" burdened with these accomplishments, with the carefree mind of a Sunday pedestrian, strolling aimlessly and awkwardly through a few thousand years of history, and then you have Wells's book, which is to replace the Marxian school.—L.T.

don. Their philosophical excogitations are apparently of no use either to Conservatives or to Liberals. They are of still less use to the working class, to whom they neither give nor explain anything. Their productions serve in the last analysis only to make clear to the Fabians themselves what is the use of the existence of Fabianism. Together with theological literature, these works seem to be the most useless, at any rate, the most boring, form of intellectual creation.

At present it is customary in England in certain fields of activity to speak with a certain contempt of the men of the "Victorian era," i.e., the outstanding figures of the time of Queen Victoria. Everything has changed since then in England, but the Fabian type has perhaps been preserved even more intact. The insipid, optimistic Victorian epoch, in which it was believed that tomorrow will be somewhat better than today and the day after tomorrow still better than tomorrow, has found its most perfect expression in the Webbs, Snowden, MacDonald, and other Fabians. They may therefore be considered as an awkward and useless survival of an epoch that has already been definitely and irrevocably destroyed. We may say without exaggeration that the Fabian Society, founded in 1884 with the object of "awakening the social consciousness," is now the most reactionary group to be found in Great Britain. Neither the Conservative clubs nor Oxford University nor the higher Anglican clergy nor other priestly institutions can begin to be compared with the Fabians. For all these are institutions of our enemies, and the revolutionary movement of the proletariat will inevitably break down their walls. But the proletariat is being restrained precisely by its own leading ranks, i.e., by the Fabian politicians and their mental offspring.

These inflated authorities, pedants, conceited and pompous cowards are systematically poisoning the labor movement, obscuring the consciousness of the proletariat, paralyzing its will. Thanks only to them, Toryism, liberalism, the Church, the monarchy, the aristocracy, the bourgeoisie, continue to maintain themselves and even to feel secure in the saddle. The Fabians, the Independents, the conservative bureaucracy of the trade unions, are now the most counterrevolutionary power in Great Britain and perhaps in the entire present stage of the world situation. The driving out of the Fabians will be equivalent to a liberation of the revolutionary energy of the proletariat of Great Britain, to socialism's conquest of the British fortress of reaction, to the freeing of India and Egypt, and to a mighty stimulus to the movement and growth of the peoples of the Orient.

Renouncing force, the Fabians believe only in the power of "ideas." The kernel of truth imprisoned by this vile, hypocritical philosophy is merely the fact that no system can be maintained by force alone. And this holds good also of the British imperialist system. In a country in which the overwhelming majority of the population consists of proletarians, the ruling Conservative-Liberal imperialist clique could not have maintained itself for a single day if the instruments of force which this clique holds in its hands were not reinforced, supplemented, and coated with pseudosocialist ideals, confusing and disintegrating the proletariat.

The French "enlighteners" of the eighteenth century[57] considered Catholicism, clericalism, the priesthood, to be their great enemy, and felt it was necessary to *ecraser l'infame* before further progress was possible. They were right in the sense that it was the priesthood, the organized system of superstition, of the Catholic mental police system, which stood in the way of bourgeois society, obstructing the growth of science, art, political ideas, economics. Fabianism, MacDonaldism, pacifism, now play precisely the same role in relation to the historical movement of the proletariat. Fabianism is the chief support of British and European imperialism, if not of the entire world bourgeoisie; we must point out to the workers the true countenance of these complacent pedants, prattling eclectics, sentimental careerists, liveried footmen of the bourgeoisie. In showing them up for what they are, we are discrediting them forever. In discrediting them we are performing an immense service to historical progress. On the day when the English proletariat frees itself from the mental baseness of Fabianism, humanity, particularly in Europe, will increase in stature by at least a head.

The problem
of revolutionary force

We have become acquainted with MacDonald's views on the use of force in revolution and have found them to be a paraphrase of Mr. Baldwin's conservative theory of gradual changes. More curious—though somewhat more genuine—is the renunciation of violence on the part of the "left" Lansbury. Lansbury, it seems, says simply that he does "not believe" in force. He also does "not believe" in the capitalist army or in armed uprisings. If he believed in force, he would not vote—he says—for the British fleet, but would join the Communists. What a brave fellow! But the fact that Lansbury, who does not believe in force, does believe in a future life makes it somewhat doubtful whether he is entirely consistent.

Nevertheless, with Lansbury's permission, certain facts in the world have been brought about with the aid of force. Whether Mr. Lansbury believes in the British navy or not, the Hindus know that this fleet exists. In April 1919, the English General Dyer, without having issued any previous warnings, gave orders to shoot at an unarmed Hindu meeting at Amritsar, with the result that 450 persons were killed and 1500 wounded. Leaving the dead out of consideration, we may feel safe in declaring that the wounded cannot afford "not to believe" in force. But even as a believing Christian, Lansbury should know enough to understand that if the cunning Hebrew priesthood, together with the cowardly Roman Proconsul Pontius Pilate, a political predecessor of MacDonald, had not applied force to Jesus Christ, we should not have had the crown of thorns, nor the resurrection, nor the ascension; and even Mr. Lansbury would not have had the opportunity to be born a good Christian and to become a bad socialist.

A disbelief in violence is equivalent to a disbelief in gravitation. All life is built up on various forms of force, on the opposition of one mode of force to another, and renunciation of the use of force for purposes of liberation is equivalent to giving support to force used for oppression, which now rules the world.

But we are of the opinion that scattered observations will not be of much avail here. The question of force and the "denial of force" by the pacifists, Christian socialists, and other sanctimonious persons, is such an extensive phenomenon in English politics, that a special, detailed treatment is necessary, adapted to the political understanding of the present-day "leaders" of the British Labour Party, for which reason we are obliged to beg the pardon of our other readers for descending to this level.

What is, at bottom, the meaning of a denial of any use of force? If—let us suppose—a burglar should break into Mr. Lansbury's house, we very much fear that this devout gentleman (we are speaking of the master of the house) would apply force or would call upon the nearest policeman to apply force. Even if Lansbury, in the fullness of his Christian mercy, should permit the burglar to depart in peace—of which we are not at all certain—it would of course only be under the obvious condition of the burglar's immediately leaving the apartment. Furthermore, the honorable gentleman could only permit himself the luxury of so Christian a gesture by reason of the fact that his premises are under the protecting supervision of British property laws, and their numerous arguses, with the result that in general nighttime visits on the part of burglars are rather the exception than the rule. If Lansbury should attempt to answer that an intrusion into a respectable private Christian home is an application of force which calls for the necessary resistance, we shall answer him that such a view is an abandonment of the renunciation of force in general, equivalent—on the other hand—to a recognition of force in principle and in practice, which may also be applied with perfect correctness to the class struggle, where we find daily intrusions by the thief-capitalist in the life of the proletariat and expropriations of surplus value which fully justify the offering of resistance. Perhaps Lansbury may reply that he does not imply every form of constraint when he uses the word "force," for our excellent social life could not get along without some such forms, but only violations of the Sixth Commandment with its injunction: "Thou shalt not kill."

In a defense of such an understanding of the question, it would be possible to adduce a great many high-sounding phrases concerning the sanctity of human life, and we should then be obliged to use the language of the parables in the Gospels, which is more accessible to the leaders of British socialism, and ask how Mr. Lansbury would act if he should behold a murderer falling upon little children with a club, if there were no other means of saving them than an immediate well-aimed shot from a revolver. If our supposed fellow-debater does not prefer to engage in absolutely empty sophisms, he will answer, I suppose, to render his position easier, that our example is a very exceptional one.

But this answer would merely be equivalent once more to an admission that Lansbury would transfer his right to the use of murder under these circumstances to his police, the special organization of force which permits him to dispense in most cases with the necessity of using his revolver and even of considering its practical destination.

But now let us ask about the case in which armed strikebreakers beat up strikers or beat them to death. Such cases are everyday matters in America and are not unusual even in other countries. The workers cannot entrust the police with the execution of their right to resist the strikebreakers, because the police in all countries defend the right of strikebreakers to beat up strikers and beat them to death; for it is well known that the law concerning the sanctity of human life does not apply to strikers. Our question is this: Have the strikers the right to resort to the use of sticks, stones, revolvers, bombs, against the fascists,[58] the bands of the Ku Klux Klan, and other hired thugs of capital? We should like to have a clear and straight answer to this question, without any evasive sanctimonious embroidery.

If Lansbury should say to us that the task of socialism is to provide the masses of the people with such training as to prevent the fascists from being fascists, to prevent scoundrels from being scoundrels, this would be pure hypocrisy. The fact that the object of socialism is the elimination of force, first in its cruder and bloodier forms, and later in its other, less obvious forms—we do not dispute. But we are not speaking of the manners and morals of the coming communist society, but of the concrete ways and means of the struggle with capitalist violence.

When the fascists break up strikes, occupy newspaper offices and seize their treasuries, beat up or beat to death the workers' parliamentary representatives, while the police surround the murderers with a protective cordon, only the most contemptible hypocrite could under these circumstances advise the workers not to give back blow for blow, by urging that there will be no room for violence in the communist society. Of course, in each given case it will be necessary to decide *how* to answer the enemy's violence, and *to what extent* to proceed in our opposition, depending on all the circumstances of the case. But this is a question of practical tactics, which has nothing to do with the recognition or renunciation of violence in general.

What is the true nature of force? Where does it begin? When is it permissible and practical for the collective action of the masses to enter the phase of violence? We very much doubt whether Lansbury or any other of the pacifists would be capable of giving a reply to this question unless it be by merely referring to the criminal code, which provides clearly what may be done and what not. The class struggle is a constant stream of overt and covert violence "regulated"—to this or that extent—by the state, which is in turn the organized apparatus of force of the most powerful of the antagonists, i.e., the ruling class.

Is the strike a form of violence? There was a time when strikes were prohibited and when every strike almost inevitably was combined with physical collisions. Later, as a result of the growth of the strike movement, i.e., as a result of the force applied by the masses against the laws, or more correctly, as a result of the constant blows struck by the masses against the violence of the laws, strikes were legalized. Does this mean that Lansbury considers the only permissible instrument of struggle to be the peaceful, "legal" strikes, i.e., those permitted by the bourgeoisie? If the workers had not inaugurated strikes at the beginning of the nineteenth century, the English bourgeoisie would not have legalized them in 1824. If we approve of the strike, which is a form of applying power or force, we must accept all the consequences, including that of the defense of strikes against strikebreakers with the aid of practical measures of counterforce.

Furthermore, if strikes by the workers against the capitalists or against single groups of capitalists are desirable, will Lansbury refuse to recognize the necessity of a general strike of the workers against the fascist government, which oppresses the workers' unions, destroys their press, and fills the ranks of the workers with provocateurs and murderers?

Of course, it must again be pointed out that the general strike should be applied not at every moment, but only in certain concrete conditions. But this again is a question of practical strategy, not a general "moral" consideration. As far as the general strike is concerned, which is one of the most decisive instruments in the struggle, it would be hard for Lansbury and those who sympathize with him to devise any other instrument that could be used by the proletariat for the attainment of so significant a goal. Lansbury will surely not fall so low as to recommend the workers to wait until the spirit of brotherly love will have won the hearts—let us say—of the Italian fascists, who, by the way, are for the most part pious Catholics. And if we recognize that the proletariat has not only the right, but the obligation, to resort to a general strike against the fascist regime, we are also obliged to draw the necessary conclusions from this admission.

The general strike, unless it be a mere demonstration, is an extraordinary upheaval of society, and in any case calls for strength on the part of the revolutionary class. The general strike may only be applied when the working class, and particularly its vanguard, is ready to prosecute the struggle to the bitter end. But of course, fascism also is not prepared to yield to any peaceful strike manifestation. In a case of real immediate danger, the fascists will set all their forces in motion, will resort to provocations, murder, incendiarism, on an unheard-of scale. We now ask: Is it permissible for the leaders of the general strike to create little bands for the defense of the strikers from violence, for disarming and

dispersing the fascist bands? And as no one has ever succeeded, at least within our memory, in disarming savage
enemies with the aid of religious hymns, it will obviously
be necessary to equip the revolutionary detachments with
revolvers and hand grenades until such time as they may be
able to take possession of rifles, machine guns, and cannons.
Or is this perhaps the stage where the domain of inadmissible violence begins?

But if we pursue this argument, we shall become definitely
involved in childish and shameful contradictions. A general strike which does not defend itself against violence and
destruction is a demonstration of cowardice and is doomed
to destruction. Only a madman or a traitor could call to
arms under such conditions. An "unarmed" strike struggle,
by the logic of conditions that do not depend on Lansbury,
would bring about armed conflicts. In economic strikes this
frequently is the case; in a revolutionary political strike it
is absolutely inevitable where the strike has the object of
overthrowing the existing order. He who renounces force
should renounce the struggle altogether, i.e., should really
stand in the ranks of the defenders of the triumphant violence of the ruling classes.

But this is not all. Our hypothetical general strike has
as its object the overthrow of the fascist power. This object
can be attained only by gaining the upper hand over this
power by means of armed forces. Here again two courses
are possible: outright military victory over the forces of reaction or the winning over of these forces to the side of the
revolution. Neither of these two methods can be applied exclusively, in its pure form. A revolutionary uprising carries
off the victory if it succeeds in defeating the firmest, most
resolute, and most reliable troops of the reaction, and wins
over to its side the other armed forces of the system. This is
possible, again, only under the condition that the vacillating
troops of the government become convinced that the work-

ing masses are not merely demonstrating their dissatisfaction, but are firmly determined this time to overthrow the government at any cost, and will not recoil from the most uncompromising forms of conflict. The hesitating military forces can only be brought over to the side of the people by impressing them with this fact. The more procrastinating, vacillating, yielding the policy of the managers of the general strike, the less vacillation will there be among the troops, the more firmly will they support the existing power, the greater will be the latter's chance of carrying off the victory in the crisis, thereupon to let loose upon the heads of the working class all the scorpions of bloody retaliation.

In other words, when the working class is obliged, in order to secure its liberation, to resort to a general political strike, it must first thoroughly understand that the strike will inevitably produce detached as well as general, armed and half-armed conflicts; it must also thoroughly understand that the strike will fail to be immediately defeated only if it is able to offer the necessary resistance to the strike-breakers, provocateurs, fascists, etc.; they must understand in advance that the government, whose existence is called in question, will inevitably, sooner or later in the struggle, call its armed forces into the streets, and that the destinies of the existing system will depend on the outcome of the collisions between the revolutionary masses with these armed forces, and consequently also the fate of the proletariat. The workers must first make use of every method in order to win over the soldiers to the side of the people by means of preliminary agitation; but the working class must also foresee that the government will always have left a sufficient number of dependable or half-dependable soldiers, which it can call out to suppress the uprising; and consequently, the question will be finally decided in armed clashes, for which it is necessary to be prepared by means of the most thorough preliminary plan, and which must be conducted with the fullest revolutionary resoluteness.

Only great boldness in the revolutionary struggle can strike the weapons from the hands of reaction, shorten the period of civil war, and diminish the number of its victims. He who is not prepared to go so far should not take up arms at all; he who will not take up arms should not inaugurate a general strike; he who renounces the general strike should not think of serious resistance at all. The only thing that would remain would be to educate the workers in the spirit of complete submission, which would be a work of supererogation, as it is already being performed by the official schools, the governing party, the priests of all the churches, and . . . the socialist preachers of the impropriety of force.

But here is an interesting point: just as philosophical idealists in practical life eat bread, meat, and base material things in general, and, forgetting the fact that they have immortal souls, make every effort to escape being run over by automobiles, so these pacifists, impotent opponents of violence, moral "idealists," in all cases when they find it consonant with their interests, invoke political violence and directly or indirectly make use of it. As Mr. Lansbury is apparently not without a certain amount of temperament, such cases occur with him more often than with others. In the parliamentary debates on the question of the unemployed (House of Commons session of March 9, 1925), Lansbury declared that the law on unemployment insurance in its present form was introduced in 1920 "not so much in order to safeguard the lives of the workers and their families as—to use the words of Lord Derby—in order to prevent revolution." "In 1920," continued Lansbury, "all the workers serving in the army were included in the number of those insured, because the government was at that time not quite sure that these workers would not turn their rifles in a direction not at all to the liking of the government" (*Times*, March 10, 1925).

After these words, the minutes of Parliament record "applause from the opposition benches," i.e., the Labour Party, and cries of "Oho!" from the cabinet benches.

Lansbury does not believe in revolutionary force, but he nevertheless recognizes—following Lord Derby—that the fear of revolutionary violence gave birth to the law for government insurance of the unemployed. Lansbury resists all efforts to abolish this law: he believes, therefore, that the law born from the fear of revolutionary violence has a certain value for the working class. But this almost mathematically proves the utility of revolutionary force, for with Lansbury's permission, if there were no such thing as violence, there would be no fear of violence; if there were no actual possibility (and necessity) for turning one's rifles against the government under certain conditions, the government would never have reason to fear such a possibility. Consequently, Lansbury's so-called disbelief in force is pure folly. As a matter of fact, he is making use of force, at least in the form of an argument, every day. And furthermore, he is actually utilizing in practice the achievements of revolutionary violence in past decades and centuries. He merely refuses to put two and two together in his own mind. He renounces revolutionary force for the seizure of power, i.e., for the full liberation of the proletariat, but he is on excellent terms with force and uses it in the struggle so long as the matter does not transcend the bounds of bourgeois society. Mr. Lansbury believes in force retail but not wholesale. He resembles the vegetarian who became reconciled to devouring the meat of ducks and rabbits, but renounced the slaughter of large cattle with pious disgust.

However, we predict that Mr. Lansbury, or some more diplomatic and hypocritical sympathizer of his, will answer us: yes, against the fascist regime, in fact against all despotic governments, force may in the last analysis, we do not deny

it, be used to a certain extent, so to speak; but force is entirely out of place in a democratic system. For our own part,
we should at once register this statement as a surrender of
the position in principle, for we were not speaking of the
conditions under which force was permissible or desirable,
but of whether force was permissible in general, from the
somewhat abstract humanitarian-Christian socialist point
of view.

When we are informed that revolutionary force is inadmissible only under a system of political democracy, the
whole question is at once shifted to another plane. This does
not mean, however, that the democratic opponents of force
are more profoundly and more intelligently Christian or
humane. We can easily show this to be the case.

Is it true that the question of the advisability and admis-
sibility of revolutionary force can be decided on the basis of
the greater or less democracy in the *form* of bourgeois rule?
A negative answer is implied in all the experience of history. The struggle between revolutionary and conciliatory,
legalistic, reformist tendencies within the workers' movement begins long before the establishment of republics or
the introduction of universal suffrage. In the time of Chartism, and down to 1868, the workers of England were absolutely deprived of the suffrage, this fundamental weapon of
"peaceful" development. However, there was a split in the
Chartist movement between the advocates of physical force,
with the masses behind them, and the advocates of moral
force, consisting chiefly of petty-bourgeois intellectuals and
the aristocracy of the workers.

In Hohenzollern Germany, with an impotent parliament, there was a struggle within the Social Democracy
between the advocates of parliamentary reform and the
preachers of a revolutionary general strike.[59] Finally, even
in czarist Russia, under the regime of June 3, the Mensheviks abandoned revolutionary methods, under the slogan

of the "struggle for legality."[60]

Thus, to speak of the bourgeois republic or universal suffrage as a fundamentally reformist and legalistic method is merely an expression of theoretical ignorance, short memory, or downright hypocrisy. As a matter of fact, legalistic reformism means the submission of the slaves to the institutions and laws of the slaveholders. Whether these institutions include in their number the general right of suffrage or not, whether they are headed by a king or a president, this question is of secondary importance even for the opportunist. The opportunist is always on his knees before the idol of the bourgeois state and consents to advance to his "ideal" only through the asses' gates constructed for him by the bourgeoisie. And these gates are so made that no one can get through them.

What is political democracy and where does it begin? In other words, where, by what countries has the stage been reached where force is inadmissible? For instance, can we call a state democratic if it includes monarchy and an aristocratic upper house? Is it permissible to use revolutionary methods for the overthrow of these institutions? One may perhaps reply that the English House of Commons is strong enough, if it should find it necessary, to dismiss the royal power and the House of Lords, and that the working class has at its disposal a peaceful means of achieving a democratic system in its own country. Let us admit this for a moment. How does the case stand with the House of Commons itself? Can this institution really be called democratic, even from the formal point of view?

By no means. Important portions of the population are actually deprived of the suffrage right. Women have the vote only after thirty, men only after twenty-one. A lowering of the age limit is, from the point of view of the working class, in which the working life begins early, a rudimentary demand of democracy. And, to cap the climax, the boundaries of the election districts in England are fixed in such an outrageously unjust manner that there are twice as many votes corresponding to one Labour delegate as to one Conservative.

In raising the age limit, Parliament is actually excluding the active young people of both sexes, and entrusting the destinies of the nation predominantly to the older generations, who are more tired of life and whose eyes are directed rather to the ground than to the future. That is the mission of the high age limit. The vicious geometry of the election districts gives a Conservative vote twice as much weight as a worker's vote. Thus, the present English Parliament is a crying distortion of the will of the people, even if we understand the latter in the bourgeois-democratic sense.

Has the working class a right, still standing on the ground of the principles of democracy, to demand vigorously from the present privileged and, at bottom, usurping House of Commons the immediate introduction by the latter of a truly democratic suffrage? If Parliament should answer unfavorably, which we consider inevitable, for Baldwin's government recently refused even to make the age limit the same for men and women, would the proletariat then have the "right" to obtain from the usurping Parliament, by means of a general strike, the introduction of a democratic suffrage system?

Even if we should further admit that the House of Commons—in its present usurping form or in some more democratic form—should decide to dismiss the royal power and the House of Lords—of which there is not the slightest hope—this would not at all mean that the reactionary classes, recognizing that they had a minority in the Parliament, would submit unconditionally to this decision. Only a short time ago we saw the Ulsterite reactionaries resort to open civil war under the leadership of Lord Carson[61] when their opinion differed with that of the British Parliament on the question of the governmental system of Ireland, and the English Conservatives openly supported the Ulster rebels. But we shall be told that this was an open uprising on the part of the privileged classes against the democratic Parliament, and this mutiny should of course have been put down with the aid of government forces. We subscribe to this view but ask only that certain practical conclusions be drawn from it.

Assuming for a moment that a Labour majority in Parliament may be returned in the next elections, which will proceed by legal methods to decree that the lands of the landlords shall be transferred without compensation to the farmers and to those chronically unemployed, that there shall be a high capital levy, and that the king, the House of Lords, and some other indecent institutions must go. There is no doubt that the possessing classes will not yield without a fight, particularly when we remember that they have the entire mechanism of the police, the courts, and the army and navy in their hands. We have already had a case of civil war in England, in which the king was supported by a minority of the Commons and a majority of the Lords against the majority of the Commons and a minority of the Lords. This was in the 1640s. Only an idiot—we repeat—only a sorry idiot could seriously imagine that a repetition of a civil war of this kind (on the basis of the new class conditions) is impossible in the twentieth century, by reason of the obvious progress in the last three centuries in the Christian view of life, humanitarian feelings, democratic tendencies, and a lot of other fine things. The Ulster example alone should show us that the possessing classes do not trifle when Parliament, their own parliament, is forced to limit their privileged position even to the slightest extent.

Those who prepare to seize power must necessarily prepare also for all the consequences that will result from the inevitable opposition of the possessing classes. We must firmly grasp this fact: if a real workers' government should come to power in England, even by the most extremely democratic means, civil war would be inevitable. The workers' government would be obliged to put down the opposition of the privileged classes. It would be impossible to do this by means of the old governing apparatus, the old police, the old courts, the old militia. A workers' government created by the parliamentary method would be obliged to create for itself new revolutionary organs, drawing their strength from the trade unions and the workers' organizations in general. This would lead to an immense increase in the activity and independent action of the working masses. On the basis of the immediate struggle with the exploiting classes, the trade unions would be actively welded together, not only in their upper ranks, but also in the masses, and would find it absolutely necessary to create local gatherings of delegates, i.e., soviets of workers' deputies. The true workers' government, i.e., the government which is entirely devoted to the interests of the proletariat, would thus be obliged to destroy the old government apparatus as an instrument of the possessing classes and would oppose it with workers' soviets for that purpose. This means that the democratic origin of the workers' government—if such a thing be at all possible— would lead to the necessity of opposing the strength of the revolutionary class to its reactionary opponent.

We have already pointed out that the present English Parliament is a monstrous distortion of the principles of bourgeois democracy, and that without applying revolutionary force, it is hardly possible in England to obtain even an honest allotment of election districts or the abolition of the monarchy and the House of Lords. But let us assume for a moment that these demands could be realized in one way or another. Would this mean that we should have a truly democratic Parliament in London? By no means. The London Parliament is a slaveholders' Parliament. Even though it is said to represent in an ideal formal-democratic way 40 million people, the English Parliament passes laws for 300 million people in India and has control of financial resources which are obtained by the rule of England over her colonies. The population of India has no part in the legislation which determines that country's fate.

The English democracy resembles that of Athens in the sense that the equality of democratic rights (in reality nonexistent) is concerned only with the "free-born," and is based on the absence of rights in the "lower" nations. There are about nine colonial slaves for each inhabitant of the British Isles. Even if we consider that revolutionary force is not in place in a democracy, this principle cannot in any way be made to apply to the peoples of India, who do not rebel against democracy but against the despotism that oppresses them. This being the case, even an Englishman, if he be truly democratic, cannot consider binding the democratic force of British laws as far as India, Egypt, etc., are concerned. And since the entire social life of England, as a colonial power, is based on these laws, it is obvious that all the activity of the Westminster Parliament, as a concentration of a predatory colonial power, is antidemocratic at its very basis. From a consistent democratic point of view, we should be obliged to state: As long as Hindus, Egyptians, etc., have not been given full rights of self-determination, i.e., the right of secession, as long as Hindus, Egyptians, etc., do not send their representatives to the imperial Parliament, with rights equivalent to those of Englishmen, the Hindus and Egyptians, as well as the English democrats, have the right to rebel against the predatory government created by a parliament which represents an insignificant minority of the population of the British empire. That is the state of things for England, if we approach the question of the use of force from purely democratic criteria, actually applying them consistently, however.

The denial by the English social reformers of the right of the oppressed masses to use force is a shameful renunciation of democracy, a contemptible support of the imperialist dictatorship of a small minority over hundreds of millions of enslaved persons. Before undertaking to teach communists the sacredness of democracy and to criticize the Soviet power, Mr. MacDonald should rather sweep before his own door.

We have approached the question of force first from the "humanitarian," Christian, clergyman's point of view and have shown that the social pacifists in their search for an escape from an inescapable contradiction are actually obliged to surrender their position and to recognize that revolutionary force is permissible even after passing the threshold of democracy. We have further shown that it is as difficult for the deniers of force to base themselves on the democratic point of view as on the Christian point of view. In other words, we have completely shown the untenable, lying, sanctimonious nature of social pacifism, judged on its own terms.

But this by no means signifies that we are ready to recognize these terms. In solving the question of revolutionary force, the parliamentary-democratic principle is by no means the highest instance in our eyes. Humanity does not exist for democracy, but democracy is one of the auxiliary tools on the path of human development. As soon as bourgeois democracy becomes an obstacle, it should be destroyed. The transition from capitalism to socialism does not emanate from formally democratic principles standing above society, but from the material conditions of the development of society itself, from the growth of the productive forces, from the ineluctable capitalist contradictions, domestic and international, from the sharpening of the struggle between the proletariat and the bourgeoisie. A scientific analysis of the entire historical process and the political experience of our own generation, which includes the imperialist war, all bear unanimous witness that our civilization is threatened with stagnation and decay. Only the proletariat, led by its revolutionary vanguard and followed by all the toiling and oppressed masses both of the home country and the colonies, can accomplish the transition to socialism.

Our highest criterion in all our activity, in all our political decisions, is the interests of the revolutionary struggle of the proletariat for the seizure of power and the reconstruction of society. We consider it reactionary pedantry to judge the movement of the proletariat from the point of view of the abstract principles and legal paragraphs of democracy. We consider the only proper method to be to judge democracy from the point of view of the historical interests of the proletariat. We are interested not in the shell, but in the kernel of the nut. The talk of our Fabian friends about the inadmissibility of a "narrow class point of view" is pure balderdash. They would subordinate the problem of the social revolution brought about by the proletariat to the scholastic rules of pedants. By the solidarity of mankind they mean an eclectic philistinism corresponding to the *narrow class horizon of the petty-bourgeois.*

The bourgeoisie has placed the screen of democracy between its property and the revolutionary proletariat. Socialist pedants say to the workers: we must take possession of the means of production, but meanwhile we must introduce certain apertures and channels in this screen by legal methods. But why should we not throw down the screen? Oh, do not think of that! Why not? Because, if we should save society by this method, we should be overthrowing the complicated system of government force and deception which the bourgeoisie has taught us to consider as holy democracy.

Having been forced out of its first two positions, the opponents of force may retire to a third line of defense. They may consent to throw overboard Christian mysticism and democratic metaphysics, and attempt to defend the reformist-democratic, peaceful, parliamentary method by means of considerations of mere political expediency. Some of them may say, for example: of course, the teachings of Christ do not provide for a method of escaping from the contradictions of British capitalism; likewise, even democracy is not a holy institution, but only a temporary and useful product of the historical development; but why should the working class not make use of the democratic parliament and all its methods as a legislative apparatus for the actual seizure of power and for the reconstruction of society? For this is a perfectly natural and, in view of the present circumstances, a more economical method for the accomplishment of the social revolution.

We Communists are by no means disposed to advise the English proletariat to turn its back on Parliament. On the contrary, when a number of English Communists displayed a tendency in this direction, they encountered opposition from our side in the international congresses.[62] The question therefore is not whether it is worthwhile to use the parliamentary method at all, but what is the place of Parliament in the evolution of society; whether the strength of the classes is in Parliament or outside of Parliament; what is the form and the field in which these forces will clash; is it possible to use Parliament, created by capitalism in the interests of its own growth and preservation, as a lever for the overthrow of capitalism?

To answer these questions, we must try to picture to ourselves, at least with some degree of definiteness, the future course of English political evolution. Of course, any such attempt to look into the future can only be hypothetical and general in character. But without such efforts, we should be obliged to grope in the dark altogether.

The present government has a solid majority in Parliament. It is not impossible, therefore, that it may remain in power for three or four years, although the time may be much shorter. In the course of this period, the Conservative government, beginning with the "conciliation" speeches of Baldwin, will reveal that it is called upon, after all, to conserve all the contradictions and disabilities of postwar England. On the subject of the most menacing of these distempers, chronic unemployment, the Conservative Party itself has no illusions. There can be no hope of any serious improvement in exports. The competition of America and Japan is growing; German industry is reviving. France is exporting with the aid of its declining currency. Baldwin declares that statesmen cannot provide any alleviation for industry, which must find its own remedy within itself. New efforts to reestablish the gold currency mean new sacrifices on the part of the population, and consequently also of industry, thus bringing about a further growth of discontent and unrest. The radicalism of the English working class is rapidly advancing.

All this prepares for the Labour Party's coming to power. But we have every reason to fear, or rather to hope, that this process will provide much dissatisfaction not only to Baldwin but also to MacDonald. We may expect, above all, increased industrial conflicts, and with them a greater pressure exerted by the working masses on their parliamentary representation. But neither can be to the taste of such leaders as applaud the conciliation speeches of Baldwin and express their sorrow at Curzon's death. The internal life of the parliamentary fraction, as well as its position in Parliament, will thus be made harder and harder.

On the other hand, there can be no doubt that the capitalist tiger will soon cease purring about gradual changes and will start to show its claws. Will MacDonald, under these conditions, succeed in preserving his leadership until the new elections? In other words, may we expect a shifting of the party leadership to the left, right away, during the party's opposition stage? This question, of course, is not a decisive one, and the answer to it may only be in the nature of a conjecture. At any rate, we can and should expect a further sharpening of the relations between the right and the so-called left wing of the Labour Party and—much more important—a strengthening of the revolutionary tendencies in the masses.

The possessing classes are beginning to follow everything that goes on in the ranks of the working class with increasing uneasiness, and are preparing for the elections long in advance. The election campaign should under these conditions show considerable tension. The last elections, featuring a forged document, raised as an emblem by the campaign managers and circulated throughout the bourgeois press and at all meetings, was only a feeble harbinger of the coming elections.

One of three things is possible as a result of the elections, unless we assume that the latter will immediately bring about civil war (which, generally speaking, is by no means impossible): either the Conservatives will again be returned to power, with a considerably curtailed majority; or neither of the parties will have an absolute majority, and we shall have a repetition of the parliamentary condition of last year, but under political circumstances far less favorable for the conciliation tendency; or finally, the Labour Party may have an absolute majority.

In the case of a new victory of the Conservatives, the restlessness and indignation of the workers will inevitably be increased. The question of the mechanism of elections, with their crooked allotment of election districts, must at once be faced in all its nakedness. The demand of a new, more democratic parliament will resound in greater strength. For a time, this may retard to a certain extent the internal struggle in the Labour Party, but it will create more favorable conditions for the revolutionary elements.

Will the Conservatives make peaceful concessions in this

question which may involve their very existence? It is hardly probable. On the contrary, if the question of power is sharply raised, the Conservatives will attempt to split the workers by utilizing the Thomases on top and those trade unionists who refuse to pay the political contributions at the bottom. It is not at all impossible that the Conservative government may even attempt to bring about isolated clashes, in order to put them down by force, frighten the leaders of the Labour Party, the Liberal philistines, and thus force back the movement.

Can this plan succeed? That also is not impossible. By leading the Labour Party with their eyes closed, without any breadth of view, without any understanding of social reality, these leaders make it easier for the Conservatives to deliver a blow to the movement at its next and higher stage. Such an event would involve a temporary more or less serious defeat of the laboring class, but would of course not have anything in common with parliamentary methods as they are depicted by the "conciliators." On the contrary, such a defeat would prepare for a renewal of the class struggle at the next stage, in more decisive revolutionary forms, and consequently under a new leadership.

If neither of the parties should have a majority after the next elections, Parliament would fall into a state of prostration. A repetition of the Labour-Liberal coalition could hardly take place after their recent experience, and furthermore, under circumstances of new, more bitter interclass and interparty relations. A Conservative-Liberal government seems more probable, but this would in its essentials resemble the above-discussed variant of a Conservative majority. And, if it should be impossible to attain agreement, the only parliamentary solution would be a revision of the electoral system. The question of the election districts, of by-elections, etc., would be an immediate subject of contention in the fight for power of the two principal parties. Would Parliament be capable, divided between parties of which none can obtain power, of passing a new electoral law? It is more than doubtful. At any rate, immense pressure would be needed from below. The weakness of Parliament without a sure majority would afford favorable occasion for such pressure. But here again we are faced with revolutionary possibilities.

However, this temporary situation has no importance for us as such, for it is evident that the unstable condition of Parliament must sooner or later be succeeded by a shift in one direction or the other, either a Conservative or a Labour government. We have already considered the former case. The latter also is very interesting from our point of view. The question, consequently, stands as follows: May we assume that the Labour Party, having secured an absolute parliamentary majority in the elections, and having set up its government, will enforce by peaceful measures a nationalization of the most important branches of production, and develop socialist construction within the framework and the methods of the present parliamentary system?

In order not to render this question too complicated, let us assume that the Liberal-conciliation alignment of MacDonald will still retain the official leadership of the party in its hands at the next elections, with the result that the victory of the workers will lead to the creation of a MacDonald government. This government will, of course, not be a mere repetition of the former MacDonald government: in the first place, because we are assuming it to have behind it an independent majority; in the second place, the interparty relations will inevitably become more strained in the impending period, particularly in the case of a Labour Party victory. At present, the Conservatives, having a solid majority in their hands, are inclined to treat MacDonald, Thomas, and Company with a certain patronizing condescension. But since the Conservatives are made of sterner stuff than the pseudosocialists, they will immediately show their teeth and their claws when left in the minority. We may therefore not doubt that if the Conservatives cannot in one way or other—parliamentary or otherwise—prevent the creation of an independent government by the Labour Party—and this would perhaps be more favorable from the point of view of the peaceful development of the situation—the Conservatives left in the minority will do everything in their power to sabotage all the measures of the Labour government with the aid of the officialdom, the courts, the armed forces, the House of Lords, and the nobility.

The Conservatives, as well as the remnants of the Liberals, will be faced with the task of compromising at any cost the first independent government of the working class. For this is a life-and-death struggle. We shall no longer be dealing with the old fight between the Liberals and the Conservatives, the differences between them remaining in the "family" of the possessing classes. Any reasonable, serious reforms by the Labour government in the domain of taxation, nationalization, and true democratization of administration, would cause an immense outburst of enthusiasm on the part of the working masses, and since appetite increases with eating, successful *moderate* reforms would inevitably serve as a stimulus for more *radical* reforms.

In other words, each additional day would lessen the Conservatives' possibility of returning to power. The Conservatives could not fail to be fully aware of the fact that they are not facing an ordinary change of government, but the beginnings of the socialist revolution by parliamentary methods. The resources of government obstruction, of legislative and administrative sabotage, in the hands of the possessing classes are very large, for regardless of the parliamentary majority, the entire governing apparatus from top to bottom is indissolubly bound up with the bourgeoisie. The latter owns the entire press, the most important organs of local government, the universities, the schools, the churches, countless clubs, and voluntary associations in general. In its hands are the banks and the entire system of national credit—the mechanism of transportation and trade—with the result that the daily food supply of London, including that of the Labour government, will depend on the great capitalist organizations. It is self-evident that all these gigantic instruments will be set in motion with furious energy in order to block the activity of the Labour government, paralyze its strength, frighten it, introduce dissension in its parliamentary majority, in short, to bring about a financial panic, interruptions in the food supply, lockouts, to terrorize the upper ranks of the workers' organizations, and cripple the proletariat. Only the most complete idiot could fail to understand that the bourgeoisie will move heaven, earth, and hell itself if a workers' government should really come to power.

The so-called English fascism of the present day has thus far been of interest only as a curiosity, but this curiosity is nevertheless quite symptomatic. The Conservatives are today too firmly in the saddle to need the aid of the fascists, but an aggravation of the interparty conditions, a growth of the firmness and aggressiveness of the working masses and the prospects of a victory of the Labour Party will inevitably call forth a growth of the fascist tendencies in the Conservative right wing. In a country that has been getting poorer year by year, its petty and middle bourgeoisie becoming gradually impoverished, with chronic unemployment, there will be no lack of elements for the creation of fascist bands.

We therefore cannot doubt that by the time the Labour Party obtains victory in the elections, the Conservatives will have behind them not only the official government apparatus, but also the unofficial bands of fascists. They will begin their work of provocation and blood-letting before the Parliament has a chance to hear the reading of the first bill for nationalizing the coal mines. What can the workers' government then do? Either capitulate shamefully or offer resistance. The latter decision is not entirely a simple matter. The experience of Ireland has shown that to be able to offer resistance, it is necessary to have real material strength and a strong governmental apparatus. The Labour government will have neither. The police, the courts, the army, the militia, will be on the side of the disorganizers, the saboteurs, the fascists. It will be necessary to break down the bureaucratic apparatus, substituting Labour Party members for the reactionaries. There is no other way. But it is perfectly obvious that such sharp government measures, though they be entirely "legal," will extraordinarily aggravate the legal and illegal opposition of the united bourgeois reaction. In other words, this is the path to civil war.

But perhaps the Labour Party, once it is in power, will approach its task so cautiously, so tactfully, so ingeniously, that the bourgeoisie—how shall we put it?—will not feel the necessity of offering any active resistance? Of course, such a supposition is ludicrous; yet we must not forget that precisely this is the fundamental hope of MacDonald and his friends. When the present pseudoleader of the Independents says that the Labour Party will introduce only such reforms as are "scientifically" proved to be possible (we know MacDonald's "science"), he means that the Labour government will look questioningly into the eyes of the bourgeoisie before it takes any step in reform. Of course, if everything depended on the goodwill of MacDonald and his "scientifically" founded reforms, things would never come to the pass of civil war, for the bourgeoisie would have no reason for resorting to such action. If the second MacDonald government should be like the first, we should have no reason for taking up the question of bringing about socialism by a parliamentary method, for the budget of the City has nothing in common with the budget of socialism.

However, the policy of the Labour government, even if it should retain its present membership, would suffer some changes. It would be absurd to imagine that the powerful surge of labor, capable of lifting MacDonald into power, would at once recede respectfully after this accomplishment. No, the demands of the working class would grow enormously, for it would no longer feel that it depended on Liberal votes. The opposition of the Conservatives, the House of Lords, the bureaucracy, the monarchy, would redouble the energy, the impatience, the spirit of the workers. The calumnies and intrigues of the capitalist press would drive them on. Even the most unfaltering energy displayed by their own government under these conditions will seem insufficient. But to expect MacDonald, Clynes,[63] and Snowden to display revolutionary energy is as reasonable as to expect fragrance from rotten mangold roots. Between the revolutionary onslaught of the masses and the fierce opposition of the bourgeoisie, the MacDonald government will be thrown from side to side, antagonizing some elements, failing to satisfy others, angering the bourgeoisie with their half measures, redoubling the revolutionary discontent of the workers, kindling civil war and making every effort, at the same time, to deprive it of the necessary leadership on the proletarian side.

Meanwhile, the revolutionary wing will inevitably become strengthened and more farsighted; resolute and revolutionary elements of the working class will come to the top. On this path, the MacDonald government sooner or later, owing to the alignment of power outside of Parliament, will have to yield place either to a Conservative government, with fascist and not with conciliation tendencies, or to a revolutionary government truly capable of putting the thing through. In either case, a new outburst of civil war, a sharp clash between the classes, is inevitable all along the line. In the case of a victory of the Conservatives, there will be merciless destruction of the workers' organizations; in the case of a victory of the proletariat, the opposition of the exploiters will be crushed by measures of revolutionary dictatorship.

You do not like this, gentlemen? What can we do about it? The fundamental springs of action are as little dependent on us as on you. We are "decreeing" nothing; we are merely analyzing the situation.

Among the "left" half-supporters, half-opponents of Mac-Donald, who, like MacDonald, stand on a democratic basis, there are some who will probably say: of course, if the bourgeois classes attempt to offer resistance to the democratically elected Labour government, the latter will not recoil from methods of the harshest compulsion, but this will not be a class dictatorship, but the force of the democratic state which . . . etc., etc.

There is no use pursuing the argument on this plane. To imagine, indeed, that the destinies of society may be determined by the election to Parliament of either three hundred and seven Labour delegates, i.e., a minority, or three hundred and eight, i.e., a majority, and not by the actual alignment of power at the moment of the stern collision of classes fighting for their existence, would be equivalent to a complete surrender to the fetishism of parliamentary arithmetic.

But—we ask—suppose the Conservatives, faced with a growing revolutionary audacity and with the danger of a Labour government, should not only refuse to democratize the election system, but on the contrary, should introduce further limitations of it? "Not very probable!" reply those simpleminded folk who do not know that in matters of life and death *anything* is probable.

In England there is already a tremendous preliminary scurry with regard to the reorganization and strengthening of the House of Lords. In this connection, MacDonald recently said that he could understand the concern felt by certain Conservative Lords, but he "could not understand why the Liberals should work in the same direction." The sage does not grasp why the Liberals are strengthening a second line of trenches against the advance of the working class! He does not understand this because he is himself a Liberal, but of the highly provincial, petty, narrow-minded type. He does not understand that the bourgeoisie means business, that it is preparing for mortal combat, that the Crown and the House of Lords will play a prominent part in this combat. If they are successful in reducing the rights of the House of Commons, i.e., in putting through a legal coup d'etat, the Conservatives, in spite of all the difficulties attending this enterprise, will be in a far more favorable position than if they were obliged to organize opposition against a successful Labour government in process of consolidation.

"Well, in that case, of course," some "left" bigmouth might exclaim, "we shall call upon the masses to offer resistance." You mean revolutionary violence? We must infer, therefore, that revolutionary force is not only admissible but even inevitable in case the Conservatives accomplish a preventive government coup d'etat, by *legal parliamentary methods*. Would it not be a plainer way of putting it to say that revolutionary force is useful whenever and wherever it strengthens the position of the proletariat, weakens or repels the enemy, accelerates the socialist evolution of society?

However, heroic promises to hurl thunderbolts of resistance if the Conservatives should "dare," etc., are not worth a single bad penny. It is futile to lull the masses to sleep from day to day with prattling about peaceful, painless, parliamentary, democratic transitions to socialism and then, at the first serious punch delivered at one's nose, to call upon the masses for armed resistance. This is the best method for facilitating the destruction of the proletariat by the powers of reaction. In order to be capable of offering revolutionary resistance, the masses must be prepared for such action mentally, materially, and by organization. They must understand the inevitability of a more and more savage class struggle, and its transformation, at a certain stage, into civil war. The political education of the working class and the selection of the leading members must be in accordance with this understanding. The illusion of conciliation must be fought from day to day, all-out war must be declared against MacDonaldism. That is the present state of the question.

Disregarding concrete conditions, for the moment, it can be said that MacDonald did in the past have an opportunity to facilitate considerably the transition to socialism, and to reduce to a minimum the upheavals of civil war. This was on the occasion of the Labour Party's first accession to power. If MacDonald had confronted Parliament at once with a resolute program (liquidation of the monarchy and House of Lords, a high capital levy, nationalization of the most important instruments of production, etc.) and after having dissolved Parliament, had appealed to the country with revolutionary courage, he might have hoped to catch the possessing classes, to a certain extent, unawares, before they could gather their strength, to crush them under the onslaught of the working masses, to conquer and reconstruct the government apparatus before British fascism could succeed in organizing itself, and thus to bring about the revolution through the portals of Parliament, "legalize it," and lead it to victory with a firm hand.

But it is perfectly clear that such a possibility is merely theoretical. For such a purpose, you would need a different party with different leaders, and this would in turn presuppose entirely different circumstances. If we set up this theoretical possibility in the case of the past, it is only in order to show the more clearly its impossibility in the future. The first experience of a Labour government, in all its cowardly emptiness, was nevertheless an important historical warning to the governing classes. It is hopeless to take them unawares, they are now following everything that goes on among the workers with much greater farsightedness. "Under no circumstances will we shoot first," the most humane, pious, and Christian Baldwin declared most unexpectedly in his parliamentary speech of March 5. And a few donkeys on the Labour benches actually applauded these words. Baldwin does not doubt for a moment that there will be shooting, but wishes only to shift the responsibility for the impending civil war in advance—at least in the eyes of the intermediate classes—to the shoulders of the enemy, i.e., the workers. This is precisely the method used by the diplomacy of each country when war is impending; each country attempts to transfer the guilt to the opposite side.

Of course, the party of the proletariat is also interested in throwing the responsibility for civil war on the capitalist leaders, and in the last analysis, the Labour Party has and will have much more political and moral justification for this procedure. We may assume that the assault of the Conservatives on the House of Commons would be one of the "favorable" motives for agitation, but this is after all a matter of third or fifth importance. We are here not considering the question of the methods preceding revolutionary conflicts, but that of the methods of seizing the government with the object of securing a transition to socialism. Parliament will in no way assure a peaceful transition: the revolutionary force of the class will be necessary and inevitable. We must expect and prepare for this situation. The masses must be trained and tempered for revolutionary action. The first condition for such training is an uncompromising struggle with the corrupting spirit of MacDonaldism.

On March 25, 1925, a committee of the House of Lords solemnly proclaimed that the title of Duke of Somerset should pass to a certain Mr. Seymour, who thus obtains the right to legislate in the House of Lords, which decision had depended on the solution of another parliamentary question: when in 1787, a certain Colonel Seymour married, in order to give Great Britain a new lord after the lapse of several generations, was his wife's first husband still living, or had the latter died in Calcutta?

This question, it appears, was of very great importance for the destinies of English democracy. In the same issue of the *Daily Herald* which reports this instructive episode in the life of the first husband of the ancestress of legislator Seymour, the editors defend themselves against the accusation of desiring to introduce a soviet system in England; no, by no means; we are only for trade with the Soviets, not at all for a soviet system in England.

And what could be so very bad, we ask, about the application of the soviet order to English technology and English industry, to the cultural habits of the English working class? Let the *Daily Herald* consider the consequences of the introduction of a soviet system in Great Britain.

In the first place, the royal power would be abolished, and Mrs. Snowden would be relieved of the necessity of bemoaning the superhuman exertions put upon the members of the royal family. In the second place, the House of Lords would be abolished, together with Mr. Seymour, now obliged to legislate by virtue of a mandate given him by the timely death of the first husband of his great-grandmother in Calcutta. In the third place, the present Parliament would be liquidated, concerning whose dishonesty and impotence even the *Daily Herald* reports every day. The agrarian parasitism of the landlords would be destroyed forever. The basic branches of industry would pass into the hands of the working class, which constitutes in England an overwhelming majority of the population. The powerful apparatus of the Conservative and Liberal newspapers and publishing houses could be utilized for the education of the working class. "Give me a dictatorship over Fleet Street [London's newspaper row] for a single month, and I shall destroy the hypnosis!" cried Robert Williams in 1920. Williams himself has since changed, but Fleet Street is still waiting for its proletarian master. . . .[64]

The workers would elect their representatives not on the basis of the dishonest election districts into which England is at present divided, but in their works and factories. The soviets of workers' deputies would renew the governing apparatus from top to bottom. Privileges of birth and wealth would disappear, together with the false democracy based on the banks. A true workers' democracy would rule, combining the government of industry with the political administration of the country. Such a government, for the first time in the history of England, truly based on the people, would establish free, equal, and fraternal relations with India, Egypt, and other colonies. It would immediately conclude a powerful political and military alliance with workers' and peasants' Russia. Such an alliance would be designed for many years to come. The economic plans of the two countries would be adjusted to each other, in their corresponding divisions, a number of years at a time. The exchange of resources, products, and services between these two countries, each supplementing the other, would raise to an unprecedented height the material and mental well-being of the toiling masses of both countries.

That would not be so bad, would it? Why, therefore, defend oneself against the accusation of a desire to introduce the soviet order in England? By terrorizing the social opinion of the workers, the bourgeoisie wishes to inspire them with a wholesome fear of any attack on the present British system, and the Labour press instead of mercilessly unmasking this policy of reactionary hypnosis is basely adapting itself to the latter and thus supporting it. This also is MacDonaldism.

The English as well as the continental opportunists have more than once said that the Bolsheviks arrived at their dictatorship only by the logic of their position and in spite of all their principles. In this connection, it would be extremely instructive to trace the evolution of Marxian thought, as well as of revolutionary thought in general, on the question of democracy. We shall content ourselves here with two cursory quotations. As early as 1887, Lafargue, Marx's closest disciple and related to Marx by close personal ties,[65] outlined the general course of revolution in France in the following broad strokes:

> The working class will rule in the industrial cities which will all become revolutionary centers and will form a federation in order to win over the villages to the side of the revolution and put down the resistance that may be organized in such trading and seaport cities as Havre, Bordeaux, Marseilles. In the industrial cities, the socialists must seize power in the local institutions, arm the workers, and organize them in a military way; he who has the rifle also has the bread, said Blanqui.[66] They will open the doors of the jails, in order to release the petty thieves, and will put under lock and key such great thieves as bankers, capitalists, great industrialists, large property-holders, etc. Nothing will be done to these men, but they will be considered as hostages, responsible for the good conduct of their class. The revolutionary power is built up by the method of simple seizure and only when the new power is in full control of the situation will the socialists turn for a consolidation of their activities to the suffrage which is called universal. The bourgeoisie hesitated so long to admit the indigent classes to the ballot box that they should not be too much surprised to find all the former capitalists deprived of the suffrage right until such moment as the revolutionary party is assured of its victory. [Paul Lafargue, *Complete Works*, Vol. I, Russian edition, p. 330]

The destinies of the revolution are not decided for Lafargue by appealing to any constituent assembly, but by the revolutionary organization of the masses in the process of their struggle with the enemy.

> When the local revolutionary institutions have been established, they must organize, by the method of delegation or otherwise, a central power, upon which will be imposed the obligation to take general measures in the interest of the revolution and to prevent the formation of a reactionary party. [Lafargue, loc. cit.]

Of course, we do not find in these few lines any fully formulated characterization of the soviet system, for the latter is not at all an a priori principle, but a deduction from revolutionary experience. Yet the construction of a central revolutionary power by the method of sending delegates from the local revolutionary organs which are engaged in the struggle with reaction is a close approximation of the idea of the soviet system. And at any rate, as far as formal democracy is concerned, Lafargue's attitude on this subject is indicated with remarkable clearness. The working class may only attain power by the path of revolutionary *seizure*. "The suffrage which is called universal," Lafargue ironically remarks, "may be introduced only after the proletariat is in control of the apparatus of the state." But even then, the bourgeoisie is to be deprived of the suffrage right, and the great capitalists are to be reduced to the status of hostages.

Anyone even slightly aware of the character of the relations between Lafargue and Marx will be fully convinced that Lafargue developed his opinions on the dictatorship of the proletariat on the basis of many conversations with Karl Marx. If Marx himself did not dwell exhaustively on the expounding on these questions, it is probably only for the reason that the character of the revolutionary dictatorship of the class appeared self-evident to him. At any rate, Marx's own words on this subject, not only in 1848–49, but also in

1871 on the occasion of the Paris Commune,[67] do not leave any doubt as to the fact that Lafargue is merely developing Marx's thought on the subject.

However, Lafargue is not alone in favoring a class dictatorship in opposition to democracy. This idea was advanced with considerable fullness as long ago as the time of Chartism. In the periodical *The Poor Man's Guardian,* in connection with a proposed extension of the suffrage right, the following "sole true reform" was advanced: "It is but common justice that the people who make the goods should have the sole privilege of making the laws" (quoted in Max Beer's *History of British Socialism,* Vol. I, p. 307). The significance of Chartism is precisely in the fact that all the subsequent history of the class struggle is recapitulated concisely in the decade of its history. After this time, the movement in many ways lay dormant. It extended its base and acquired new experience. On its new and higher basis, it will inevitably return to many of the ideas and methods of Chartism.

Two traditions: the Great Rebellion and Chartism

The editor of the *Daily Herald* not long ago expressed his doubts as to whether Oliver Cromwell might be called the "pioneer of the labor movement." One of the newspaper's writers supporting the editor's doubts mentions the harsh lesson given by Cromwell to the Levellers.[68] These thoughts and questions are extremely characteristic of the historical learning of the leaders of the Labour Party. We need not waste a single word to prove that Oliver Cromwell was the pioneer of *bourgeois* society and not of *socialist* society. This great revolutionary bourgeois was opposed to the universal suffrage right, for he saw in it a danger to private property. From this the Webbs literally conclude the "incompatibility" of democracy with capitalism, closing their eyes to the fact that capitalism later learned how to get along well with democracy and to manage the instrument of the universal suffrage right as well as the instrument of its stock exchange.* Nonetheless, the English

---

* It is amusing to note that two centuries later, in 1842, the historian

workers may learn incomparably more from Cromwell than from MacDonald, Snowden, the Webbs, and the rest of the conciliation brethren. Cromwell was the great revolutionist of his time, who learned *to hesitate at nothing* to defend the interests of the new bourgeois social order against the old aristocratic order. This must be learned from Cromwell; in this sense, the dead lion of the seventeenth century stands infinitely higher than many dogs still alive.

Following those contemporary anything-but-lions who write editorials for the *Manchester Guardian* and other Liberal papers, the leaders of the Labour Party customarily contrast democracy with all despotic governments, such as the "dictatorship of Lenin" or the "dictatorship of Mussolini."[69] The historical ignorance of these gentlemen is nowhere expressed more clearly than in this juxtaposition. Not because we are inclined to deny that the "dictatorship of Lenin" did exist; in actual fact, Lenin's power over the entire course of events of a great state was unique.

But can we really speak of a dictatorship without considering its social-historical content? History records the dictatorship of Cromwell, the dictatorship of Robespierre, the dictatorship of Arakcheyev, the dictatorship of Napoleon I, the dictatorship of Mussolini.[70] A fool might consider the dictatorship of Robespierre and of Arakcheyev to be of the same type; we shall not argue with such a man. Various classes, in various situations, and for various purposes, find themselves obliged, in certain extremely critical and responsible periods of their history, to assign exclusive power and authority to such of their leaders as most clearly and fully advocate their fundamental interests in the given epoch. In speaking of dictatorship, we must first make clear what interests, of what particular classes, are historically expressed

---

Macaulay, then a member of Parliament, protested against the general right of suffrage on precisely the grounds advanced by Cromwell.—L.T.

in this dictatorship. Oliver Cromwell for one epoch, Robespierre for another, expressed the historically progressive tendencies in the evolution of bourgeois society. William Pitt, also quite close to the practice of personal dictatorship, defended the interests of the monarchy, of the privileged classes, of the upper bourgeois circles, against the revolution of the petty bourgeoisie, which found its highest expression in the dictatorship of Robespierre.

The Liberal churls usually declare that they are opposed to dictatorship from the left as well as to dictatorship from the right, although in actual practice they rarely neglect an opportunity to support a dictatorship from the right. For us, the question is decided by the fact that one dictatorship pushes society forward while another holds it back. The dictatorship of Mussolini is the dictatorship of the prematurely decaying, impotent, diseased Italian bourgeoisie: it is a dictatorship with a broken nose. The "dictatorship of Lenin" expressed the powerful onward sweep of a new historical class and its superhuman struggle with all the forces of the old society. If Lenin must be compared with anyone, it is surely not with Bonaparte, and still less with Mussolini, but with Cromwell and Robespierre. We may say with a certain justification that Lenin is the proletarian Cromwell of the twentieth century. This comparison will serve as the best possible apology for the petty-bourgeois Cromwell of the seventeenth century.

The French bourgeoisie, distorting the Great Revolution, adopted it and, having reduced it to petty coin, put it into general circulation. The English bourgeoisie has erased even the memory of the revolution of the seventeenth century, and recasts its entire past in the form of "gradual changes." The vanguard of the English workers should discover the British Revolution and should find in it, under its ecclesiastical garment, the powerful conflict of social forces. Cromwell was by no means a "pioneer of labor," but in the drama of the seventeenth century, the English proletariat may find great precedents for revolutionary action. This tradition, which is also "national," is fully justifiable and fully in place in the arsenal of the working class.

The proletariat also has another great tradition in the Chartist movement. An acquaintance with these two epochs is indispensable to every class-conscious English worker. An explanation of the historical thought of the seventeenth century and of the revolutionary content of Chartism is one of the most important tasks devolving upon English Marxists.

A study of the revolutionary epoch in the history of England, which extends, let us say, from the compulsory convocation of Parliament by Charles Stuart to the death of Oliver Cromwell, is particularly necessary for the purpose of acquiring an understanding of the place of parliamentarism and of "law" in general, in living—not imaginary—history. The great "national" historian Macaulay distorts the social drama of the seventeenth century by veiling the internal conflict by means of commonplaces, sometimes interesting, always superficial. The French conservative Guizot goes deeper into these events. In any case, no matter whose exposition we may accept, any man who is able to see under the cloak of history the living real bodies, classes, factions, will be convinced precisely by the experience of the English Revolution of the extremely subsidiary, subordinate, conditional role played by law in the mechanism of the social struggle, particularly in a revolutionary epoch, i.e., when *basic* interests of *basic* classes of society come into the foreground.

In the 1640s in England, we find Parliament based on a grotesque election law, and yet considering itself the representative of the people. The lower house represented the nation, the bourgeoisie, and therefore also the national wealth. In the reign of Charles I, it was ascertained, not without astonishment, that the House of Commons was three times as rich as the House of Lords. The king now dissolves the Parliament and then summons it to assemble anew under the pressure of financial necessity. Parliament creates an army for its defense. The army gradually concentrates within it all the most active, valiant, resolute elements. Just because of this fact, Parliament capitulates to the army. We repeat: *just because of this fact*. By this we mean that Parliament capitulates not merely to armed force (it did not surrender to the king's army), but to the Puritan army of Cromwell, which voiced the demands of revolution more boldly, more resolutely, more consistently, than did Parliament.

The adherents of the Episcopalian, or Anglican (half-Catholic) Church, were the party of the court, the nobility, and of course the higher clergy. The Presbyterians were the party of the bourgeoisie, the party of wealth and education. The Independents and the Puritans in general were the party of the petty bourgeoisie, and the petty independent land-owners. The Levellers were the incipient party of the left wing of the petty bourgeoisie, the plebs. Under the integument of ecclesiastical disputes, under the form of a struggle for the religious structure of the Church, there proceeded a social self-determination of classes, a regrouping of classes on new, bourgeois foundations. In politics, the Presbyterian party stood for a limited monarchy, the Independents, also sometimes called "root and branch men," or—in the language of our day—"radicals," were for a republic. The lukewarm nature of the Presbyterians was fully in accord with the contradictory interests of the bourgeoisie, vacillating between the nobility and the plebs. The party of the Independents, which had dared to carry its ideas and slogans to their logical conclusion, naturally supplanted the Presbyterians in the towns and villages which were the centers of the awakened petty-bourgeois masses, who had become the most important force of the revolution.

The course of events evolved empirically. Fighting for

power and for property interests, both sides were hiding under the cloak of legality. Guizot presents this situation rather neatly:

> Then commenced between the Parliament and the king [Charles I] a conflict previously unexampled in Europe. . . . Negotiations were still continued, but neither party expected any result from them, or even had any intention to treat. It was no longer to one another that they addressed their declarations and messages; both appealed to the whole nation, to public opinion; to this new power both seemed to look for strength and success. The origin and extent of the royal authority, the privileges of the Houses of Parliament, the limits of the fidelity due from subjects, the militia, the petitions for the redress of grievances, and the distribution of public employments became the subjects of an official controversy, in which the general principles of social order, the various nature of governments, the primitive rights of liberty, the history, laws, and customs of England were alternately quoted, explained, and commented upon. In the interval between the disputes of the two parties in Parliament and their armed encounter on the field of battle, reason and learning interposed, as it were, for several months, to suspend the course of events and to put forth their ablest efforts to obtain the free concurrence of the people. . . . When the time came for drawing the sword, all were astonished and deeply moved. . . . Now, however, both parties mutually accused each other of illegality and innovation, and both were justified in making the charge; for the one had violated the ancient rights of the country and had not abjured the maxims of tyranny; and the other demanded, in the name of principles still confused and chaotic, liberties and a power which had until then been unknown. [Guizot, *History of Charles*

I and the English Revolution, revised edition, translated
by Andrew R. Scoble, Vol. I, pp. 356–58]

As the civil war came nearer and nearer, the more active
royalists deserted the Westminster House of Commons and
the House of Lords, and escaped to York to Charles's headquarters: the Parliament was split, as in all great revolutionary epochs. Whether the "legal" majority in one case or another happens to be on the side of revolution or of reaction,
it is not a decisive element in such situations.

At the decisive moment, the political history of the destinies of "democracy" depended not on Parliament, but—
what a frightful thought for the scrofulous pacifists!—on
the cavalry. In the first period of the struggle, the royalist
cavalry, the most significant arm of the service in those days,
put the fear of the Lord into the parliamentary horsemen. It
is of interest to note that we find similar situations in later
revolutions, particularly in the Civil War in the United States
of America, where the Southern cavalry in the first stages
was indisputably superior to the Northern horse, and finally,
in our revolution, in whose early stages the White Guard
cavalrymen inflicted a number of hard blows upon us before
our workers learned to sit firmly in the saddle.

By reason of its origin, cavalry is the most aristocratic
branch of the army. The royalist cavalry was therefore more
close-knit and resolute than the parliamentary horsemen
who had been gathered hastily and at random. The cavalry
of the Confederate states was, so to speak, the native arm
of the Southern planter troops, while the trade-industrial
North had to learn to ride a horse. Finally, in our country,
the natural training-ground for the cavalry was the southeastern plains, the Cossack Vendee.[71] Cromwell very quickly
learned that the destinies of his class were being decided by
horsemen. He said to Hampden:[72] "I will raise such men as
have the fear of God before them, and make some conscience

of what they do; and I warrant you they will not be beaten"
(Ibid., Vol. II, p. 36).

The words addressed by Cromwell to the free landhold-
ers and artisans picked by him are very interesting: "I will
not cozen you by perplexed expressions in my commission
about fighting for King and Parliament. If the King chanced
to be in the body of the enemy, I would as soon discharge
my pistol upon him as upon any private man; and if your
conscience will not let you do the like, I advise you not to
enlist yourselves under me" (Ibid., Vol. II, p. 37). In this
manner, Cromwell constructed not only the army, but also
a party; his army was to a great extent an armed party,
and precisely this element gave it its strength. In 1644, the
"holy" battalions of Cromwell were already winning splendid victories over the royalist horsemen, earning for themselves the name "Ironsides." Revolutions are always in need
of "Ironsides." The English workers may learn much from
Cromwell in this connection.

The remarks made by the historian Macaulay on the army
of the Puritans are not without interest:

A force thus composed might, without injury to its
efficiency be indulged in some liberties which, if allowed
to any other troops, would have proved subversive of all
discipline. In general, soldiers who should form themselves
into political clubs, elect delegates, and pass resolutions on
high questions of state, would soon break loose from all
control, would cease to form an army, and would become
the worst and most dangerous of mobs. Nor would it be
safe, in our time, to tolerate in any regiment religious
meetings, at which a corporal versed in scripture should
lead the devotions of his less gifted colonel, and admon-
ish a backsliding major. But such was the intelligence, the
gravity, and the self-command of the warriors whom
Cromwell had trained, that in their camp a political orga-

nization and a religious organization could exist without destroying military organization. The same men who, off duty, were noted as demagogues* and field-preachers, were distinguished by steadiness, by the spirit of order, and by prompt obedience on watch, on drill, and on the field of battle. . . . In his camp alone the most rigid discipline was found in company with the fiercest enthusiasm. His troops moved to victory with the precision of machines, while burning with the wildest fanaticism of Crusaders" (Macaulay, *History of England*, New York, Harper and Brothers, Vol. I, p. 120).

All historical analogies must be drawn with the greatest possible care, particularly when we are comparing the seventeenth and twentieth centuries; nonetheless, there is no harm in pointing out a few of the obvious traits of resemblance in the mode of life and character of the army of Cromwell and the Red Army. To be sure, in the former case everything was based on the belief in predestination and on a harsh religious morality; here, in our country, we are animated by a militant atheism. But under the religious mantle of Puritanism, there proceeded a preaching of the historical meaning of the new class and the doctrine of predestination was the religious prelude to historical causality.

Cromwell's warriors felt themselves to be in the first place Puritans, in the second place soldiers, as our warriors feel themselves to be in the first place revolutionists and communists and in the second place soldiers. But the traits of difference are even greater than those of similarity.

The Red Army, created by the party of the proletariat, is the latter's armed organ. Cromwell's army, embracing his party within it, was itself a decisive force; we have seen how

---

* Macaulay means revolutionary agitators.—L.T.

the Puritan army begins to adapt Parliament to itself and to revolution. The army succeeds in excluding from Parliament eleven Presbyterians, i.e., representatives of the right wing. The Presbyterians, the Girondists[73] of the English Revolution, try to raise an insurrection against the English Parliament. The truncated Parliament seeks safety with the army and thus subordinates itself still more to the latter; under the pressure of the army, particularly of its left, more resolute wing, Cromwell is obliged to execute Charles I. The axe of the revolution is curiously wreathed with psalms; but the axe is more convincing. Then Cromwell's Colonel Pride surrounds the Parliament building and drives forth eighty-one Presbyterian members by force. Only the rump of Parliament is left. It consists of Independents, i.e., those sympathizing with Cromwell and his army; but for this very reason, Parliament, having inaugurated an immense struggle with the monarchy, at the moment of success ceases to be the source of any independent thought and power.

The focus of both is on Cromwell alone, whose strength is in the army directly; but in the last analysis, his decisive strength is drawn from his bold solution of the fundamental problems of revolution. A fool, an ignoramus, or a Fabian may see in Cromwell *only* the personal dictator. As a matter of fact, we here find, under conditions of profound social upheaval, that the dictatorship of a class assumes the form of personal dictatorship, which alone is capable of freeing the kernel of the nation out of the ancient impediments. The English social crisis in the seventeenth century unites within it the traits of the German Reformation of the sixteenth century and those of the French Revolution of the eighteenth century. In the person of Cromwell, Luther clasps hands with Robespierre.[74]

The Puritans were not averse to calling their enemies philistines, but the actual matter at issue was the class struggle. Cromwell's task was to inflict as many crushing blows as possible on the absolute monarchy, the court dignitaries, and the half-Catholic Church, which had been reduced to serve the needs of the monarch and the dignitaries. For such a blow Cromwell, the true representative of the new class, was in need of the strength and passion of the masses of the people. Under his leadership, the revolution acquires all the scope it needs. Whenever it exceeds—for instance, among the Levellers—the limits of the demands of the renovation of bourgeois society, Cromwell mercilessly berates the "madmen." After his success, Cromwell begins to construct a new state law, combining biblical texts with the pikes of the "holy" soldier; the decisive word being spoken always by the pikes.

On April 19, 1653, Cromwell threw out the remnants of the Long Parliament. Conscious of his historical mission, the Puritan dictator hurled biblical epithets at the retreating miscreants: "Thou art a drunkard," he shouted to one; "thou art an adulterer!" he reminded another. Thereupon Cromwell created a Parliament of the representatives of the God-fearing elements, i.e., essentially a class Parliament; the God-fearing people were the middle class, which, with the aid of an austere morality, had achieved the work of accumulation—and with the text of holy writ on their lips, were proceeding to appropriate the world for themselves. But even this fastidious "Barebone's Parliament"[75] hampered the dictator, depriving him of the necessary liberty of action in the difficult internal and international situation. At the end of l653, Cromwell again purifies the House of Commons with the aid of soldiers.

If the remnant of the Long Parliament, driven out in April, was inclined to lean to the right, to the side of the remnants of the Presbyterians, the "Barebone's Parliament" was inclined in certain questions to follow in too straight a line the path of Puritan virtue and thus rendered more difficult for Cromwell the achievement of a new social equilibrium. The revolutionary realist Cromwell was building a new society. Parliament was not an end in itself; law is not an end in itself; Cromwell himself and his "holy" troops considered the realization of divine commands to be the true end, but in reality the latter were merely the ideological conditions for the construction of bourgeois society. Dispersing Parliament after Parliament, Cromwell thus revealed as little reverence for the fetish of "national" representation as he revealed an insufficient respect for the monarchy by the grace of God in his execution of Charles I.

Nevertheless, it was Cromwell who paved the way for the parliamentary and democratic methods of the two succeeding centuries. In revenge for Cromwell's execution of Charles I, Charles II had Cromwell's body suspended on a gibbet. But no Restoration could reestablish the pre-Cromwellian society. The work of Cromwell could not be liquidated by the predatory legislation of the Restoration. For the pen can never eradicate that which has been written by the sword. This reversal of the popular proverb is much more correct, particularly when we speak of the axe of revolution.

As an illustration of the relation between "right" and "might" in epochs of social upheavals, the history of the Long Parliament will always be of exceptional interest. This Parliament for twenty years experienced all the vicissitudes of events: it served as a target for the impact of class forces, was driven to the right and to the left, first rose against the king, and then suffered suppression on the part of its own armed servants, was twice dispersed and twice reconstituted, it dictated and was humiliated, before it was finally enabled to pass the resolution abolishing itself.

We do not know whether the proletarian revolution will have its "long" Parliament; it is quite probable that it will content itself with a *short* Parliament. However, it will achieve this end the more surely, the better it learns the lessons of Cromwell's era.

Of the second tradition, which is purely proletarian in nature, we shall only say a few words.

The period of Chartism is immortal for the reason that in the decade of its existence it affords us an abbreviated and systematic view of practically the entire course of the proletarian struggle—from petitions to Parliament down to armed insurrection. All the fundamental questions of the class movement of the proletariat—the relations between parliamentary and extraparliamentary activities, the part played by the universal suffrage right, the trade unions and cooperatives, the importance of the general strike and its relation to armed insurrection, even the mutual relations between the proletariat and the peasantry—were not only crystallized in practice in the history of the Chartist mass movement, but found their answer in it as far as principles are concerned. Theoretically this answer is not always well-founded, the threads are not always properly united, the entire movement, as well as its theoretical expressions, present much of immaturity, of the unachieved. But the revolutionary slogans of Chartism to this day—if examined critically—are infinitely higher than the cloying eclecticism of the Mac-Donalds and the economic obtuseness of the Webbs.

If we may resort to a rather farfetched comparison, we might say that the Chartist movement may be compared with the prelude, which gives in undeveloped form the musical themes of the entire work. In this sense, the English working class can and should read in Chartism not only its past, but also its future. Just as the Chartists discarded the sentimental preachers of "moral action," having gathered the masses under the banner of revolution, so the English proletariat will be obliged to cast out from its midst the reformers, democrats, and pacifists, and rally around the flag of a revolutionary action.

Chartism failed, not because its methods were incorrect, but because it appeared too early on the scene. It served only as a historical prophecy. The revolution of 1905 also lost the battle. But its traditions were born anew after twelve years, and its methods were victorious in October 1917. Chartism is by no means disposed of. History is liquidating liberalism and preparing for the liquidation of pseudo-labor pacifism for the very purpose of recreating Chartism on new, incomparably higher historical foundations. This is the true national tradition of the English labor movement.

Trade unions and Bolshevism

The fact that it is absurd to evaluate and define the fundamental tasks of a labor movement from the formal and ultimately legal point of view of democracy, is particularly clear from the most recent history of England itself, especially from a study of the question of the political contributions of the trade unions. This question, at first glance merely a practical one, is nevertheless of immense importance in principle, and this importance is—we fear—by no means understood by the leaders of the Labour Party.

The trade unions have as their object the improvement of the working and living conditions of wage laborers. For this purpose, the members of the unions contribute certain fees. In political matters, the trade unions have been considered—at least in form—as neutral; in actual fact, they have often followed in the train of the Liberal Party. Needless to say, the Liberals, as well as the Conservatives, who sell honors of all kinds to the rich bourgeois in return for generous contributions to their party treasury, have not needed the financial aid of the trade unions, but only their votes. The situation changed as soon as the workers, through the trade unions, had created the Labour Party. Once having brought the latter to life, the trade unions were obliged to finance their party. Additional contributions were needed for this purpose from the trade union organizations of the workers.

The bourgeois parties unanimously raised a howl against this "crying violation of individual liberty." "The worker is not only a worker, but also a citizen and a man," MacDonald profoundly instructs us. "Precisely so," is the echo from Baldwin, Asquith,[76] and Lloyd George. In his quality as a citizen, the worker, whether he supports the trade unions or not, has the right to vote for any party he likes. To collect from him a compulsory contribution to the Labour Party is a violation not only of his purse, but also of his conscience. And finally, it is an outright violation of the democratic constitution which forbids any form of compulsion in the matter of support given to this party or that! As a matter of fact, these conclusions must have considerably impressed the leaders of the Labour Party, who would gladly have renounced the compulsory anti-Liberal, almost Bolshevist methods of the trade union organizations, had it not been for this cursed need of shillings and pounds, without which it is impossible to obtain a representative's mandate even in the Arcadia of democracy. And it is the sad destiny of democratic principles that shillings and pounds are the weapons that give black eyes and bloody noses. Such is the imperfection of this best of all worlds.

The history of the question of political contributions by the trade unions is already quite full of turning points and dramatic episodes, which we shall not enumerate here. Only recently, Baldwin relinquished (for the present!) the new effort on the part of his Conservative friends to forbid the collection of political contributions. The parliamentary law of 1913, still in force, which forbids the unions from collecting political contributions, gave each member of a trade union the right to refuse to pay this contribution and simultaneously forbade the trade unions to prosecute such members, drop them from their lists, etc. If we may believe the report in the *Times* (March 7, 1925), about 10 percent of all the members of the trade union organizations of the workers have taken advantage of their right to refuse to pay the political contributions. Thus the principle of individual liberty has been saved at least in part. A full victory of "liberty" would be attained only if the contributions could be collected only from those members who should declare their willingness to contribute.

At present, wherever resolutions have been passed by the unions, all the members are obliged to pay the contribution, only such being exempted as have duly declared their intentions in the proper form. In other words, the Liberal principle has been transformed from a triumphant rule to a tolerated exception. And even this partial application of the principle of personal liberty was realized—alas!—not by the will of the workers but by the compulsion brought to bear by bourgeois legislation on the organizations of the proletariat.

This condition gives rise to the question: How does it happen that the workers, who constitute the great mass of the English population, and consequently of the English democracy, are driven by the very nature of their struggle into violations of the principles of "personal liberty"; while the legislating bourgeoisie, particularly the House of Lords, appears in the role of a champion of liberty, now by categorically forbidding "compulsion" against the persons of the trade unionists (decision of the House of Lords in 1909 in the Osborne case), now by seriously limiting this "compulsion" (Act of Parliament, 1913)! The essence of the matter is, of course, in the fact that the workers' organizations, having established their anti-liberal "despotic," Bolshevik rule of compulsory collection of political contributions, are in this manner fighting for an actual, real, not merely metaphysical possibility of a parliamentary representation of labor; while the Conservatives and Liberals, who advance the principle of "personal liberty," are actually attempting to disarm the workers materially and thus to drive them over to the bourgeois parties.

It is sufficient to consider the distribution of roles: the trade unions are for the unconditional right of compulsory collection of political contributions; the House of Lords is for the unconditional prohibition of such collections, in the name of the sacred principle of personal liberty; finally, the House of Commons forces a concession from the trade unions, which amounts in fact to a rebate of 10 percent in favor of the principles of liberalism. Even a blind man can here perceive the purely class character of the principle of personal liberty which in the present concrete conditions means nothing more or less than an attempt by the possessing classes to expropriate the proletariat politically, by reducing its party to nothing.

The Conservatives defend against the trade unions the "right" of the worker to vote for any party he may wish, these same Tories who for centuries refused to grant the worker any suffrage right at all. And though we have lived and seen much, we cannot read without considerable indignation the history of the struggle for the Reform Bill in the early 1830s. With what extraordinary stubbornness, with what tenacity, with what impudence, the slaveholding class of landlords, bankers, bishops, in a word, the privileged minority, fought off the attack on the parliamentary citadel by the bourgeoisie and the workers in its train. The reform of 1832 was instituted only when it was no longer possible to avoid it, and the extension of the suffrage right was introduced as a matter of direct calculation, for the purpose of separating the bourgeoisie from the workers. There was in reality nothing that divided the Conservatives from the Liberals, who, having attained the electoral reform of 1832, left the workers in the lurch. When the Chartists demanded from the Tories and Whigs the granting of the right of suffrage to the workers, the opposition of the parliamentary monopolists became positively furious. And when the workers finally secured the vote, the Conservatives come out in defense of their "individual liberty" against the tyranny of the trade unions.

And this vile, disgusting hypocrisy is not appreciated at its true value in Parliament. On the contrary, the Labour members thank the prime minister who benevolently declines to place a financial noose upon the necks of the workers but fully and absolutely reserves the right to do so at some more appropriate moment. Windbags who may be fed with such terms as "democracy," "equality," "individual liberty," should be sent back to school and made to study the history of England, particularly the history of the struggle for the extension of the right of suffrage.

The Liberal Cobden[77] once declared that he would rather live under the authority of the Bey of Algiers than under that of the trade unions. Cobden was thus expressing his Liberal indignation against the "Bolshevist" tyranny involved in the very nature of the trade unions. From his standpoint, Cobden was right. The capitalist who falls into the hands of the trade unions will fare very badly. The Russian bourgeoisie can tell a few tales in this connection.

But the essence of the matter is that the worker actually has over him a permanent Bey of Algiers in the person of his employer, and the tyrannical power of this Bey can be weakened only through the activity of the trade unions. Of course, the worker must make some sacrifice for this purpose, not only in money, but also personally. However, "individual liberty" will in the last analysis gain incomparably more than it loses through the intermediation of the trade unions.

This is the class point of view from which it is impossible to get away, and which is the basis of the right to collect political contributions. The bourgeoisie, in the mass, at present considers it necessary to *reconcile itself* with the existence of the trade unions, but it wishes to keep their activities below the line where the struggle with the various groups of capitalists becomes a struggle with the capitalist state.

The Conservative member, Macquisten, pointed out in Parliament that the refusal of the trade unions to pay political contributions is observed chiefly in the small and scattered branches of industry, while in the concentrated branches of industry, he regrets to say, there is observed "moral pressure and mass intimidation." This observation is extremely interesting! How characteristic of the English Parliament that it should be spoken by an extreme Tory, the author of the proposed prohibitive legislation, and not by a socialist. This observation means that the refusal to pay political contributions is found in the most backward branches of industry, in which a powerful petty-bourgeois tradition and consequently also petty-bourgeois conceptions of individual liberty, are found usually coupled with voting for the Liberal and even for the Conservative Party. In the newer, more modern branches of production, class solidarity and proletarian discipline are found, which impresses the capitalists and their servants, the deserters from the workers, as terrorism.

A certain Conservative member, trembling with rage, declared that in one trade union the secretary had threatened to post publicly a list of members refusing to pay the contributions to the party. The Labour members began indignantly to demand the name of this dishonorable secretary, and yet every trade union should have been advised to act in this manner. Of course, bureaucrats who, among the howls from both bourgeois parties, attempt to eject Communists from labor organizations, will never do this. As soon as

Communists are concerned, solicitude for individual liberty ceases; then we only hear talk of the security of the state. It is wrong to admit to the Labour Party Communists who deny the holiness of democracy.

Yet, during the debates concerning the political contributions, the author of the prohibitive legislation, Macquisten, who has already been mentioned, made a remark on the subject of this same democracy which was received by the opposition with gay laughter, but which should, as a matter of fact, not only be engraved on the walls of Parliament, but proclaimed and expounded at every workers' meeting. Elucidating with figures the significance of the political contributions of the trade unions, Macquisten declared that before the Liberal Bill of 1913, the trade unions had expended annually only about 10,000 pounds for political purposes, while now, owing to the legalization of the political contributions, they have in their hands a fund of 250,000 pounds. "Of course," says Macquisten, "the Labour Party has become strong. *When you have 250,000 pounds of annual income, you can create a party for any purpose.*"

The infuriated Tory said somewhat more than he intended. His remark is a frank recognition that parties *can be made,* that they can be made with the aid of *money,* that funds play a *decisive part* in the mechanism of democracy. Must we point out that the financial resources of the bourgeoisie are incomparably more plentiful than those of the proletarians? This simple fact should be sufficient to disperse the hypocritical vapors of democracy. Every wide-awake English worker should say to MacDonald: "It is not true that the supreme criteria for our movement are the principles of democracy. These very principles are under the thumb of financial resources, and may be distorted and falsified at will."

Yet we must admit, even adhering to the formally democratic point of view, and operating with the understanding of the ideal citizen, not the proletarian, capitalist, landlord, that the most reactionary gorillas of the upper house are far more consistent. Every citizen of course has the right to support freely with his purse and his vote the party indicated by his conscience. The only trouble is that this ideal British citizen does not exist in nature, being merely a legal fiction. Nor has he ever existed. Yet the petty and middle bourgeois to a certain degree has approached this ideal conception. The Fabian at present considers himself to be the standard of this ideal variety of citizen; he regards the capitalist and the proletarian merely as "deviations" from the ideal type of citizen. But there are not so many Fabian philistines in the world, although there are more than there should be. In general, the electors may be divided into the wealthy, the exploiters, on the one hand, and the proletarians, the exploited, on the other hand.

The trade unions are—in spite of all the subtleties of Liberal casuistry—a class organization of wage workers for combating the greed and avarice of capitalists. One of the most important weapons of the trade unions is the strike. Members' contributions go to support strikes. In times of strikes, the workers are engaged in a fierce struggle with strikebreakers, who are the product of another Liberal principle, that of the "right to work." In any great strike, the union needs political support, it must turn to the press, the parties, the parliament. The hostile attitude of the Liberal press toward the trade union struggle was one of the causes impelling the latter to create a Labour Party.

If we examine the history of the origin of the Labour Party, it will become clear that from the point of view of the trade unions, the party is their political section. It needs a strike fund, an organization of reliable men, a newspaper, dependable members of Parliament. Expenditures on the election of members of Parliament are for these unions as legally necessary and obligatory an expenditure as that which goes to clerical and secretarial work. The Liberal or

Conservative member of the trade union may say: "I pay regularly my customary trade union dues, but I refuse to pay the contribution for the Labour Party, since I vote, by reason of my political convictions, for the Liberals (or the Conservatives)," whereupon the representative of the trade union might say to him: "In times of strike for the improvement of working conditions—and that is the object of our organization—we need the support of the Labour Party, of its members in Parliament, of its press; but the party you vote for (Liberals or Conservatives) under such circumstances always falls upon us, tries to compromise us, sows dissension in our ranks, or even goes so far as to organize strikebreakers. Members who support strikebreakers are of no use to us!" Thus, what may appear from the point of view of capitalist democracy to be personal liberty, appears from the point of view of proletarian democracy to be the liberty of political strikebreaking.

The 10 percent rebate obtained by the bourgeoisie is by no means such an innocent matter. It signifies that one out of every ten members of the trade unions is a conscious political (i.e., class) opponent. Of course, some of these may be won over, but the remainder may be a priceless weapon in the hands of the bourgeoisie, in the case of a real struggle, against the workers. We must therefore inevitably fight, in the further course of our struggle, against the breaches torn in the wall of the trade unions by the Act of Parliament of 1913.

Generally speaking, we Marxists hold that any honest, straightforward worker, regardless of his political, religious, and other convictions, may be a member of a trade union. We consider the trade unions, on the one hand, as militant economic organizations, and as a school of political education, on the other hand. Although we favor, as a general rule, the admission of backward and non-class-conscious workers to the trade unions, we do not start from the abstract principle of liberty of opinion, liberty of conscience, but from considerations of revolutionary expediency. But these very considerations tell us that in England, where 90 percent of the workers organized in trade unions pay the political contributions, some because of their direct desire to do so, others because they do not wish to disturb the spirit of solidarity, and where only 10 percent decide to disregard the open appeal of the Labour Party, a systematic struggle becomes necessary against these 10 percent. They must be made to feel that they are deserters, and the trade unions must be given the right to exclude them as strikebreakers. In the last analysis, if the abstract citizen has the right to vote for any party he pleases, the workers' organizations have the right to refuse to admit to their ranks such citizens as show by their political conduct that they are hostile to the interests of the working class. The struggle of the trade unions for the exclusion of unorganized workers from the factories is already known as a manifestation of "terrorism" or—in present-day parlance—Bolshevism. Precisely in England, these methods can and should be transferred to the Labour Party, which is a direct continuation of the trade unions.

The debates already mentioned by us, which took place in the English Parliament on March 6, 1925, on the subject of the political contributions, are extremely interesting as an indication of the nature of parliamentary democracy. Only in the speech of Prime Minister Baldwin do we observe guarded references to the real danger which is founded in the class structure of England. The old relations have passed away. There no longer exist any of the good old English enterprises with their patriarchal customs—Mr. Baldwin himself managed such an enterprise in his youth. Industry is concentrating and combining. The workers are uniting into trade unions, and these organizations may be a danger to the state itself.

Baldwin spoke of united employers as well as of the labor

unions. But of course he sees a real danger to the democratic state only in the trade unions. What the so-called struggle against the trusts amounts to, we have already learned from the example of America. The noisy antitrust agitation of Roosevelt[78] was mere empty gesturing. The trusts, under Roosevelt and after him, became stronger and stronger, and the American government turned out to be their executive organ in a much more direct manner than the Labour Party is the political organ of the trade unions. If the trusts in England, as a form of organization, do not play the same great role as in America, the capitalists play a part which is equally important. The danger from the trade unions consists in the fact that they—hitherto only partly, irresolutely, and in a half-and-half manner—are advancing the principle of a workers' government, *which is impossible without a workers' state*, as opposed to the capitalists' government, which can continue its existence at present only under the guise of democracy. Baldwin fully agrees with the principle of "individual liberty," which is the basis of the prohibitive bill introduced by his friends in Parliament. He also considers the political contributions of the trade unions as a "moral evil" but he does not wish to disturb the peace.

The struggle, once it has begun, may have serious consequences: "We shall under no circumstances shoot first." And Baldwin concludes: "Give us peace in our time, O Lord!" Almost the entire chamber greeted this speech with applause, including many Labour members; the prime minister, according to his own declaration, had made a "gesture of peace." Thereupon the Labour member Thomas rose, who is always on the spot when a gesture of abject servility is required; he congratulated Baldwin; he pointed out the truly human note in Baldwin's speech; he declared that both employers and workers had much to gain from a close cooperation between them; he referred with pride to the fact that not a few left workers in his own union had refused to pay the political contributions by reason of the fact that their secretary was the great reactionary Thomas himself. And all the debates on this question, in which the life interests of conflicting classes are in constant contact, are conducted in this tone of hypothetical statement, half-truths, official lies, purely English parliamentary cant.

The half-truths of the Conservatives have the quality of Machiavellianism; the half-truths of the Labour Party are the child of contemptible cowardice. The representation of the bourgeoisie resembles the tiger which hides its claws and cuddles amiably. The Labour leaders of the Thomas type are more like the beaten dog with his tail between his legs.

The hopelessness of the economic situation of England is best expressed in the trade unions. On the day after the conclusion of the war, when it seemed in the heat of the moment that Great Britain had become the unlimited ruler of the destinies of the world, the labor masses, awakened by the war, poured into the trade unions by the hundred thousands and millions. The peak was reached in 1919: then began the descent. At present the number of members of the trade unions has fallen very low and is still falling.

John Wheatley, a "left" member of the MacDonald cabinet, at one of the meetings last March in Glasgow, said something to the effect that the trade unions are now a mere shadow of their former selves, and that they are equally incapable either of fighting or of conducting negotiations. Fred Bramley, general secretary of the Trades Unions Congress, came out boldly against this opinion. The discussion between these two men, who theoretically are equally helpless antagonists, is, however, of extraordinary symptomatic interest. Bramley referred to the fact that the political movement being "more promising," i.e., offering greater opportunities for career-making, draws away from the trade unions their most valuable workers. On the other hand, Bramley asks, what would the party be without the political contributions of the trade unions? At bottom, Bramley does not deny the decline in the economic power of the trade unions, which he explains with a reference to the economic situation of England.

But we should seek in vain in the general secretary of the Trades Unions Congress for any indication of an escape from this blind alley. His ideas do not transcend the bounds of the concealed rivalry between the apparatus of the trade unions and the apparatus of the party. And yet, the important question is by no means this. Underlying the radicalization of the laboring classes and consequently the growth of the Labour Party, we find the same causes which have dealt such severe blows to the economic power of the trade unions. One doubtless will soon develop at the cost of the other. But it would be extraordinarily careless to draw the conclusion that the role of the trade unions is a thing of the past. On the contrary, there is still a great future in store for the industrial unions of the English working class. For the very reason that within the framework of capitalist society, in the present situation of Great Britain, there are no great prospects for the trade unions, the industrial labor unions will be obliged to enter the path of a socialist reorganization of the economy. Having reconstructed the latter in accordance with this need, the trade unions will become the principal lever for the economic reconstruction of the country.

But a necessary presupposition for this is the seizure of power by the proletariat—not in the sense of the sad and wretched farce of the MacDonald ministry, but in the real, material, revolutionary, class sense. The whole apparatus of the government must become an apparatus in the service of the proletariat. The working class, being the sole class interested in a socialist revolt, must be enabled to dictate its will to the entire society. The entire administration, all the judges and officials, must be as profoundly imbued with the socialist spirit of the proletariat as the present-day officials and judges are permeated with the spirit of the bourgeoisie. Only the trade unions can furnish the necessary human personnel. Finally, the trade unions alone will supply from their midst the organs for the management of the nationalized industry.

In the near future, the trade unions will become schools of education for the proletariat in the sense of socialist production. Their future role is therefore of infinite proportions. But they are at present undoubtedly in a blind alley. There is no possibility of escaping this situation by means of palliatives and half-measures. The decomposition of English capitalism inevitably produces the impotence of the trade unions. Only revolution can save the English working class, and with it its organizations. In order to seize power, the proletariat must have at its head a revolutionary party. In order to make the trade unions capable of undertaking their future function, they must be freed from conservative office-holders, from superstitious fools, who ignorantly expect "peaceful" miracles from somewhere. In short, from the agents of large-scale capital, from the renegades of the Thomas type. A reformist, opportunist, liberal-labor party can only weaken the trade unions by paralyzing the activity of the masses. A revolutionary labor party based on the trade unions will, however, be a powerful weapon in their improvement and growth.

The compulsory, anti-Liberal, "despotic" collections of political contributions contain, as the future stalk and ear are contained in the grain, all those Bolshevik methods against which MacDonald tirelessly sprinkles the holy water of his aroused mental limitations. The working class has the right and duty to place its deliberate class will higher than all the fictions and sophisms of bourgeois democracy. It should act in the spirit of revolutionary self-confidence with which Cromwell filled the young English bourgeoisie. Cromwell exhorts his Puritan recruits, as we have already seen, as follows: "I will not cozen you by perplexed expressions in my commission about fighting for King and Parliament. If the King chanced to be in the body of the enemy, I would as soon discharge my pistol upon him as upon any private man; and if your conscience will not let you do the like, I advise you not to enlist yourselves under me." These are not the words of bloodthirsty despotism, but the consciousness of a great historical mission, permitting its bearer to annihilate all obstacles in his path. A young progressive class, first realizing its mission, speaks through the lips of Cromwell. If we must seek national traditions, then let the English proletariat borrow this spirit of revolutionary self-confidence and aggressive manhood from the old Independents. The MacDonalds, Webbs, Snowdens, etc., are borrowing from Cromwell's fellow-fighters only their religious prejudices, and combine them with truly Fabian cowardice.

The proletarian vanguard must unite the revolutionary manhood of the Independents with the clarity of the materialist conception of the universe.

The English bourgeoisie is not mistaken in its view that the chief danger threatens it from the trade union side, and that only under the pressure of the mass organizations will the Labour Party, having radically altered its leadership, be able to transform itself into a revolutionary force.

One of the new methods of struggle against the trade unions is the independent organization of the administrative-technical staff (engineers, managers, foremen) into a "third party in industry." The *Times* is conducting a very ingenious and clever struggle against the theory of the community of interests between physical and mental labor. In this as in other cases, the bourgeois politicians are artfully utilizing the very ideas that Fabianism has inspired in them. The opposition of labor to capital is ruinous for national growth, says the *Times*, together with all the leaders of the Labour Party, and the *Times* draws the inference that the engineers, managers, administrators, and technicians, who stand between capital and labor, are more capable of grasping the interests of industry "as a whole" and of establishing peace in the relations between employers and employees. For this very reason, the administrative-technical staff should be segregated into a third party in industry.

At bottom, the *Times* is working directly into the hands of Fabianism. The basic principle in the position of the latter, which is a reactionary utopian opposition to the class struggle, coincides best of all with the social position of the petty-bourgeois and middle-bourgeois intellectual, engineer, administrator, who stands between capital and labor and who is, in the last analysis, an instrument in the hands of capital, but who wishes to consider himself independent and therefore all the more emphasizes his independence from the proletarian organizations, all the more falls into the hands of the capitalist organizations. We may without difficulty predict in advance that as its inevitable exclusion from the trade unions and the Labour Party proceeds, Fabianism will more and more unite its destinies with those of the intermediate elements of industry, the trade and governmental-bureaucratic apparatus. The Independent Labour Party, after its present temporary elevation, will inevitably be cast down and, having become a "third party in industry," will find itself lost between capital and labor.

A forecast of the future

When Mrs. Lloyd George, wife of the former British prime minister, lost a valuable necklace, the *Daily Herald*, the official organ of the Labour Party, called the attention of its readers to Liberal leaders who desert to the enemy's side and present their wives with costly necklaces. The following instructive inference is contained in this newspaper's leading article: "The existence of the Labour Party depends on its success in preserving labor leaders from pursuing this ruinous path." Arthur Ponsonby, a despairing Liberal, who has not ceased to be a Liberal though he has entered the Labour Party, in the same issue of the *Daily Herald* gives free rein to his reflections on the destruction of the great Liberal Party by such leaders as Asquith and Lloyd George. "Yes," the editorial writer repeats after him, "the Liberal leaders have dropped their simple ways in exchange for the manners of the rich in whose company they constantly move; they have borrowed the arrogance of the latter toward the lower classes," etc., etc.

As a matter of fact, there is nothing surprising in the bourgeois mode of life of the Liberal Party leaders, since the Liberal Party is one of the two bourgeois parties. But the liberals in the Labour Party regard liberalism as an abstract system of lofty ideas, and the Liberal ministers who purchase necklaces for their wives as traitors to Liberal ideas.

It is instructive to read the reflections on how to preserve Labour leaders from entering on this path of ruin. Of course these reflections are merely timid and halting reminders addressed to semiliberal Labour leaders by semiliberal Labour journalists, who must pay some attention to the opinions of their readers. It is not difficult to observe the presence of the careerist distemper in the ministerial elite of the British Labour Party! It is sufficient to state that Mrs. Lloyd George herself, in a letter of protest written to the editor of the *Daily Herald,* mentions such incidents as the "royal" gifts bestowed upon MacDonald by his capitalist friend, after having been reminded of which the editor held his peace. Utterly childish seems the thought that the conduct of the leaders of the Labour Party may be guided by the use of moral tales about Mrs. Lloyd George's necklace, as if politics in general could be patterned after abstract moral precepts. On the contrary, the morality of the class and of its party and leaders is an outgrowth of policy, in the widest historical sense of the word. This is nowhere more visible than in the very organizations of the British working class.

The *Daily Herald,* in its profound musings, has discovered the dangers of permitting Labour Party "leaders" to hobnob with the bourgeoisie, entirely overlooking the fact that such relations depend altogether on the *political* attitude toward the bourgeoisie. If we assume the point of view of an irreconcilable class struggle, there will be no fraternization of any kind. Labour leaders will not enter into bourgeois circles, nor would the bourgeoisie let them in. But the leaders of the Labour Party actually defend the idea of collaboration between classes and rapprochement between their leaders. "Cooperation and mutual confidence between employers and workers," as Mr. Snowden said, for example, in one of his parliamentary speeches this year, "are the most essential requirements for the country's prosperity." Similar speeches have been delivered by Clynes, the Webbs, and all the other luminaries. The attitude of the trade-union leaders is the same; we hear nothing from their mouths but reminders of the necessity of frequent meetings of employers and representatives of the workers around the "green table."

However, the policy of constant "friendly" relations between the Labour leaders and the bourgeois magnates, in their effort to obtain a common ground, i.e., the elimination of what separates them, does constitute, as the *Daily Herald* says, a danger not only to the conduct of the leaders, but to the development of the party also. What else could be expected? When John Burns deserted the proletariat,[79] he began to say: "I have no more use for a special workers' point of view than for the workers' boots or the workers' oleomargarine." No one will doubt the fact that John Burns, when he became a bourgeois minister, considerably improved both his butter and his boots, but it may hardly be said that his evolution into a bourgeois was likely to improve the boots of the dockworkers who had lifted Burns into power. Morality flows from policy. In order that Snowden's budget may please the City, it is necessary for Snowden himself, both in his standard of living and in his moral conduct, to resemble bankers more than Welsh miners.

And how about Thomas? We have already mentioned the dinner given by the railroad magnates, at which Thomas, secretary of the Railroad Workers' Union, declared that his soul did not belong to the working class, but to "the truth," and that it was in search of this truth that he, Thomas, had come to the dinner. It is worthy of note that this vile nonsense is all duly recorded in the *Times*, while the *Daily*

Herald prints not a word of it. That unhappy paper prefers to moralize more abstractly. But you will never succeed in chastising Thomas with parables about Mrs. Lloyd George's necklace. Thomas must be cast out, and that cannot be accomplished by keeping silent about Thomas's embraces with the enemy at dinners and elsewhere, but by shouting them out loud, revealing them in all their nakedness, and calling upon the workers to purify their ranks ruthlessly. A change of morality will require a change of politics.

As I write these lines (April 1925), the official policy of England stands under the sign of compromise, in spite of the fact that the government is Conservative: "cooperation" is needed between the two factors of industry, mutual concessions must be made, the workers must be made to "participate" in one form or another in the profits of industry, etc. This frame of mind on the part of the Conservatives is illustrative of both the strength and the weakness of the English proletariat, which has forced the Conservatives to base their policy on an "acceptance" of the creation of an independent labor party. But the proletariat, in putting such men as MacDonald and Thomas at the head of the Labour Party, enables the Conservatives to build their hopes on this "acceptance."

Baldwin delivers speech after speech on the necessity of mutual patience, in order that the country may emerge *without a catastrophe* from the difficulties of its present position. Labour "leader" Robert Smillie states that he is in complete agreement with these speeches: "a splendid summons to patience on both sides!"[80] Smillie promises to follow the call implicitly, expressing the hope that the captains of industry will take a more humane course with regard to the demands of the workers. "This is a perfectly legal and sensible desire," assures the *Times*, with a straight face. And all these honeyed utterances are made in a period of industrial difficulties, chronic unemployment, with British orders going to German shipyards, threatening conflicts in many branches of industry, and this in England, with all England's experience of class wars. Surely the memory of the toiling masses is short, and the hypocrisy of the rulers is without parallel! The historical memory of the bourgeoisie is in the traditions of its rule, in the country's institutions and laws, in the cumulative art of government. The memory of the working class is in its party; the reform party is the party of poor memory.

While the Conservatives' policy of harmony is hypocritical, it is nonetheless based on sound reasons. The main efforts of the ruling parties in Europe are at present directed toward the maintenance of internal and external peace. The so-called reaction against the war and the methods of the early postwar period cannot be explained by psychological motives alone. The power and elasticity of the capitalist system, as revealed by the war, gave rise to the specific *illusions of military capitalism*. A bold, centralized leadership in the economic life, military conquest of lacking economic resources, living on debts, unlimited issues of paper money, the elimination of social dangers by means of bloody reprisals on the one hand and all sorts of concessions on the other—it began to appear in the heat of the moment as if such methods could solve all questions and overcome all obstacles.

But economic reality soon clipped the wings of the illusions of military capitalism. Germany approached the brink of ruin. The government of wealthy France finds it impossible to escape from its thinly disguised bankruptcy. The English government is obliged to maintain an army of unemployed almost twice as numerous as the army of French militarism. The wealth of Europe has been found to have limits. The continuation of the war and the upheavals would have meant the inevitable destruction of European capitalism. Hence the eagerness for "orderly" relations between governments and classes.

The English Conservatives gambled precisely on this fear of upheavals, in the last elections. Now in power, they are for conciliation, agreement, social benevolence. "Security, that is the key to the situation," says the Liberal Lord Grey, seconded by the Conservative Austen Chamberlain.[81] The English press of both bourgeois camps lives on repetitions of such words. The desire for a state of peace, the establishment of "normal" conditions, the safeguarding of the gold standard, the resumption of commercial treaties, will not of themselves solve a single one of the contradictions that brought about the imperialist war and have been further aggravated by the war. But these efforts, and the political groupings based upon them, are sufficient to indicate the present internal and foreign policy of the ruling parties in Europe.

It is hardly necessary to point out that these pacific tendencies again and again encounter the obstacle of the postwar economic conditions. The English Conservatives have already begun to undermine the Unemployed Insurance Act. English industry, *as it is now,* cannot be rendered more capable of meeting competition except by lowering wages. And this is impossible if unemployment insurance be retained, for this insurance strengthens the opposition of the working class. Vanguard skirmishes have already taken place in this field, and they may lead to serious struggles. At any rate, in this as in other fields, the Conservatives will soon be obliged to come out under their true colors, and the situation of the Labour Party heads will thus be made more and more difficult.

It is well to speak here of the conditions produced in the House of Commons after the elections of 1906, when a large Labour membership first appeared in Parliament. For the two succeeding years, the Labour delegates were treated with every consideration, but the third year things changed for the worse. In 1910, Parliament was already "ignoring" the

Labour members, not by reason of any irreconcilable attitude on the part of the latter, but because the working masses who were not in Parliament were becoming more and more exacting. Having elected many members to Parliament, they expected that real changes would be made in their own lives, an expectation that constituted one of the factors producing the powerful strike wave of 1911–13.

These facts provide us with conclusions that are applicable to the present. The flirtation with the Labour members now being carried on by the Baldwin majority will turn into its opposite the more rapidly, as the pressure of the workers on their parliamentary representatives, on capital, and on Parliament itself becomes more persistent. We have already spoken of this in connection with the question of the role of democracy and revolutionary force in the mutual relations between the classes. We shall now consider the same question from the point of view of the *internal development of the Labour Party itself.*

The leading part in the British Labour Party is of course played by the heads of the Independent Labour Party, led by MacDonald. Not only before the war, but during its progress, the attitude of the Independent Labour Party was pacifistic, "condemning" social-imperialism and occupying in general a centrist position. Its platform was "opposed to militarism in any form." The war ended; the Independent Labour Party seceded from the Second International.[82] As resolved in the 1920 conference, the Independents even began a correspondence with the Third International, proposing to the latter twelve questions, each more profound than the other. The seventh question ran: "May communism and the dictatorship of the proletariat be brought about only by armed force, or may parties also be admitted to the Third International which consider this question still open?" It is an instructive point of view; the butcher has his big knife, but the doomed calf has an open mind. At that critical time, however, the

Independent Labour Party was considering the question of joining the Communist International, while now it excludes Communists from the Labour Party.

The contradiction between the Independent Labour Party's policy of yesterday and that of the Labour Party of today, particularly in the months during which it enjoyed power, is truly amazing. Today even the politics of the Fabians in the Independent Labour Party are different from the politics of the same Fabians in the Labour Party. These contradictions are a feeble reflection of the struggle between centrist and social-imperialist tendencies. These tendencies meet and are conjoined in MacDonald himself, and we therefore find the Christian pacifist building light cruisers in anticipation of the time when he may build heavy ones.

The chief trait of socialist centrism is its noncommittal, irresolute, and uncertain position. Centrism maintains itself so long as it is not obliged to draw the final conclusions, to give outright answers to straight questions. In a peaceful "organic" epoch, centrism may maintain itself as the official doctrine of even a large and active labor party, as was the case with the German Social Democracy before the war, for in that period the decision of the fundamental questions in the national life did not depend on the party of the proletariat. Generally speaking, however, centrism is most appropriate to small organizations, which, by reason of their insignificant influence, are freed from the necessity of giving a clear answer to all the questions of policy and of bearing the practical responsibility for such answers. Such was the centrism of the Independent Labour Party.

The imperialist war showed only too clearly that the labor bureaucracy and the labor aristocracy had during the preceding period of capitalist expansion undergone a profound petty-bourgeois transformation, both in the sense of its habits of life and in its intellectual makeup. But the petty bourgeois will preserve the *appearance* of independence until the first blow is struck.

The war, by a single stroke, revealed and consolidated the political dependence of the petty bourgeois on the big bourgeois and the biggest bourgeois. Social-imperialism was the form assumed by this dependence within the labor movement. Centrism, therefore, insofar as it was retained or reborn in the war period and the postwar period, was an expression of the terror of the petty bourgeois among the labor bureaucracy in the presence of their complete, and on the whole, frank surrender to imperialism.

The German Social Democracy, which for many years, even under Bebel,[83] had been carrying on a fundamentally centrist policy, precisely because of its great strength, could not maintain itself in this position during the war; it either had to come out straight against the war, i.e., enter upon an essentially revolutionary path, or for the war, i.e., go over to the camp of the bourgeoisie. The Independent Labour Party in England, a propagandist organization within the working class, was not only able to preserve but temporarily even to strengthen its centrist qualities during the war, "renouncing all responsibility," engaging in platonic protests, pacifistic preachings, thinking not one of its thoughts through to the end, and providing not the slightest serious difficulty to the warring state. The opposition of the Independents in Germany was also of centrist character; they also "renounced all responsibility," which did not prevent Scheidemann and Ebert, however, from placing the entire strength of the labor organizations at the disposal of warring capitalism.[84]

In England, we have witnessed since the war a very unusual "compatibility" of the social-imperialist and centrist tendencies in the labor movement. The Independent Labour Party, as the reader already knows, was remarkably well adapted for the role of an irresponsible centrist opposition, constantly criticizing, but causing no true embarrassment to those in power. Yet, the Independents were destined to become a political power within a short period, and thus changed simultaneously both their role and their physiognomy.

The strength of the Independents was due to two coexisting causes: in the first place, to the fact that history had faced the working class with the necessity of creating its own party; in the second place, because the war and the postwar period, having awakened the many-millioned masses, for the moment created favorable conditions for the reception of the ideas of a labor pacifism and reformism. Of course, the minds of the English workers were filled with plenty of democratic-pacifistic illusions even before the war. The difference, however, is a tremendous one.

In the past, the English proletariat, insofar as it participated in political life, was attached, by reason of its democratic-pacifistic illusions—particularly during the second half of the nineteenth century—to the activities of the Liberal Party. The latter did "not justify" these hopes, and lost the faith of the workers. A separate labor party then grew up, a priceless historical achievement, which even now can never be nullified. But we must not overlook the fact that the working masses were disillusioned rather as to the goodwill of the Liberals than as to the democratic-pacifistic methods of solving social questions, the more since new generations, new millions, were for the first time being drawn into political life. They transferred their hopes and illusions to the Labour Party. For this reason, and for this reason only, the Independents were given an opportunity to head the party.

Behind the democratic-pacifistic illusions of the working masses stands *their awakened class will, their profound dissatisfaction with their conditions, their readiness to support their demands by all the means that circumstances may require.* But the working class can build a party out of those ideological and individual leading elements who have been prepared by the entire preceding evolution of the country, by its entire theoretical and political culture.

Here, generally speaking, is the source of the great influence of the petty-bourgeois intelligentsia, including of
course the labor aristocrats and bureaucrats. The establishment of the British Labour Party became a necessity for the
very reason that the masses of the proletariat were undergoing a profound shift to the left. The political formulation
of this change devolved upon those representatives of the
impotent conservative-Protestant pacifism who happened
to be available. But having transferred their general staff
to a basis consisting of several million organized workers,
the Independents were no longer able to remain themselves,
or even to impress their centrist stamp on the party of the
proletariat. Having suddenly become the leaders of a party
of millions of workers, they no longer could content themselves with centrist commonplaces and pacifist passivity;
they had, first in their capacity as a responsible opposition,
and then in their capacity as a government, to pronounce a
straight yes or no in answer to the most ticklish questions in
the national life. From the moment that centrism became a
political force, it had to pass beyond the bounds of centrism,
i.e., it had either to draw revolutionary conclusions from its
opposition to the imperialist government, or frankly serve
that government.

Of course, it did the latter. The pacifist MacDonald began to build cruisers, jail Hindus and Egyptians, engage in
diplomatic manipulations with the aid of forged documents.
Having become a political power, centrism as such was reduced to zero. The profound move to the left on the part of
the English working class, which had brought MacDonald's
party into power with astonishing swiftness, produced in
that party an open shift to the right. Such is the relation
between yesterday and today, and such is the cause which
enables the small Independent Labour Party to look with
amazement upon its success and to try to transform itself
into a centrist party.

The practical program of the British Labour Party, led by the Independents, is at bottom of Liberal character and, particularly in its foreign policy, is a belated repetition of the Gladstone impotence. Gladstone was "forced" to seize Egypt, just as MacDonald was "forced" to build cruisers. Beaconsfield represented the imperialist demands of capital more truly than Gladstone.[85] Free trade no longer decides issues. The giving up of the plan to fortify Singapore is meaningless when viewed from the point of view of the entire imperialist system of Great Britain. Singapore is a key to two seas. Whoever wishes to keep the colonies, i.e., to continue the policy of imperialist domination, must have this key in his hands.

MacDonald stands on the ground of capitalism; he introduces a few cowardly corrections which solve nothing at all, which mean nothing at all, but which increase all the difficulties and dangers. As to the question of the destinies of English industry, there are no essential differences between the three parties. The fundamental trait of this policy is a confusion born of the fear of social upheavals. All three parties are conservative and fear nothing so much as industrial conflicts. The Conservative Parliament refuses the miners the fixing of a minimum wage. The members elected by the miners say that the conduct of Parliament is an "outright call to revolutionary action," although not one of these members seriously thinks of revolutionary action. The capitalists propose to the workers that they study together the condition of the coal industry, hoping thus to prove that which needs no proof, namely, that under the present system of the coal industry, disorganized by private ownership, it is expensive to mine coal even when wages are low. The Conservative and Liberal press sees salvation in this investigation. The Labour leaders pursue the same path. Everyone is afraid of strikes which may strengthen the preponderance of foreign competitors. And yet, if any sort of rational production is still possible in general, under capitalist conditions, it can never be attained except with the aid of the pressure exerted by great strikes of the workers. Paralyzing the working masses through the trade unions, the leaders are supporting the process of economic stagnation and decay.

One of the most outspoken reactionaries in the leadership of the British Labour Party, Dr. Haden Guest, a chauvinist, militarist, protectionist, gloated mercilessly in Parliament over the line followed by his own party as to the question of free trade or protection: MacDonald's position, according to Guest, is purely negative in character and does not present any escape from the economic impasse. As a matter of fact, the impossibility of free trade is perfectly clear: yet the overthrow of the free-traders also involves overthrowing liberalism.

But England has just as little to hope for from protectionism. For a young capitalist country just beginning to grow, protectionism may be an inevitable and desirable stage in its development; but for an old industrial country, whose industry has been planned to fill the demands of a world market, which has been aggressive and belligerent in character, a resort to protectionism is an historical confession of an incipient process of dissolution, and is practically equivalent to supporting those branches of industry which are less capable of maintaining themselves under the present world conditions, at the expense of other branches of English industry that are better adapted to the conditions of the world market and the domestic market. The program of the outlived protectionism of Baldwin's party cannot be opposed by the equally outlived and hopeless free-traders, but only by the practical program of a socialist transformation. But in order to proceed to this step, the party must first be purified not only of its reactionary protectionists like Guest, but also of its reactionary free-traders like MacDonald.

From what beginning and by what path can the transformation of the policy of the Labour Party, which is inconceivable without a radical transformation of leadership, take place?

As the absolute majority in the executive committee and in other important institutions of the British Labour Party belongs to the Independent Labour Party, the latter is the ruling faction in the Labour Party. This mutual relation within the English labor movement affords—it must be said—extremely valuable material on the question of the "dictatorship of the minority," for it is precisely in this way, i.e., as a dictatorship of the minority, that the leaders of the British party picture the role of the Communist Party in the Soviet Republic. However, we find that the Independent Labour Party, counting about 30,000 members, obtains a dominant position in an organization based—through the trade unions—on millions of members. But this organization, i.e., the Labour Party, thanks to the numerical strength and the part played by the English proletariat, comes to power. Thus, an insignificant minority of 30,000 members gains the power in a country having 40 million inhabitants and ruling over hundreds of millions. The most outright "democracy" therefore leads to a party dictatorship of the minority.

To be sure, the "dictatorship" of the Independent Labour Party is worth, in the class sense, not a single bad penny, but that is already an entirely different question. If, however, a party with 30,000 members, without a revolutionary program, without the experience of struggle, without serious traditions, merely through the intermediary of a heterogeneous Labour Party, based on the trade unions, can attain power by the methods of bourgeois democracy, why should these gentlemen be so displeased or surprised when the Communist Party, tempered by theory and practice, with entire decades of heroic struggle at the head of the masses of the people behind it, a party with a membership of hundreds of thousands, should come to power, based on the mass organizations of the workers and peasants? In any case, the obtaining of power by the Independent Labour Party is incomparably less grounded and rooted in the conditions than was the obtaining of power by the Communist Party in Russia.

But the vertiginous career of the Independent Labour Party is of interest not only from the point of view of polemics against considerations concerning the dictatorship of the communist minority. It is far more important to evaluate the swift rise of the Independents from the point of view of the future destinies of the English Communist Party. Certain conclusions force themselves upon us.

The Independent Labour Party, born in a petty-bourgeois environment and close to the circles of the trade union bureaucracy in its feelings and tendencies, naturally headed—together with the latter—the Labour Party, when the masses by their pressure obliged their secretaries to create such a party. And the Independent Labour Party, in its fabulous emergence, in its political methods, in all its functions, is preparing and clearing the road for the Communist Party. In the course of decades, the Independent Labour Party succeeded in gathering about 30,000 members. But when the profound alteration in the international situation and in the internal structure of English society gave birth to the Labour Party, an unexpected demand for leadership by the Independents was at once displayed. The same course of political evolution is preparing for a still more powerful "demand" for communism at the next stage of development.

At the present moment, the Communist Party is extremely small. In the last elections it had altogether 53,000 votes—a figure which, when compared with the 5½ million votes of the Labour Party, might seem distressing if we did not understand the logic of the political evolution of England. To imagine that the Communists in the course of subsequent decades will increase step by step, acquiring at each new parliamentary election a few tens of thousands or hundreds of thousands of votes more, would be a radical misunderstanding of the development of the future. Of course, during a certain comparatively prolonged period, communism will develop rather slowly, but then there will ensue an ineluctable crisis: *the Communist Party will occupy the position in the Labour Party which is now held by the Independents.*

What is needed in order to bring this about? The general answer is quite clear. The Independent Labour Party owes its unprecedented boom to the fact that it enabled the working class to create a third party, i.e., its own party. The last elections show with what enthusiasm the English workers regard the instrument created by them. But a party is not an end in itself. The workers expect from it action and results. The English Labour Party was born almost overnight, as a party aiming directly to seize power, and it already has had some success in this. In spite of the profoundly compromising character of the first "Labour" government, the party at the new elections obtained more than one million new votes. However, there arose within the party the so-called left wing, amorphous, spineless, without any independent future. But the very fact of the arising of an opposition bears witness to the growth of the demands of the masses and to the parallel growth of nervousness in the upper circles of the party. Even a slight acquaintance with the qualities of the MacDonalds, Thomases, Clyneses, Snowdens, and all the rest is quite sufficient to prove to us how catastrophically the contradictions between the demands of the masses and the obtuse conservatism of the leading upper circles of the Labour Party will grow, particularly if this party should come to power again.

In sketching this prospect, we start with the assumption that the present international and domestic situation of English capitalism will not only not improve but—on

the contrary—will grow worse and worse. If this prognosis should turn out to be wrong, if the English bourgeoisie
should succeed in strengthening the empire, in giving back
to it its former position on the world market, in reviving industry, giving work to the unemployed, raising wages, the
political evolution would of course have a different character: the aristocratic conservatism of the trade unions would
again be strengthened, the Labour Party would go down-
hill, its right wing would be fortified, and the latter would
move closer to liberalism, which in turn would experience
a certain accession of living forces.

But there is not the slightest foundation for such a conception of the future. On the contrary, whatever may be the
partial fluctuations in the economic and political situation,
everything speaks in favor of a progressive sharpening and
deepening of the difficulties which England is now passing
through, and therefore, simultaneously, of a further accel-
eration of the speed of its revolutionary development. Under these circumstances, a new obtaining of power by the
Labour Party in one of the coming stages seems extremely
probable, and already a conflict between the working class
and the Fabian leaders at its head is absolutely inevitable.

The present role of the Independents is due to the fact
that their path intersected that of the proletariat. This by
no means signifies that these paths will continue to coincide. The swift growth of the influence of the Independents
is only an evidence of the exceptional strength of the impact
of the working class; but this very impact, conditioned by
all the circumstances, will bring the English workers into a
clash with their Independent leaders. In the measure as this
occurs, the revolutionary *quality* of the British Communist
Party—assuming that it follows a correct policy—will be
transformed into a *quantity* of many millions.

A certain analogy may be drawn between the destinies of
the Communist Party and those of the Independent Labour

Party. Both look back upon a long record as propagandist organizations, rather than as parties of the working class. Then,
in a profound crisis in the historical evolution of England,
the Independent Labour Party headed the proletariat. For a
certain interval, the Communist Party will, in our opinion,
undergo a similar boom.* The path of its development will
coincide at a certain point with the great historical road of
the English proletariat. However, this combination will be
effected in an entirely different way than was the case with
the Independent Labour Party; with the latter, the combining element was the bureaucracy of the trade unions. The
Independents may head the Labour Party as long as the
trade union bureaucracy weakens, neutralizes, distorts the
independent class pressure of the proletariat. The Communist Party, on the other hand, can only stand at the head of
the working class by virtue of the latter's adopting an irreconcilable opposition to the conservative bureaucracy in
the trade unions and in the Labour Party. The Communist
Party will prepare itself for the function of leadership only
by a merciless criticism of the entire dominating staff of the
English labor movement, only by a constant unmasking of
its conservative, anti-proletarian, imperialist, monarchic,
lackeyish function in all fields of social life and the class
movement.

The left wing of the Labour Party represents an effort
to re-create centrism within the social-imperialist party of
MacDonald. It thus reveals the nervousness of a portion of
the labor bureaucracy as to their relations with the masses
moving to the left. It would be a monstrous illusion to imagine that these left elements of the old school are capable of

---

* Of course, prognoses of this kind are hypothetical and general in character and may in no case be compared with astronomical predictions of
lunar or solar eclipses. The actual course of evolution is always more
complicated than the necessarily schematic outline of prophecy.—L.T.

heading the revolutionary movement of the English proletariat and its struggle for power. They represent an accomplished formation. Their elasticity is extremely limited.
Their leftism is throughout opportunistic. They will not
and cannot lead the masses to struggle. Within the limits of
their reformist narrow-mindedness, they reproduce the old
irresponsible centrism, which does not prevent but which
rather aids MacDonald in holding the responsibility for the
leadership of the party, and, in certain cases, for the destinies of the British Empire.

This picture was presented clearest of all in the Glouces-
ter congress of the Independent Labour Party (Easter 1925).
Carping at MacDonald, the Independents approved the so-
called "activity" of the Labour government by a vote of 398
against 139. And even the opposition could permit itself the
luxury of censuring the government only for the reason that
the majority for MacDonald was already assured. The dissatisfaction of the lefts with MacDonald is the dissatisfaction of
centrism with itself. MacDonald's policy cannot be improved
by means of minor alterations. Centrism, having obtained
power, will necessarily carry out a MacDonald (i.e., capitalist) policy. Serious opposition to the MacDonald method can
be offered only by the method of a socialist dictatorship of
the proletariat. It would be completely erroneous to imagine
that the Independent Labour Party is capable of developing
into a revolutionary party of the proletariat. The Fabians
must be driven out, "removed from their posts." This can
be accomplished only by the method of an uncompromising
struggle with the centrism of the Independents.

The more clearly and acutely the question of the seizure
of power is put, the more will the Independent Labour Party
attempt to evade the answer by substituting for the fundamental revolutionary problems certain bureaucratic lucu-
brations as to the best parliamentary and financial modes
of nationalizing industry. One of the committees of the In-

188 / LEON TROTSKY ON BRITAIN

dependent Labour Party arrived at the conclusion that the purchase of lands, works, and factories is preferable to confiscation, since in England, according to the feelings of the committee, nationalization will take place gradually, by the Baldwin method, step by step, and it would be "unjust" to deprive one group of capitalists of their profits while another group was receiving dividends on its capital. "It would be another matter," says the committee's report (we are quoting the *Times*), "if socialism were to come not gradually but suddenly, as a result of a catastrophic revolution; then the arguments against confiscation would lose most of their force. But we," says the report, "do not think that this contingency is likely to arise, *and we do not feel called upon to discuss it in the present report.*"

Generally speaking, there is no reason for objecting in principle to a purchase of lands, factories, and works. Unfortunately, however, the political and financial opportunities for such an operation never coincide. The condition of the finances of the United States of America makes such an operation quite feasible, yet, in America this is not at all a practical question, and there is not a single party that would dare seriously to propose it. And by the time such a party would appear, the economic situation of the United States would already have suffered very sharp changes. On the contrary, in England, the question of nationalization is now put in all its baldness as the question of saving English industry. But the state of the national finances is such that it is more than doubtful whether this purchase is possible.

Besides, the financial side of the question is of secondary importance. The principal task is to create the political conditions for nationalization, whether by purchase or without purchase, that is of no importance. In the last instance, it is a matter of life and death for the bourgeoisie. Revolution is inevitable for the reason that the bourgeoisie will never permit itself to be strangled by Fabian banking operations.

Even a partial nationalization can be undertaken by bourgeois society in its present form only by surrounding it with such conditions as would render the success of these measures extremely doubtful, thus compromising the principle of nationalization and with it the Labour Party. The bourgeoisie would oppose as a class every straightforward attempt at even a partial nationalization. The other branches of industry would resort to lockouts, to sabotage, to a boycott of the nationalized industry, i.e., bring about a life-and-death struggle. However guarded the first steps might be, the task will nevertheless lead to the necessity of breaking the opposition of the exploiters. When the Fabians assure us that they do not feel themselves "called upon" to discuss "this condition," we feel constrained to remark that these gentlemen are mistaken altogether as to their calling. It is quite possible that their most active leaders may be useful in some office or other of the future Labour government, in which accountings are made of the various elements in the socialist balance sheet. But they are of no use at all when it is a question of how to create the Labour government, i.e., the fundamental condition of socialist economy.

In one of his weekly reviews in the *Daily Herald* (April 4, 1925), MacDonald by a slip of the pen delivers himself of a few rather realistic words: "The condition of the party in our days is such that the struggle will become hotter and fiercer. The Conservative Party will fight to the death, and as the power of the Labour Party becomes more threatening, the pressure of the reactionary members will become more violent (Conservative Party)."[86]

This is quite true. The more immediate the danger that the working class will come to power, the stronger will become the influence of such men as Curzon (it was quite right for MacDonald to term him a "model" for future leaders) in the Conservative Party. MacDonald has this time given us a correct estimate of the future. But, as a matter of fact, the leader of the Labour Party does not himself understand the significance and import of his words. His reference to the fact that the Conservatives will fight to the death, and more fiercely as time goes on, was made only in order to show the inexpedience of interparty parliamentary committees. In the last analysis, the prognosis offered by MacDonald not only speaks against interparty parliamentary committees, but cries out against the possibility of solving the entire present social crisis by parliamentary methods. "The Conservative Party will fight to the death" (quite right!), but this means that the Labour Party will never defeat it except by displaying its own readiness for struggle. We are dealing here not with the rivalry between two parties, but with the destinies of two classes. And when two classes are fighting a life-and-death struggle, the question is never decided by counting votes. History presents no such case, and will present none while classes exist.

But the important point is not MacDonald's general philosophy, nor his occasional slips of the tongue, i.e., not the way in which he explains his activity to himself, nor his desires, but what he does and how he does it. If we approach the question from this angle, we shall find that the entire activity of MacDonald's party is paving the way for a proletarian revolution in England, of gigantic dimensions and extraordinary harshness. For it is MacDonald's party that is strengthening the self-confidence of the bourgeoisie and simultaneously testing the patience of the proletariat to the utmost. And when this patience breaks, the proletariat will be brought face to face in its rebound with the bourgeoisie, which has only been strengthened by the party of MacDonald in the consciousness of its omnipotence. The longer the Fabians succeed in holding up the revolutionary development of England, the more ominous and dangerous will be the break.

The English bourgeoisie has been trained to mercilessness by all the conditions of its insular position, its Calvinist moral philosophy, its colonial practice, its national arrogance. England is being forced more and more into the background. This inevitable process is also creating a revolutionary situation. The English bourgeoisie, obliged to humiliate itself before America, to make concessions, to maneuver, to watch and wait, is being filled with extraordinary fury, which it will reveal in frightful forms in the civil war. Similarly, the hoodlums of the French bourgeoisie, having been defeated in the Franco-Prussian War, took their revenge on the Communards; similarly, the officers' corps of the shattered Hohenzollern army took its revenge on the German workers.

The cold cruelty displayed by ruling England in its relations with the Hindus, Egyptians, and Irish, which has seemed to be an arrogance of race, will in the case of civil war reveal its true class character when directed against the proletariat. On the other hand, the revolution will inevitably awaken in the English working class the most unusual passions, which have hitherto been so artificially held down and turned aside, with the aid of social training, the Church, and the press, in the artificial channels of boxing, football, racing, and other sports.

The actual course of the struggle, its duration, its outcome, will depend entirely on the internal and particularly on the international situation at the moment the conflict breaks out. In the decisive struggle against the proletariat, the English bourgeoisie will receive the most powerful support from the bourgeoisie of the United States, while the English proletariat will draw its strength in the first place from the working class of Europe and the subject nations in the British colonies. The character of the British empire will inevitably impart to this gigantic struggle the scale of a worldwide conflict. It will be one of the most impressive spectacles of world history. The destinies of the English proletariat will be bound up in this struggle with the destinies of all mankind. The entire world situation and the role of the English proletariat in production and in society assures it of the victory, provided its leadership be truly and resolutely revolutionary. The Communist Party will expand and come to power as the party of the proletarian dictatorship. There is no roundabout way. He who believes in and preaches any such way will merely deceive the English workers. That is the most important lesson to be drawn from this analysis.

Part 2

Where is Britain going? Part 2

Editorial note

The collection that Trotsky entitled *Kuda idet Angliya? 2 vypusk (Where Is Britain Going? Part II)* was published by the State Publishing House, Moscow-Leningrad, in the second half of 1926, following the British general strike in May.

An English translation of the first chapter, "Problems of the British Labor Movement *(In Lieu of a Preface),"* was printed in *Communist International,* no. 22, 1926. That translation is used here, after stylistic changes and the restoration of certain phrases critical of British "leftists" that were deleted by *Communist International* for political reasons.

The second, third, and fourth chapters were translated for this volume from the Russian by Julia Drayton. Portions of chapters two and four appeared in English in *International Press Correspondence (Inprecorr)* on March 11 and June 5, 1926, respectively.

The four chapters in Part 2 have also been published in Britain by New Park Publications under the title *Problems of the British Revolution,* translated by R. Chappell, 1972. This pamphlet, however, omits all the material collected by Trotsky as appendixes for his work.

Following the four chapters, the editors have included all the material collected by Trotsky as appendixes to his work. Wherever possible, the original English, German, and Yiddish versions have been used for these appendixes; those that could not be located in the original language have been retranslated from the Russian by Julia Drayton, and are identified accordingly.

The excerpting of the selections in the appendixes follows the Russian edition, except in the case of the MacDonald and Williams articles, which we have chosen to print in full. In some of these selections, Trotsky's critics quote from the American translation of his book *(Whither England?);* in others they quote from the British translation *(Where Is Britain Going?).* We have not attempted to make them uniform.

Problems of the British labor movement

(In lieu of a preface)

MAY 19, 1926

The present article is a collection of fragments written at different times dating from the end of last year [1925]. These fragments were primarily intended to be used as material for a more complete work. The general strike,[1] like all epoch-making events at once changed perspective and gave prominence to some problems while relegating others to the background. From the point of view of understanding and evaluating the general strike and its outcome, it would seem more expedient to print these fragments as they were written, hot on the trail of facts and events, i.e., in chronological order.

DECEMBER 22, 1925

We have already mentioned that we have at our disposal two letters from a British "left" socialist, written at an interval of but a few weeks. The first letter was written prior to the Liverpool conference of the Labour Party (September 1925), and the second after.

"The most controversial question in the present political world," wrote our author in his first letter, "is undoubtedly the question as to what will happen at the annual Labour Party conference in Liverpool. . . . The Liverpool conference in all probability will not only rescind its last year's resolution to exclude Communists, but may even lay the basis for a definite split in the ranks of the Labour Party itself."[2] As we already know, things turned out just the other way about. The right wing scored a complete victory, while the left wingers presented a sorry picture of helplessness and confusion. The exclusion of the Communists was confirmed and reinforced.

In the second letter, written after the conference, our correspondent makes the following admission: "With regard to the Liverpool conference, at which I was not present, I can now make only one observation. The right wingers maintained the upper hand, while the lefts once more disclosed inadequate unity. The Communists also gained a victory. *The right wingers played right into the hands of the Communists. . . .*" It is hardly likely that our author himself understands what this means, though the logic of the facts is simple: if you want a victory over the MacDonaldites, over organized treachery, over systematic betrayal, then act not in the spirit of the "lefts" but in the Bolshevik spirit.[3] In that sense alone do the right wingers play into the hands of the Communists.

The working class, in the words of this same critic, "is encumbered by both extreme wings." Excellently put! What the "left" calls the right wing is the official leadership of the Labour Party. The political will of the British proletariat, whether it likes it or not, passes through the Thomas-MacDonald clearing house. The opposite wing, i.e., the Communists, are a small persecuted minority in the labor movement. In what way can the working class be "encumbered" by them? Either it wants to listen to them or it does not. They do not possess any means whereby to impose a hearing for themselves. Thomas and MacDonald have the entire machinery of the capitalist state to back them. MacDonald excludes the Communists; Baldwin throws them into jail.[4] One thing is the corollary of the other.

The working class can shake off MacDonald only when it really wants to shake off Baldwin. The working class is becoming more and more burdened by its dependency upon the conservative Fabian bourgeois politicians. How to get rid of them, what path to choose—this it does not yet know.

The left wingers reflect the discontent of the British working class. As yet it is ill-defined, and they express its profound and persistent endeavor to break away from Baldwin-MacDonald in left oppositional phrases entailing no obligations whatsoever. They transform the political helplessness of the awakening masses into an ideological maze. They constitute an expression of the forward move, but also act as a brake on it.

We have already heard the prophecy that the Liverpool conference would lay the foundation for a definite split in the ranks of the Labour Party, and we see how cruelly real life ridiculed this prophecy. An imperialist war was needed to compel the centrists to split away temporarily from the social-imperialists. No sooner had the pressure of events weakened than the centrists retraced their steps. Centrism is not capable of an independent policy. Centrism cannot be the leading party of the working class. The essence of centrism is that it does not decide to decide—and even when it does, that is only when events definitely force it to do so. But in Great Britain things have not yet got to that stage: that is why there was no split whatever at Liverpool.

What would have happened, however, if such a split had

taken place? Here, too, our author does not leave us without an explanation: "As a result of such a split, two parties would have ultimately had to be formed out of the former Labour Party; one a left-liberal party, and the other a genuine socialist party. . . . Even if one allows that that development will lead to economic upheavals and revolution, the socialist party arising out of this split could assume the leadership of the revolution, and Trotsky does not even take this into account."

In this argument, scraps of truth are lost in confusion. It stands to reason that for centrists like our critic, to split away from the Fabian bourgeoisie would not be without effect on the labor movement. But to bring about such a split now, sagacity and will would be necessary, which are just the qualities of which there is not a trace in the British "opposition." Even if the centrists do split, this will be at the last moment when there is no other way out.

But a party which is hatched at the "last moment" cannot lead a revolution. This does not mean that centrists who have split away cannot temporarily "lead" the masses, like the German Independents and even the Social Democrats at the end of 1918,[5] like our Mensheviks, and Social Revolutionaries after February 1917. Such a stage in the development of the British revolution is not out of the question. It will even be inevitable if the ferment of social antagonisms proceeds more rapidly than the formation of the Communist Party.

Under pressure of a general strike and a victorious rising, a certain section of the "left" leaders might even get into power—with something of the same feelings and moods as a calf going to the slaughter. Such a situation, however, would be of short duration. The "independents," despite their entire policy, might get into power, but they could not maintain power. Power would either have to go from the centrists to the communists or else be returned to the bourgeoisie.

Raised to power by the revolution, against their own will,

the German Independents immediately shared this power with Ebert and Scheidemann. Ebert immediately entered into negotiations with General Groener[6] to suppress the workers. The Independents criticized the Spartacists, the Social Democrats hounded them down, while the officers shot Liebknecht and Luxemburg.[7] Then events took their own logical course. The coalition between the Social Democrats and Independents was replaced by a coalition of capitalists and Social Democrats. Then the Social Democrats were no longer needed. Ebert died just in time. The revolution, which started out against Hindenburg,[8] ended with the election of Hindenburg as president of the republic. By that time the Independents had already returned to the banner of Ebert.

In Russia, the Mensheviks and Social Revolutionary patriots, who opposed the revolution by every possible means in the name of defense, were brought to power by the revolution. The Bolshevik Party, despite fifteen years of unexampled training, organization, and militant work, was at first an insignificant minority. Ready at any moment to act on the left flank against all attempts at counterrevolution, the party at the same time pursued a ruthless ideological struggle against the parties which against their will found themselves "heading the revolution." It was only this that made October possible.

A split between the British "Independents" and MacDonald and Thomas five minutes before the bell is not out of the question. And with a stormy development of events, the accession of the centrists to power is also not impossible. There need be no doubt that in this case they will beseech MacDonald and Webb to share the burden with them. Nor need there be any doubt that MacDonald—himself or through Thomas—will at the same time conduct negotiations with Joynson-Hicks.[9] A powerful apparatus for liquidating the proletarian semi-victory will be set in motion. It is very possible that among the left wingers a new split will set in.

But the development will proceed along a "Russian" and not a "German" path only if there be in existence a mass Communist Party armed with a clear comprehension of the entire trend of events.

DECEMBER 25, 1925

A foreign communist who knows England well, and only recently left there, wrote to me a few days ago:

> During my sojourn in England I had many talks with certain prominent left leaders on the theme of the British revolution. The impression I came away with was approximately as follows: they are certain that in the near future they will secure a parliamentary majority and will commence the cautious but decisive realization of the maximum demands of the working class, such as the nationalization of the mines and certain other branches of industry and of the banks, etc. "If the industrial magnates and bankers dare to resist, oh well, they will be immediately arrested and their enterprises nationalized." To my question: "What would the fascist bourgeoisie, in whose hands are the army and navy, do in such an event?" I was answered: "In the event of the armed resistance of the fascists, they will be outlawed, and the British people in their overwhelming majority will follow the Labour Party in defense of lawful government." When I pointed out: "Since it is inevitable that they will resort to arms, the working class should already be preparing now for such an event, so that the armed forces of the bourgeoisie will not take them unawares," they replied: "Such a preparation would be a premature signal for civil war and would prevent the Labour Party from getting a majority in Parliament."

To the question: "On what side of the barricades will MacDonald, Snowden, Thomas, and their friends be?" they replied: "Most probably on the side of the bourgeoisie."

"Why then do you work together with them against the Communists to strengthen a party leadership which will betray the working class at the critical moment?" The answer to this was: "We think that in any case we shall succeed in retaining a majority in Parliament, and that the splitting away of MacDonald and his Liberal friends absolutely does not threaten the successful outcome to a peaceful revolution."

This little page of personal impressions and thoughts is really priceless. These people were firmly decided in advance to get into power no other way than over the asses' bridge which had been pointed out to them by an enemy armed to the teeth and keeping guard over this bridge. If they, the lefts, take power (over the bridge indicated), and if the bourgeoisie rises up against the lawful authority, then the good British people will not tolerate this. And if MacDonald and Thomas, whom the wise left wingers carry on their backs, prove by chance to be in conspiracy with the armed bourgeoisie against the unarmed workers, this should not instill fear into anyone, as the left wingers have provided for victory in this case also.

In short, these courageous and wise fellows have firmly decided to beat the bourgeoisie in all possible eventualities, and at the same time maintain the best relations with Parliament, the law, the courts, and the policemen. It is a pity that the bourgeoisie does not intend giving the lefts a prerogative for the legal expropriation of power. The more energetically the fascist wing is pushed forward, and the more direct the threat of civil war becomes, the more the bourgeoisie will find adequate means of provocation, of a legal coup d'etat, etc. For after all, the question is not who best interprets laws and traditions, but who is master in the house.

*

The heated discussion which was recently carried on in the British labor press on the question of self-defense is extremely significant. The question itself arose not as a problem of an armed rising for the seizure of power, but as a problem of strikers resisting blacklegs and fascists.

We have already pointed out elsewhere how trade unionism by the very logic of development—particularly under the conditions of the decline of capitalism—will inevitably break outside the bounds of democracy. Class conflicts cannot be arbitrarily postponed until a parliamentary majority is won. Hard pressed by its own decline, the bourgeoisie brings pressure to bear on the proletariat. The latter defends itself. Hence, inevitable strike collisions. The government prepares blackleg organizations in dimensions hitherto unprecedented. The fascists are linked up with the police. The workers raise the question of self-defense. Here already we have the basis of a civil war.

A worker writes in *Lansbury's Labour Weekly:* "Fascism is purely and simply a military organization and is not amenable to argument. It can only be successfully countered by a similar organization on the other side." The author recommends taking the military organization of fascism as an example. Quite right: the proletariat can and should learn military methods from the enemy.

From the same source—the objective sharpening of class antagonisms—there develops the desire of the workers to win the soldiers onto their side. Agitation in the army and navy is the second powerful element in civil war, the development of which is not in direct connection with the conquest of a parliamentary majority. The transfer of a considerable section of the armed forces onto the side of the workers would ensure the conquest of power by the proletariat even without a parliamentary majority. The greatest possible majority in parliament can be reduced to nought if armed force is in the hands of the bourgeoisie. Whoever does not understand that is not a socialist, but a blockhead.

The left-wing wiseacres have scraped together all the prejudices and commonplaces of the past few centuries against the slogan for arming the workers: the preeminence of the moral factor over violence, the advantages of gradual reforms and the anarcho-pacifist idea of a peaceful strike, which they require not as a means of struggle but as an argument against insurrection, and heroic preparedness . . . to allow violence in the so-called "extreme eventuality when it is forced on us," i.e., evidently when the enemy, having taken us unawares, pins us unarmed against a wall.

DECEMBER 28, 1925

The left critic accuses us just because we back the British Communist Party as winner. That does not mean that he completely rejects it himself. No, the position of a left winger—without rudder and without sails—consists of not recognizing anything completely and not denying anything entirely. Here we are compelled once more to quote him.

> Instead of trying to regenerate the masses, they [the Communists] have endeavored to drive them on with a big stick, and the masses are definitely discontented with this. A striking testimony of the correctness of the principles they defend is the fact that despite all their hopelessly wrong tactics, despite their scurrilous attacks against friends and enemies, despite their profound ignorance of those masses whom they declare to lead, they nevertheless have great influence. If the workers adhere

to them, they do this *out of despair*, because they do not see any other way out—not because they approve the party as it is at present, but because they are compelled to accept its conclusions.

Those words are truly remarkable as the involuntary testimony of an opponent in favor of the ideas and methods against which he struggles. The inner force of communism is so great that larger numbers of workers adhere to it, despite the "scurrilous" nature of the Communists. But the workers do so out of despair!—exclaims our critic, who also seems to be rather desperate.

It is quite true that the workers are really getting into a state of "despair"—and this will continue to become aggravated more and more as a result of worthless, treacherous, cowardly, or aimless leadership. One cannot even conceive that the British workers with their age-long traditions of liberal politics, parliamentarism, compromise, national self-conceit, etc., could consciously take the path of revolution other than by utterly despairing of the very same policy which formerly gave them something, or which at any rate successfully deceived them. Here the critic has got himself into a quandary. The strength of the Communist Party lies in the fact that despite its numerical weakness, inexperience, and errors, the situation compels the working masses to listen to it more and more.

Australian Prime Minister Bruce, defending his policy of deporting revolutionary labor leaders, said on the eve of the last elections: "The Communist Party in Australia has a membership of less than a thousand. But it is able to direct 400,000 workers in the Commonwealth." The *Times* cites these words with great praise (see the lead article of November 12, 1925). Speaking of Australia, the London *Times* has of course Great Britain in view. In order to emphasize this, the paper states with crude frankness: "The truth is that the great majority of those Labour leaders in Australia who are moderate in their ideas are equally moderate in their ability. The control of the party is passing more and more into the hands of its 'wild men.'" In Russia this is called blaming the cat for stealing the milk.

We are quite ready to agree with the *Times* that the capabilities of the official leaders of the British Labour Party (at which the *Times* is hinting) are as moderate as their views. But as a matter of fact no special capabilities have been demanded of them: they have transmitted the will and ideas of the bourgeoisie amongst the working class. They were "skillful" so long as the bourgeoisie was all-powerful. We have to say that even the wise *Times,* when it mumbles on about the mutual relations between the United States and Great Britain, displays an irrelevance which results from an inner consciousness of weakness, a desire to preserve the appearance of strength, and an effort to restrain the gnashing of teeth. In the final analysis, the reason for the *Times*'s discovery of the modest capacities of MacDonald is the bad trade balance and the bad bank balance of Great Britain. And as powerful historic forces are working for the ruin of the British balance of payments, one need not doubt that the workers will fall more and more into despair with their old leaders and fall under the influence of the "wild men."

JANUARY 5, 1926

In the American publication *Freiheit,* which has pretensions to Marxism and even communism, I am rebuked on the ground that, in criticizing the British centrists, I have lost sight of the "revolution" which has already taken place in the British trade unions.

There is no need to refer here to the fact that the causes and perspectives of the evolution of the trade unions have been discussed in the chapter "Trade Unions and Bolshevism." There is no need to repeat here the elementary conception that without a swing around of the working class, and consequently of the trade unions, onto a revolutionary path, there cannot even be any talk of the proletariat conquering power.

But it would be the greatest ignominy to shirk a struggle against opportunism in the leadership by references to the profound revolutionary processes that are taking place within the working class. This seemingly "deep" approach arises entirely from not understanding the role and importance of the party in a working class movement, particularly in the revolution. Indeed it is always the centrists who have screened and will continue to screen opportunist sins by profoundly thoughtful references to objective tendencies of development. Is it worthwhile wasting time and energy on a struggle with hopelessly confused people such as Wheatley, Brailsford, Purcell, Kirkwood, etc.,[10] once revolutionary tendencies are already growing up amongst the proletariat, once the trade unions are already swinging around towards collaboration with the Soviet trade unions, etc.? In reality, this pretended revolutionary objectivism only expresses a desire to elude revolutionary tasks by transferring them onto the shoulders of a so-called historic process.

The danger of tendencies of this kind is particularly great in England. Yesterday we had to prove that objective conditions were working there in a revolutionary direction. To keep repeating this over and over again today is like knocking at an open door. The growing preponderance of America; the burden of debts and war expenses; the industrialization of the colonies, dominions, and in general of the more backward countries; the economic strengthening of the Soviet Union and the growth of its magnetic revolutionary forces; the liberation movement in the oppressed nations—all these are factors in a growing process. Through inevitable conjunctural fluctuations, British capitalism is moving toward a catastrophe. It is clear what advances in the correlation and consciousness of classes this implies. But the objective prerequisites of the proletarian revolution are being prepared and are maturing much more rapidly than the subjective prerequisites. That fact must be understood especially *today*.

The danger is not that the bourgeoisie will once more pacify the proletariat, nor that an epoch of Liberal-Labour politics will open up again before the trade unions: the United States has monopolized for itself the possibility of a privileged position for wide circles of the proletariat. The danger lies in the other direction: *the forming of the proletarian vanguard might lag behind the development of the revolutionary situation.* Faced with the necessity for decisive action, the proletariat might be unable to find the necessary political leadership. It is a question of the *party*. This is the question of questions. The most mature revolutionary situation without a revolutionary party of the necessary dimensions, without correct leadership, is just like a knife without a blade. We saw this in the autumn of 1923 in Germany.[11] A Bolshevik party in Great Britain can only be built up in the process of a permanent and irreconcilable struggle against the centrism which is taking the place of Liberal-Labour policy.

JANUARY 6, 1926

The struggle for a united front is of such great significance in England because it responds to the elementary demands of the working class for a new orientation and grouping of forces. This being the case, the struggle for the united front raises the question of leadership, i.e., of program and tactics, and this means the question of the party.

But the struggle for the united front itself does not solve

this problem, it only creates certain conditions for its solution. The ideological and organizational formation of a really revolutionary (i.e., Communist) party, on the basis of a mass movement, is only conceivable under conditions of a continuous, systematic, unwavering, untiring, and naked denunciation of the muddles, the compromises, and indecision of the quasi-left leaders of all shades.

It would be the most profound error to think (and such a tendency is to be observed) that the task of the united front consists in securing the victory of Purcell, Lansbury, Wheatley, and Kirkwood over Snowden, Webb, and MacDonald. Such an aim would contain an inner contradiction. The left-wing muddlers are not capable of power; and if in the course of events power got into their hands, they would hasten to hand it over to their elder brothers on their right. They would act in the government in exactly the same way as they do now in the party.

The history of the German Independents—let us recall it once more—gives very instructive lessons in this respect. In Germany the process took place at a very much more rapid rate, in accordance with the directly revolutionary nature of the past few years in German history. But the general tendencies of development are one and the same; we call MacDonald Ebert, or christen Wheatley and Cook as Crispien and Hilferding.[12] The fact that the commonplace, petty-bourgeois Hilferding still cites Marx, while Wheatley gives preference to the holy Pope of Rome, arises from the peculiarities of England and Germany in the past, but it is only of tenth-rate significance for the present day.

JANUARY 7, 1926

The left faction in the higher trade union organs has the General Council in tow on a number of questions. This is most clearly expressed in respect to the Soviet trade unions and Amsterdam.[13] But it would be erroneous to overestimate the influence of these left wingers over the trade unions as organizations of the class struggle. This is not because the trade union masses are insufficiently radical; on the contrary, the masses are immeasurably more left than the left wingers themselves. In the British labor movement, international questions have always been the line of least resistance for the "leaders." Regarding international matters as a kind of safety valve for the radical moods of the masses, these esteemed leaders are prepared to a certain extent even to bow to a revolution (elsewhere) so that they can take still more revenge on questions of the internal class struggle. The left faction of the General Council is distinguished by its complete *ideological* shapelessness and therefore is incapable of *organizationally* assuming the leadership of the trade union movement.

The impotence of the left wingers inside the Labour Party is explained in the same manner. The Labour Party after all is based on these very same trade unions. It would seem that the left faction "leading" the General Council would also have laid its hands on the Labour Party. But in reality we see something quite different. The party continues to be led by extreme right wingers. This is explained by the fact that the party cannot be restricted to various left ventures, but is bound to have a generalized system of politics. The left wingers have no such system, their very nature prevents this. The right wingers have a system: they have behind them tradition, experience, routine; and most important of all, bourgeois society as a whole is thinking for them and thrusts ready-made decisions under their noses. MacDonald has only to translate Baldwin's or Lloyd George's suggestions into the Fabian language. The right wingers are victorious despite the fact that the lefts are more numerous. The weakness of the left wingers comes from their lack of cohesion and this arises from their ideological shapelessness. In order to rally their ranks, the left wingers will first of all have to collect their thoughts. The best of them are only capable of doing this under the blows of ruthless criticism based on the everyday experiences of the masses.

JANUARY 12, 1926

Not only our "left" critic in his letter, but also more responsible left leaders like Purcell, Cook, and Bromley[14] were predicting as far back as September 27 [1925], that the Labour Party conference would be marked by a big move to the left. Things proved to be just the contrary: only a few weeks after the Scarborough trades union congress, the Liverpool conference gave a complete victory to MacDonald. To ignore this fact, to hush it up, to minimize it or explain it away by chance secondary causes would mean playing the fool and going headlong towards defeat.

Fundamentally the Labour Party has the same base as the trade union leaders. But the General Council, whose powers are extremely limited, has no authority over the individual trade unions, let alone over the whole country. The Labour Party, however, has been in power and once more is preparing to take the reins of government. There lies the crux of the matter.

The Liberal *Manchester Guardian*, writing on the Scarborough congress, stated that the influence of Moscow was only to be seen in the left phraseology, but that in practice the trade unions remain under the leadership of wise and experienced leaders. Of course the Liberal paper needs consolation; nevertheless there is no small degree of truth in its assertions. The more left the congress decisions are, the further away they are from immediate practical tasks.

Of course the leftism of the decisions is symptomatic,

and marks an about-face in the consciousness of the masses. But to think that the leaders of the Scarborough congress could become leaders of a revolutionary upheaval would be lulling oneself to sleep with illusions. It is enough to recall that there were 3,802,000 votes in favor of the right of the oppressed nationalities to self-determination even including separation, against only 79,000. What a colossal revolutionary move this would appear to be! Meanwhile, for the creation of factory committees—not for an armed uprising or for a general strike, but for nothing more than forming shop committees, and only in principle at that—there were altogether 2,183,000 votes against 1,787,000. In other words, the congress was practically divided in half. On the question of granting increased power to the General Council, the left wingers suffered complete defeat. Is it surprising then, if, after all these left resolutions, the General Council proved to be more to the right than the old one? It should be thoroughly understood that leftism of this kind remains left only so long as it has no practical obligations. But as soon as the question of action arises, the left wingers respectfully cede the leadership to the rights.

JANUARY 13, 1926

A spontaneous radicalization of the trade unions marking a profound move amongst the masses is quite inadequate in itself to free the working class from the leadership of Thomas and MacDonald. In England, national-bourgeois ideology is a powerful force not only of public opinion, but also of institutions centuries old. "Radical" trade unionism crashes against this force and will continue to do so, so long as it is led by centrists who do not carry things out to their logical conclusion.

While the trade unions are fraternizing with the Soviet

trade unions, which are led by Communists, the British Labour Party, based on the same trade unions, hounds the Communists out of their ranks at Liverpool, thereby preparing the destruction of their organizations by the government and fascists. It would be criminal to forget for a moment that such left wingers as Brailsford and even Lansbury in substance approved the decision of the Liverpool conference, blaming the Communists for everything. It is true that when indignation at the reactionary police spirit of the Liverpool conference was revealed from below, the "left" leaders slightly changed their course. But in order to get a proper estimation of them, we must take both factors into consideration. Revolutionaries need a good memory. The "left" gentlemen do not have a policy of their own. In the future also, they will swing to the right under the pressure of the bourgeois-Fabian reactionaries, and to the left under the pressure of the masses. In difficult moments these most pious Christians are always prepared to play the role, if not of Herod, at least of Pontius Pilate, and in the future many difficult moments await the British working class.

There is a movement in the Independent Labour Party in favor of the fusion of the Second and Third Internationals. But just ask these same people whether they agree not even to fusion, but just to a fighting agreement with the British Communists, and they will at once jump back in alarm. In everything that concerns the revolution, the British left wingers are dominated by "love for distance." They are in favor of the October Revolution, the Soviet system, the Soviet trade unions, and even a rapprochement with the Comintern, but under the perpetual condition that the British constitution, the parliamentary system, and the system of the Labour Party are not abandoned. The main blow must be directed against this loathsome two-faced policy of the left wingers.

We must add that the sympathy of many left wingers for

the Soviet Union (while they are hostile to their own Communists) contains a large admixture of petty-bourgeois deference to a strong state authority. This must not be forgotten. Of course, a petty bourgeois who turns round towards the Soviet Republic is more progressive than the petty bourgeois who kneels to the United States. It is a step forward. But deference is not the quality needed for the development of revolutionary perspectives.

MARCH 5, 1926 [FROM A LETTER]

. . . In Great Britain, more than in all the rest of Europe, the consciousness of the working masses, particularly of the leading strata, lags behind the objective economic situation. In this direction the main difficulties and dangers now lie. All shades of leaders of the British labor movement fear action, because the historic hopelessness of the position of British capitalism directly confronts any important problem of the labor movement.

This particularly concerns the mining industry. The present wages of the miners are maintained by a subsidy from the state which is already burdened with a budget far beyond its capacity. To continue the subsidy means accumulating and intensifying the economic crisis. To refuse the subsidy means provoking a social crisis.

The necessity for the technical and economic reorganization of the mining industry arises as a profound revolutionary problem and therefore demands the political "reorganization" of the working class. The destruction of the conservatism of the British mining industry, this foundation stone of British capitalism, can only be attained by destroying the conservative organizations, traditions, and habits of the British labor movement.

Great Britain is entering on an entire historic phase of

great upheavals. It is only the conservative British trade union leaders who can wait for an "economic" solution of the problem. But it is just because the British trade union leaders are directing their efforts towards an "economic" (i.e., peaceful, compromising, conservative) solution of the problem (i.e., are going counter to the historic process) that the revolutionary development of the working class in Great Britain will have greater overhead charges in the forthcoming epoch than in any other country. Both the right wingers and the left wingers, including of course, both Purcell and Cook, have the greatest fear of commencing the final action. Even when they verbally admit the inevitability of struggle and revolution, they hope in their heart of hearts for some kind of miracle that will deliver them from this prospect. At any rate they will themselves put a brake on the movement, will evade, will wait and see, will refer responsibility to others, and in reality will help Thomas in any really important problem of the *British* labor movement (they are more courageous in respect to *international* questions).

Hence, we may characterize the general situation as follows: the economic cul-de-sac in which the country finds itself, which is most clearly expressed in the mining industry, impels the working class to seek a way out, i.e., impels them onto the path of a more and more acute struggle. And the first stage of this struggle inevitably reveals the inadequacy of the "customary" methods of struggle. The entire present "superstructure" of the British working class—in all tendencies and groupings without exception—represents an apparatus acting as a brake on the revolution. This augurs for a long period the pressure of a spontaneous or semi-spontaneous movement against the framework of the old organizations and the formation of new revolutionary organizations on the basis of this pressure.

One of the most important tasks is to aid the Communist Party of Great Britain to understand and to think things out in the light of this perspective. In the trade union apparatus and its left wing, it is necessary to select immeasurably more energetically and decisively than hitherto elements of *action*, i.e., those elements which are capable of understanding the inevitability of great mass struggles, of not fearing them, and of making the best use of them. The united front tactics should be put forward more and more decisively in the light of this perspective.

As far as the miners' strike is concerned, it is naturally not a question of an isolated strike, however large the strike may be, but a question of the commencement of a whole series of social encounters and upheavals. In this situation we of course cannot be guided by the concepts of Purcell and others. They fear the struggle more than anyone else. For us their thoughts and words can have nothing more than symptomatic significance.

The British trade unions (through their bureaucracy and even the left wing) do not fear our "interference" in their internal affairs any less than Chamberlain.

There is an unlimited supply of restraining elements in the apparatus of the British working class. The entire situation may be summed up by saying that the alarm, discontent, and pressure of the British working masses all clash along the line against the organizational and ideological barriers of the conservative trade union apparatus. Under these conditions, to be anxious about how we can aid impatient leaders means nothing more than pouring water into the ocean.

Everything goes to show that during the coming period (I have in view one, two, or three years) the struggle will break out in England against the will of the old organizations and with complete unpreparedness of the young organizations. Of course, even with the firm revolutionary (i.e., active) intervention of the Communist Party and the best "left" elements, it should not be supposed that the proletariat will come into power as a result of the first great wave.

But the question is this: Will this left wing come through the first revolutionary stage at the head of the working masses, as we did in 1905, or will it let slip the opportunity of the revolutionary situation as the German party did in 1923? This latter danger is extremely real. It may be diminished only by aiding the left wing to find the proper orientation for action (the *real* left wing, and not Lansbury or Purcell). And in order to solve this problem (the problem of assistance in obtaining the correct orientation by the revolutionary elements in Great Britain), it must be clearly understood that all the traditions, the organizational customs, and the ideas of all existing groupings of the labor movement—in various forms and under various slogans—predispose them either to direct betrayal, or to compromise, or else to a policy of wait-and-see with reference to the compromisers and complaints about the traitors.

MAY 6, 1926

A year ago, the Conservative ministry was still only on its honeymoon. Baldwin was preaching social peace. As MacDonald had nothing to oppose to Conservatism, he competed with it in hatred for revolution, civil war, and the class struggle. The leaders of all three parties proclaimed that British institutions were quite sufficient to ensure peaceful class collaboration. It was quite natural that the revolutionary prediction for the immediate future of British imperialism made in this book should be described by the entire British press—from the *Morning Post* to *Lansbury's Labour Weekly*—as hopeless nonsense and Moscow phantasmagoria.

Now the situation has somewhat changed. England is convulsed by a huge mass strike. The Conservative government is carrying on a furious offensive policy. Everything is being done from above to provoke civil war. The contradiction between basic social factors and the falsehood of an out-of-date parliamentarism has become more manifest in England than ever before.

The mass strike arose from the contradiction between the present situation of British industry in the world market and the traditional conditions of production and relations between the classes within the country. Formally, the question at issue was a reduction of the miners' wages and longer hours of work, throwing onto the shoulders of the workers part of the sacrifices which are necessary for a real reorganization of the coal industry. Formulated in this way, the question is insoluble. It is perfectly true that the coal industry, as indeed the whole of British industry, cannot be reorganized without sacrifices, even serious sacrifices, on the part of the British proletariat. No one but a miserable fool, however, can imagine for a moment that the British proletariat will consent to submit to this sacrifice on the old bases of capitalist property.

Capitalism has been pictured as a regime of permanent progress and systematic improvement in the lot of the working masses. To a certain extent this was true for some countries in the course of the nineteenth century. The religion of capitalist progress was stronger in Great Britain than anywhere else. In fact it was this that formed the basis for the conservative tendencies in the labor movement itself, especially in the trade unions. In England, the war illusions (1914–18) were, more than in any other country, illusions of capitalist power and of social "progress."

Victory over Germany was to be the final crowning of these hopes. And now bourgeois society says to the miners: "If you want at least to ensure yourselves an existence such as you had before the war, you will have to accept for an indefinite time a reduction in your standard of living." Instead of the recently proclaimed prospect of steady social progress, it is now proposed that the workers should descend one step today so as to avoid tumbling down three or more steps all at once tomorrow. This is as good as a declaration of bankruptcy on the part of British capitalism. The general strike is the answer of the proletariat, which will not and cannot admit that the bankruptcy of British capitalism should be the commencement of the bankruptcy of the British nation and of British culture.

This answer, however, is dictated far more by the logic of the situation than the logic of consciousness. The British working class had no other alternative. The struggle—no matter what was the mechanism behind the scenes—was forced on them by the mechanical pressure of the whole situation. The world situation of British industry could not offer any material basis for a compromise. The Thomases, MacDonalds, etc., are like windmills which turn their sails when there is a strong wind, but do not yield a single pound of flour since there is no grain for them to grind. The hopeless emptiness of present-day British reformism was revealed with such convincing force that nothing remained for the reformists to do but to join in the mass strike of the British proletariat. This revealed the strength of the strike—but also its weakness.

The general strike is one of the most acute forms of class war. It is only one step from armed insurrection. This is why the general strike, more than any other form of class war, demands a clear, resolute, firm (i.e., a revolutionary) leadership.

In the present strike there is no trace of such a leadership of the British proletariat, and it cannot be expected that it will suddenly rise in a perfected form as though conjured up out of the ground. The General Council of the Trades Union Congress started out with the ridiculous declaration that the present general strike was in no way a *political* struggle, still less an attack on the state power of the bankers, the manufacturers, and the landowners, or on the sacred British Parliament. This most respectful and submissive declaration of war does not seem at all convincing, however, to a government which feels that through the effect of the strike the real instruments of power are slipping from its hands.

State power is not an "idea" but a material apparatus. If the apparatus of administration and suppression is paralyzed, the power of the state will also be paralyzed. In modern society, no one can rule without controlling the railways, shipping, post and telegraph, electric power, coal, etc. The fact that MacDonald and Thomas deny on oath that they have any political aims characterizes them as individuals, but by no means indicates the nature of the general strike which, if carried on to the end, will confront the revolutionary class with the task of organizing a new state power.

Those, however, who in the course of events have been placed "at the head" of the general strike, are fighting against this with all their strength. And herein lies the chief danger: men who did not want the general strike, who deny the political character of the general strike, who fear nothing so much as the consequences of a victorious strike, must inevitably direct all their efforts to keeping the strike within the scope of a semi-political semi-strike, i.e., to deprive it of its power.

We must face matters; the *main* efforts of the official leaders of the Labour Party and of a considerable number of the official trade union leaders will not be directed towards paralyzing the bourgeois state by means of the strike, but towards paralyzing the general strike with the aid of the bourgeois state. The government, through its most diehard conservatives, undoubtedly wants to provoke a civil war on a small scale so as to be in a position to resort to measures of terror even before the struggle develops, and thus suppress the movement.

By robbing the strike of its political program, by disintegrating the revolutionary will of the proletariat and driving the movement into a blind alley, the reformists force individual groups of workers onto the path of isolated revolts. In this sense, the reformists find themselves on the same ground as the fascist elements of the Conservative Party. Herein lies the chief danger of the fight which has begun.

It would be inopportune at this moment to make prophecies as to the duration of the fight and its development, to say nothing of its outcome. Everything must be done from the international point of view to help the fighters. We must, however, clearly recognize that success is only possible in accordance with the degree to which the British working class, in the process of the development and intensification of the general strike, realizes the necessity for changing its leaders and succeeds in so doing. The American proverb says that one should not swap horses when crossing a stream. This practical wisdom is only true within certain limits. It has never yet been possible to cross the stream of revolution on the horse of reformism, and the class which has entered the battle under opportunist leaders is compelled to change horses under fire.

In this way, the position of the really revolutionary elements of the British proletariat, particularly of the Communists, is predetermined. They will support the unity of mass action in every way, but they cannot permit any appearance of unity with the opportunist leaders of the Labour Party and the trade unions. The most important piece of work for the truly revolutionary participants in the general strike will be to fight relentlessly against every trace or act of treachery, and mercilessly expose reformist illusions. In so doing, they will not only help forward the chief and permanent task of developing revolutionary cadres, without which the victory of the British proletariat is altogether impossible, but they will also contribute directly to the success of the present strike by intensifying it, revealing its revolutionary implications, pushing aside the opportunists and strengthening the position of the revolutionaries. The results of the strike—both in immediate results and those further ahead—will be all the more important the more decisively the revolutionary will of the masses breaks down the barriers and obstacles of the counterrevolutionary leadership.

The strike in itself cannot alter the position of British capitalism, especially of the coal industry, in the world market. This requires the reorganization of the entire British economic system. The strike is only an emphatic expression of this necessity. The program of the reorganization of British industry is a program for a new power, a new state, a new class. Herein lies the fundamental significance of the general strike; it brings the question of power sharply to the forefront. A real victory for the general strike can only be found in the conquest of power by the proletariat and in the establishment of a proletarian dictatorship.

In view of the hopeless situation of British capitalism, the general strike should now less than ever be regarded as an instrument of reform or partial conquest. To put it more exactly, if the mine owners or the government were to make this or that concession under the pressure of the strike, these concessions would, in view of the whole situation, have neither a deep nor a permanent significance. This by no means implies that the present strike is faced with the alternative of all or nothing. Had the British proletariat been under a leadership which to some extent was in keeping with its class strength and the maturity of the conditions, power would have passed from the hands of the Conservatives into the hands of the proletariat in the course of a few weeks. As it is, we can hardly reckon with an outcome of this kind. This, however, does not mean that the strike is hopeless. The more widely it develops, the more violently it shakes the foundations of capitalism, the more completely it rejects the treacherous and opportunist leaders, the more difficult will it be for bourgeois reaction to take up a counteroffensive, the less the proletarian organizations will suffer, the sooner the next decisive stage of the fight will come.

The present class conflict will be a tremendous lesson and have vast consequences, quite irrespective of its immediate results. It will be clear to every worker in England that Parliament is incapable of solving the fundamental and vital tasks of the country. The question of the economic salvation of Britain will now present itself to the proletariat as a question of the conquest of power. A death blow will be given to all mediating, conciliatory, compromising and pseudopacifist tendencies. The Liberal Party, no matter how much its leaders may turn and twist, will emerge from this test even more humiliated than before it entered the fight. Within the Conservative Party, the die-hard elements will gain predominance. Within the Labour Party, the revolutionary wing will increase in influence and will find more complete expression. The Communists will push forward resolutely. The revolutionary development of Great Britain will make great strides forward.

Seen in the light of the mighty strike now developing, the questions of evolution and revolution, of peaceful development and the use of force, of reforms and of class dictatorship will, in their full intensity, occupy the consciousness of hundreds of thousands, even millions, of British workers. Of this there can be no doubt. The British proletariat, which has been kept in a state of terrible ideological backwardness by the bourgeoisie and its Fabian agents, will now spring forward like a lion.

Material conditions in England have long been ripe for socialism. The strike has made the substitution of a proletarian state for the bourgeois one a question of the day. If the strike itself does not bring about this change, it will at least greatly hasten its approach, though in what period of time we cannot of course say. We should be prepared, however, for the possibility of an early date.

MAY 13, 1926

The defeat of the general strike at the present stage is "according to the law of things," i.e., arises from all the conditions of the origin and development of the strike. This defeat could be foreseen. There is nothing discouraging in it. But we will speak of the lessons of this defeat and of the lessons of the strike itself later.

On tempos and dates
February 11, 1926

During the year that has elapsed since the book *Where Is Britain Going?* was written, events have not developed along the lines mapped out by Baldwin or MacDonald. The geniality of the Conservative prime minister has quickly evaporated. The judges of King George have thrown into prison the Communists excluded by MacDonald from the Labour Party, putting the party into a nonlegal position. The same judges pat the young fascist good-for-nothings on the shoulder encouragingly, commending the lawbreakers to join the police force whose vocation it is to protect the law. In this way, the judges prove that the difference between a fascist breach of the law and police protection of the law is one of form, in no way one of essence. The fascists are excellent citizens, but too impatient; their methods are premature. . . . The class war has not yet come to civil war.

MacDonald and Lansbury are still doing their job, restraining the proletariat with the fictions of democracy and the myths of religion. Fascism stays in the background. But the capitalist politicians understand that the matter will not be kept within the confines of democratic methods, and when he is by himself, Mr. Joynson-Hicks tries on the mask of Mussolini.

The tough repressiveness of the Baldwin government of necessity supplements its miserable economic confusion. The protectionism of the Conservative Party is as powerless as the free trade of the Liberals in the face of fresh economic facts. It was clear from the outset that attempts at protectionism would clash with the contradictory interests of the main branches of the British economy. But we never thought a year ago that the protectionist program would degenerate into such a farce. In this period, duties have been imposed on lace, gloves, musical instruments, gas-lighters, penknives, and toilet paper. In these branches of industry, not more than 10,000 workers are employed. But there are 1,231,900 miners. And there are 1,215,900 officially out of work. Isn't Mr. Baldwin over-abusing . . . "gradualism"?

The Liberal Party, whose collapse continues to be one of the most striking political expressions of the social decline of Britain, has—as far as the majority of its members is concerned—given up hope of independent power, and its right flank dreams of acting as a left-brake on the Conservatives while its left flank would like to be the right-support to MacDonald, who will need such support more and more. When old Asquith comments ironically on the speeches of Snowden and Churchill, the first of whom invites the Liberals to enter the Labour Party and the second the Conservative, Mr. Asquith is correct in his own way: between dying as an appendage of old political enemies and dying independent—there is no great difference.

The role of the MacDonald clique in the period with which we are concerned is sufficiently characterized by the simple juxtaposition of the facts. In 1924, the MacDonald government brought the Communists to trial under a penal law of

1797 (the period of the great French Revolution). At the end of 1925, MacDonald obtained the exclusion of the Communists from the Labour Party. The most reactionary minister of the Conservative government, Benito Joynson-Hicks, already mentioned above, brought the Communists to trial by the same law of 1797, and imprisoned the leaders of the party. The masses of workers protested. The MacDonald clique was forced to utter inarticulate noises of protest too. Against what? Obviously against the fact that the rival Joynson-Hicks had snatched their bit of bread from them.

Neither the economics nor the politics of Britain in the past year gives any cause for modifying in any way the conclusions of our book. There are no grounds for reacting to the gnashing of teeth of the bourgeois press of Britain and especially of America. "Leon Trotsky, under false cover of [a] new book," claims a New York newspaper, "instructs American and English people how to revolt." And the newspaper demands drastic measures against the book since the author is far away. That's all right. There is no need to answer. Events will provide the answer. The only thing I learned from the criticisms of the British bourgeois press is that Mr. Winston Churchill is not yet a lord as I had supposed erroneously . . . or at least prematurely.

The official Menshevik press says the same thing in essence, except that its call to the bourgeois police against "the preaching of force" takes a somewhat more disguised form. Here, too, there is no place for polemics. Of much greater interest to us in the present stage of developments is the left opposition in Britain. From its literary representatives, however, we hear very little. "If the irrational Moscow tendencies should take root in our soil, it could only be thanks to the self-interest of our bourgeoisie and the excessive compliance of the leaders of the Labour Party," etc., etc. That is the meaning of the articles of Lansbury, Brailsford, and others. We can predict the ready centrist cliches, thoughts, and turns of phrase. To expect a real attempt at analysis of facts and arguments from these gentlemen—is close to expecting milk from a ram.

Fortunately, we have in our hands a document distinguished by far greater directness and, so to say, freshness. A Russian comrade, in correspondence with an activist of the British workers' movement, has sent me two letters from a "left" member of the Independent Labour Party, directed against my book *Where Is Britain Going?* These letters appear to me more interesting than the articles of the British and other "leaders" of whom some have forgotten how to think and the others have never known how to. I do not at all wish to say that the author of the letters argues correctly. On the contrary, it is difficult to imagine greater chaos than that which reigns in his thoughts—in which, by the way, he sees his greatest advantage over the complete conciliators such as MacDonald, and over us "dogmatists" of revolution. We are familiar enough from Russian and international experience with confusionists of this kind. If, nevertheless, we consider the critical letters from the "leftist," not intended for publication, more instructive than the polished articles of the professional centrists, it is precisely because in the honest eclectic muddle of the letters, the political changes in the masses are more directly reflected. It goes without saying that we are using the letters with the friendly authorization of the two, Russian and British, correspondents.

The ideological groupings in the British workers' movement, and especially in its leading stratum, can be divided along three main lines. The right occupies the leading position in the Labour Party, as was again proved at the Liverpool conference. The remnants of the bourgeois theories of the nineteenth century, especially of its first half, form the official ideology of these gentlemen, who will stop at nothing in defense of bourgeois society. At the other pole is the tiny Communist minority. The British working class will gain a victory only under the leadership of a Bolshevik party. Today the party is still in its swaddling clothes. But it is growing, and it can grow quickly.

Between these two groups, different to the highest degree, as between river banks, are a vast number of shades and tendencies which in themselves have no future but prepare it. The "theorists" and "politicians" of this broad central tendency are recruited from eclectics, sentimentalists, hysterical humanitarians, and all kinds of muddleheads. For some of them, eclecticism is a complete life mission, for others, a stage of development. The opposition movement, led by the left, the semi-left and the extreme left, reflects the deep social change in the masses. But the intermediary character of the British "left," their theoretical amorphousness, their political indecision, not to speak of their cowardice, assures the mastery of the situation to the clique of MacDonald, Webb, and Snowden, which in turn is impossible without Thomas. If the summits of the British Labour Party can be compared to a bridle fastened on the working class, then Thomas is the buckle through which the bourgeoisie passes the reins.

The present stage in the development of the British proletariat, when the overwhelming majority respond sympathetically to the speeches of the "left" and support MacDonald and Thomas in power, is no accident, of course. It is impossible to skip this stage. The road of the Communist Party, as the future great mass party, goes not only via irreconcilable struggle against the agents of capital in the form of the Thomas-MacDonald clique, but also via the systematic unmasking of the muddleheads of the left through whose support alone MacDonald and Thomas are able to preserve their positions. In this lies the justification of our attention to the "left" critic.

*

There is no need to say that the critic accuses our book of rigidity, of a mechanical posing of the problem, of simplification of the reality, etc. "Through his [i.e., my] entire book runs the conviction that the decline of Britain will continue for another four to five (?!) years, before leading to serious internal difficulties," whereas, in the critic's opinion, the next twelve months will mark the apogee of the crisis after which "future development in the next ten (?!) years will proceed without serious difficulties." In this way, the critic first imputes to me a precise prediction that the crisis will intensify in the course of four to five years, and then he counterposes to it another prediction, still more precise, which divides the coming period of British history into two: twelve months of intensification of the crisis and ten years of peaceful prosperity.

The letter, unfortunately, does not contain any kind of economic justification. In order to give the prediction of a critical year and a prosperous decade any economic meaning, all we can do is assume that the author links his prognosis to the present serious financial difficulties resulting from the return to the gold standard and the settlement of the question of debts. Evidently, the author attributes the economic crisis to the deflation crisis and for that reason allows it such short duration. It is altogether probable that after the most serious difficulties of credit and finance have been overcome there will really follow a certain easing in the money market and consequently in industrial and trading turnover. But it is not possible to base a general prognosis on fluctuations of this kind which are, in substance, secondary in character. And really, in any case, his forecast of a prosperous decade does not at all follow. Britain's main difficulties are rooted, on the one hand, in the regrouping and shift of world economic and political forces, and on the other, in the internal conservatism of British industry.

The immense superiority of the industry and finances of the United States of North America over the British is a fact whose significance will only increase in the future. There are not, and there cannot be, any circumstances that can modify the fatal consequences that follow for Britain from this incomparable American superiority.

The development of the latest techniques, in particular, the growing importance of electrification, is directed immediately against the coal industry, and indirectly against the whole of the generally extremely conservative British industry, which is based mainly on coal.

The growth of the industrial and political independence of Canada, Australia, and South America, revealed in their fullest after the war, strikes ever-fresh blows against the metropolis. From a source of enrichment, the dominions have changed for Britain into a source of deficit for the national economy.

The nationalist movement in India, in Egypt, and the entire East is directed primarily against British imperialism. It is doubtful if there are any grounds at all for hoping that "in twelve months" it will become weaker.

The existence of the Soviet Union—in this it is possible to agree with the British Conservative and Liberal politicians—also implies great economic and political difficulties for Great Britain. But again there is no basis for thinking that in twelve months these difficulties will lessen.

If the so-called pacification of Europe continues, it will bring with it the revival and strengthening of German competition. But if the pacification gives place to a war or revolutionary crisis, the latter will be a blow to the economy of Great Britain.

The coming period will, in that way, create increasingly difficult conditions for British capital and thereby pose the problem of power increasingly sharply before the proletariat. I fixed no kind of date. The only remark in my book on this subject says that the revolutionary development of the British working class will be measured by periods of five years rather than of ten. I did not, of course, wish to say by this that the socialist revolution would take place "in four years" (although I did not count that excluded). My thought was that the perspective of revolutionary development should be calculated not by a number of decades, not for our children or children's children, but for the present living generation.

And so I am compelled to quote at length from the letter of the "left" critic:

Trotsky speaks almost all the time of decades. Is it possible to speak of decades with reference to an economic or even of a political situation? I think that in no case it is. It is impossible, as Trotsky himself has already said, to define and fix the precise date when a revolution begins to break out; and whereas he meant rather the impossibility of naming the precise day (?), I think it impossible even to foresee the year (?). Above all, revolution depends on economic factors; *but in the present period the economic factors which might operate for or against the revolution in Britain are innumerable.* Revolution might have broken out on August 1, 1925, as a result of the crisis in the coal industry. Revolution may break out in May of next year when the crisis is renewed. The revolution can be speeded up because of a crisis in the Far East, war, economic collapse in other countries, shortsightedness of some of the industrialists in our own country, the inability of the government to solve the problem of unemployment, crisis in other branches of industry besides coal, and also by socialist propaganda among the workers, raising their inquiries and hopes. *Each of these possibilities is altogether probable under present conditions but not one of them can be foretold even a month ahead.* The present times are characterized by extreme economic and consequently political instability; one move may spoil the whole game, but on the other hand, the existing system may be maintained artificially for many

years yet. Thus, a British revolution, if we understand by
that a political revolution, stands under the sign of the
unknown. [retranslated from the Russian]

The confusion in these lines is altogether unimaginable,
yet at the same time, it is not a personal confusion; on the
contrary, it is profoundly typical. It is the confusion of people
who, "generally speaking," recognize a revolution but who
shudder to the very marrow at it and are prepared to make
any theoretical justification for their political fear.

Let us look closely at the argument of the author, then.
He is forcing an open door when he argues that the rate of
development of the revolution, and consequently its date
also, depend on the interaction of numerous factors and
circumstances, having both an accelerating and a retarding
effect. From this he draws the conclusion, indisputable in
itself, that it is impossible to predict the date of a revolution.
However, he contrives to formulate this most elementary
thought thus: Trotsky thinks it is impossible to predict the
day of the revolution; he, however, our wise critic, thinks it
impossible to predict even the *year.* This contrasting seems
completely beyond belief in its childishness. It might even
seem that it does not on the whole merit a reply. However,
how many are there, in fact, on the "extreme left" who have
not even thought through in rough draft the most elementary questions of revolution, and for whom the very fact of
reflecting on the day or the year represents a gigantic step
forward comparable, for example, to the transition from total
illiteracy to the stage of stumbling from syllable to syllable.

If I really thought that it was only impossible to determine the day (?!) of the revolution in advance, then I would
probably have tried to determine the week, month, or year.
But it is clear that I made no such attempt. I merely pointed
out that the social development of Britain has entered a
revolutionary stage.

At the end of the last century it was only possible to speak of revolution in Britain within the limits of very general foresight. In the years immediately preceding the imperialist war it was already possible to point with confidence to a number of symptoms indicative of the coming of a turning point. After the war, this turning point arrived—and a sharp one at that. *In the past, the British bourgeoisie, oppressing the toilers and plundering the colonies, led the nation along the road of material growth and thereby ensured its own supremacy. Today, the bourgeois regime is not only incapable of leading the British nation forward, but cannot maintain for itself the level already attained.*

The British working class is struggling amidst the contradictions of the decline of capitalism. There is not one question of economic life—nationalization of the mines, the railways, the fight against unemployment, free trade or protectionism, housing and so on—which might not lead directly to the question of power. Here we have the sociohistorical basis of a revolutionary situation. Of course, it is a question of the struggle of living historical forces, and not of an automatic accumulation of quantitative magnitudes. This fact alone makes it impossible to predict passively the stages of the process and the date of the upsurge.

It remains for us to keep a finger on the pulse of British economics and politics and, not for one minute losing sight of our general perspective, to watch closely all the particular fluctuations, ebbs and flows, determining their place in the process of capitalist decline. Only on the basis of such a general orientation can the revolutionary party carry out its own politics, whose flexibility is expressed in the fact that it takes into consideration particular fluctuations but by no means loses sight of the fundamental line of development.

My "left" critic, evidently, has heard something or other— in quite a different connection—concerning the determining of the "day" of the revolution, and did not grasp that there the question was one of the moment of armed insurrection, placed on the order of the day by the revolution. These are two questions, closely bound together but nonetheless quite different. In one case, it is a question of a historically well-grounded prognosis, and of a general strategic line following from this; in the other, of a tactical plan presupposing a more or less exact determination of the place and the time.

No one, except perhaps the English procurator's office, would think of saying that in Britain at the present moment armed insurrection is on the agenda and that the working out of the plan, and hence the date, is a practical task. Meanwhile, only in such a connection would it be possible to speak of the "day" or "days." In the fall of 1923 there was such a case, namely in Germany. In Britain at the present time, the question is not one of fixing the "day" of the revolution—we are still a long way from that—but of clearly understanding that all the objective conditions are bringing this "day" nearer, are bringing it within the range of the proletarian party's educational and preparatory politics, and creating at the same time the conditions for the rapid revolutionary development of the party.

In his second letter, this same critic puts forward even more unexpected arguments to support his skepticism as regards dates (and, as a matter of fact, as regards the revolution). "The realm of economics," he argues, "speaking practically, has no limits. . . . A new invention, the regrouping of capitalist forces. . . . The other side also recognizes the danger. . . . Moreover, America might take measures against the coming crash of Britain. In a word," concludes our critic, "there are very many possibilities, and Trotsky has by no means exhausted them all."

Our "leftist" has need of all these possibilities except one, the possibility of revolution. Playing hide-and-seek with reality, he is ready to grasp at any fantasy. In what sense, for example, can a "new invention" change the social conditions of the development of Great Britain? Since the time of Marx there have been not a few inventions, as a result of which the operation of the Marxian law of the concentration of production and the intensification of class contradictions, far from being weakened has, on the contrary, become stronger. And new inventions in the future too will give advantages to the stronger, i.e., not to Great Britain but to the United States. It is undeniable that "the other side," i.e., the bourgeoisie, recognizes the danger and will fight against it with all possible means. But this very fact is a major political premise of the revolution.

Finally, his hope of America's saving hand is perfectly monstrous. It is more than likely that America will try to help the bourgeoisie in the event of civil war in Britain; but this only means that the British proletariat will have to seek allies beyond the borders of their own country. We think it will find them.

It follows from this that the British revolution will inevitably assume an international character. We least of all would argue with this. But our critic wishes to say something else. He is expressing the hope that America will alleviate the condition of the British bourgeoisie sufficiently on the whole to help it avoid revolution. It is impossible to cook up anything better than this! Each new day testifies that American capital is the historical battering ram which intentionally and unintentionally is striking the most shattering blows against the world position and the internal stability of Britain. This, however, does not at all prevent our "leftist" from hoping that American capital will politely make room for the interests of British capital. To begin with, clearly, we should expect America to waive payment of the British debt; to hand over to the British treasury without compensation the 300 million dollars which constitute the reserve of British currency; to support Great Britain's policy in China; perhaps even to transfer to the British navy some new cruisers and to give up its Canadian shares to British firms at a discount of 50 percent. In a word, we should expect the Washington government to transfer the leadership of state affairs to the hands of the American Relief Administration[15] after selecting for this the most philanthropic Quakers.

People who can give themselves pleasure with such nonsense don't dare to aspire to the leadership of the British proletariat!

Brailsford and Marxism

March 10, 1926

The London edition of the book *Where Is Britain Going?* came out with an unexpected introduction by Brailsford, a former bourgeois Radical who, after the war, joined the Independent Labour Party and now edits its organ. Mr. Brailsford, despite all his socialist sympathies, has not ceased to be a Radical. And as moderate Liberals stand at the head of the Independent Labour Party, Brailsford therefore has appeared on the left wing.

The fact that it is not in backward China, nor even in Japan (where the radical bourgeois publishing houses think it is still useful to the aim of spreading enlightenment to publish books by Russian Communists), but rather in Britain, with its glaring social contradictions, that it is possible for a Communist's book to appear with a patronizing introduction by a member of MacDonald's party—this fact alone testifies, in the eyes of every Marxist, to the incredible backwardness of British political thinking as compared with British material relations. In this opinion, which does not require evidence, is clearly contained the condemnation of such an unexpected literary bloc. We need a united front with the working masses. Unity or half-unity on a literary front with Brailsford signifies only the aggravation of that ideological chaos in which the British workers' movement is already rich, even without this.

The mistake here, however, is not Brailsford's. His historical role lies in this—that while "correcting" Thomas and MacDonald, he creates a safety valve for the discontent of the masses, slurs over distinctions, and dissolves definite ideas in amorphous "leftism." To appear with us under one jacket is politically advantageous to Brailsford whose sincerity we do not question in the least (we bear it firmly in mind, however, that the road to hell is paved with reformist intentions). The working masses of Britain are immeasurably to the left of Brailsford. By "fraternizing" with a Moscow Communist, Brailsford camouflages his membership in the party that excludes British Communists.

We have other aims. We don't need camouflage. Our first responsibility is the destruction of ideological camouflage. The British working masses are immeasurably to the left of Brailsford, but aren't yet vigorous enough to find the appropriate language for their needs. The junk of the past still divides most of the left-wing masses from the program of communism. So much the more intolerable is it to add to this junk even a thread. Fighting for the interests of the miners, the Communists are ready to take a few steps forward in this struggle side by side with Mr. Brailsford. But no ideological blocs, no united front in the sphere of theory and program! It is this very same Brailsford who, on the occasion of the American publication of our little book, expressed himself thus: "An abyss separates us from these people." Yes, yes, a thousand times yes! But there is nothing more criminal, from the standpoint of Marxism, than to throw across the political abyss literary olive branches: deceived by the camouflage, the worker will step on them and fall through.

To Mr. Brailsford, camouflage is indispensable. He makes use of a revolutionary book to attack revolution. A defender of democratic illusions and parliamentary fetishism, Brailsford says in his own introduction: Look, in our British democracy we fearlessly publish a Bolshevik book—thereby demonstrating the breadth and power of democracy.

More than this, with his own little demonstration Brailsford wants to smooth over the (for him) uncomfortable implications of the recent trial of the Communists. Brailsford himself openly admits this. The sentence passed on the British Communists—at a time when revolution is visible only as a distant perspective—shatters democratic illusions immeasurably more strikingly and convincingly than all our books and pamphlets. Brailsford understands this. Struggling to preserve democratic illusions, he "welcomes" the appearance of our book in these words: "If it may come freely from the press, if it may be discussed . . . then . . . the nightmare of this trial is dissipated." Rescuing democratic illusions at so cheap a price, Brailsford wants to suggest to the British proletariat the idea that once a revolutionary book, accompanied by a suitable dose of antidote in the form of this pacifist introduction, can appear freely in the bookshops of Britain, then by this very fact it is proved that the British bourgeoisie will bow their heads humbly when the "democrats" begin to appropriate from them the banks, fields, pits, factories, and shipyards. In other words, Brailsford unceremoniously reproves our book with considerations directly contrary to its aim, its sense, its spirit, and its letter.

No wonder Brailsford reproachfully calls ruthless polemics "Russian methods," and hopes that they will not stir up in the British readers quite that impression for which they were designed. As for that "impression," we will wait. Readers are many and various. The methods of polemic flow from the essence of politics. "Ruthlessness" is called for by the need to expose the reality beneath the conventional lie.

Nowhere in Europe does sanctimonious hypocrisy—cant—play such a role as in Great Britain. The various political groupings, even the "extremists," are accustomed in their struggle with each other not to touch upon certain questions and not to call things by their proper names. The reason for this is that from time immemorial the political struggle has been conducted in the ranks of the upper strata, who have never forgotten that the third estate is listening to them. The system of conventionality, of allusion, of reservation has taken root through the centuries from the top down, and has received its most reactionary expression in the liberal Labour Party, including its Radical oppositionist wing.

The question here is not one of literary style but of politics. Our polemic antagonizes Brailsford because it exposes utterly the basic class contradictions. It is perfectly true that in those enlightened readers who have been educated in the parliamentary tradition of political hypocrisy, such a polemic will call forth not sympathy but indignation. But—Brailsford notwithstanding—that is the very effect which the author reckoned he had the right to expect. It is perfectly true, also, that the politicians with such an upbringing nevertheless constitute a solid layer between the working class and the program of communism. However, class realities are stronger than traditional hypocrisy even in Britain. The awakening British workers, forcing their way through the crust of hereditary prejudices—from the Baldwins to the Brailsfords—will find in our polemic a little part of their own struggle. And moreover, this will be the very effect on which we are reckoning.

Brailsford's introduction offers a mixture of excessive praise and moderate reproof. The praise is for what is secondary—the form of the book. The reproof is directed against the essence. The excess of praise is meant to impart special weight to the wary attacks on Bolshevism. Brailsford acts expediently. He is following his vocation. He is concerned with camouflage. But we have need of full clarity. That is why we reject equally both Brailsford's praise and his reproof.

Brailsford acts expediently, yet he is impotent to excess. But this is no longer his fault. He cannot escape from the historical task of centrism: to obscure reality in order to maintain illusions. We have seen with what futility he discusses the lessons of the Communists' trial. This same impotence underlies the whole appraisal of our book.

On the one hand, according to him, the book is based on a knowledge of facts and an understanding of logic. On the other hand, it appears that the author of the book is "a man from another world," incapable of understanding either the character of British Protestantism or the strength of parliamentary traditions. "Not only in Parliament, but in churches, Trade Unions, and even clubs"—explains Brailsford—"this respect for the majority has been inculcated on generations of Englishmen. What can a Russian know of that? What estimate can he make of the power of tradition in our older civilization?"

Brailsford's overweening impotence lies in his method: he does not comprehend that the material bases of social development are of decisive instance. He comes to a halt before the traditions and ideological accumulations of an old struggle and thinks that this deposit is eternal. He is ignorant of the elementary laws of the dependence of ideology on class bases. To discuss with him on these themes is like persuading an inventor of perpetual motion who denies the law of the conservation of energy. It is clear to every literate Marxist that the harder the conservative forms of British society have set, the more catastrophically will the new eruptions of the social volcano blow up the hardened crust of the old traditions and institutions.

The ideas and prejudices passed on from one generation

to another are transformed into a factor of great historical force. This "independent" force of prejudices, condensed by history, is seen rather well in Brailsford himself. Nevertheless, material factors are stronger than the ideas that reflect them. It is not difficult to be convinced of this today by the edifying spectacle of the death agony of British Liberalism. Is it possible to find another tradition more powerful?

In its origin, Liberalism is bound up with the first movements of Protestantism, and consequently with the revolution of the seventeenth century which opens up the history of modern Britain. And yet this powerful Liberal tradition crumples and turns to ashes before our very eyes as a sheet of paper thrown onto a hot stove. Living facts are stronger than dead ideas. The decay of the middle classes in Britain, the decline of the world role of British capitalism—these are the material facts which ruthlessly make short shrift of the Liberal traditions. The figure of the agrarian-reformer Gracchus Lloyd George, who denies in the evening what he has said in the morning, already stands out as a splendid mockery of the Liberal tradition.

We heard from Brailsford that it is too difficult for "a man from another world" to comprehend "how deeply . . . *the instinct of obedience to the majority* [is] graven on the English mind." But the remarkable thing is that when Brailsford descends from the heights of doctrinairism to the sphere of living political facts, he himself sometimes reveals unexpectedly the secret of "obedience to the majority."

And so, in analyzing the course of the last Liberal conference which (half) accepted the charlatan Lloyd George program of "nationalization of the land," contrary to all his "traditions" and above all to his wishes, Brailsford wrote in the *New Leader* of February 26 [1926]: "The payment of expenses from the central fund (which depends on Lloyd George) and the free lunches provided to the delegates evidently created the necessary majority at the conference." The lunches *cre-*

ated the majority! From these realistic words it is obvious that the well-bred democratic instinct of obedience to the majority, inculcated on a whole series of British generations and too difficult for "a man from another world" to understand, still needs from time to time free roast-beef lunches and other subsidiary means to reveal its omnipotence.

I doubt whether Brailsford will write anything better than these words. Our idealist here runs up against what usually spoils metaphysical schemes, i.e., a chunk of reality. It has been known for a long time that the German academic followers of Kant, on their way to the realization of the categorical imperative, stumble over such obstacles as an inadequate salary, the intrigues of colleagues, or a cantankerous mother-in-law. The democratic socialist Brailsford does himself an injury with this roast beef—and moreover, a far more dangerous one than he imagines.

Of course, we, people of another world, are incapable of appreciating the noble admiration of all British people for parliamentary methods. But why confuse us with the information that within the Liberal Party, the founder of parliamentarism, the majority prevails with the help of a cash box and a series of lunches which are free but, we venture to think, quite substantial. A majority reached in such a way looks very much like a bribed or forged majority. And, as you see, for the time being it is only a question of a struggle for mandates and offices. What will happen when the question is put point-blank: To whom shall the state power belong, to the bourgeoisie or to the proletariat? And to whom the property, to the capitalists or to the people?

If, for considerations of parliamentary careerism, the leaders of the Liberal Party successfully set in motion bribery and corruption, then at what acts of violence, at what crimes will the ruling classes stop when it is a question of their whole historical fate? I very much fear that if one of the two of us appears to be a man from another world and has no understanding of the most important thing in British politics, then it is Mr. Brailsford. *He* is the man of a different epoch. The new epoch is ours.

In his introduction, Brailsford does not fail to defend religion. It is interesting that, despite this, he calls himself an agnostic. This word is sometimes used in Britain as a polite, emasculated, drawing-room term for an atheist. Even more often, it characterizes a diffident semi-atheism—i.e., that variety of idealism which on the question of God, to use parliamentary language, abstains from voting. And so we see here the force of cant, of conventionality, of the half-truth, the half-lie, of philosophical hypocrisy. Hinting at his atheism and calling himself an agnostic, Brailsford there and then takes up the defense of religion. Here are the equivocal morals and manners which British revolutionists are obliged to drive out ruthlessly from the ranks of the workers' movement. Enough of this game of hide-and-seek; call things by their names!

Brailsford defends religion by denying its class character. No Russian, you see, can understand what English religion is like, "with its long tradition of open discussion, the democratic form of its 'free' churches, . . . its relative freedom from other-worldliness" and so on and so on. No democratic priest could have delivered a more apologetic speech in defense of religious dope than our agnostic. His testimony on behalf of the Church is meant to carry greater weight because he declares he is an unbeliever. Duplicity and hypocrisy at every step.

Trying to disprove the bourgeois character of Protestantism, Brailsford, the prosecutor, asks whether Trotsky was ever in a Dissenting chapel in a mining district, had ever read Bunyan or glanced at the revolutionary history of the Anabaptists and Fifth Monarchy men.[16] I must admit that I have never been in a miners' Dissenting chapel and that I have insufficient knowledge of the historical facts of which

Brailsford speaks. I promise to visit the mining districts and their chapels as soon as Brailsford's party takes power and allows me, in accordance with the principles of democracy, an unhindered journey through the domains of His Majesty. I shall try to become acquainted with Bunyan and the history of the Anabaptists and Fifth Monarchy men earlier than the date mentioned.

But Brailsford is sadly mistaken if he thinks that the facts and circumstances enumerated by him can change the appraisal of religion in general, and of Protestantism in particular. Together with Lenin and N.K. Krupskaya,[17] I once visited a "free church" in London, and there listened to socialist speeches in the intervals between the psalms. A composer, returned from Australia, was the preacher. He spoke about social revolution. In the psalms, the people begged God to establish such a regime that there would be neither rich nor poor. This was my first practical acquaintance with the British workers' movement, almost a quarter of a century ago (1902). What role, I asked myself then, do the psalms play in relation to revolutionary speeches? The role of a safety valve. The condensed steam of discontent escapes through the valve of the church and even higher to heaven. This is the fundamental function of the church in class society.

Of course, different churches carry out this task in different ways. The Orthodox [Russian] Church, unable to cope with primitive peasant mythology, turned, as time went on, more and more to the formal bureaucratic apparatus alongside the apparatus of czarism. The priest went hand in hand with the village policeman, and replied to every development of dissent by religious sects with repression. And that is why the roots of the Orthodox Church proved to be so weak in the consciousness of the people, especially in the industrial centers. Having rid themselves of the bureaucratic church apparatus, the Russian workers, in their overwhelming mass, accompanied moreover by the young generation of the peasants, rid themselves of religion too.

Protestantism is quite another matter: it rose to power as the banner of the bourgeoisie and the small people of town and country struggling against the Crown, the nobility, the privileged, and the lords of the established Church and the bishops. The origin and development of Protestantism is so closely bound up with the development of urban culture and with the struggle of the bourgeoisie for a firmer and more stable position in society that indeed there is no need to prove this. The bourgeoisie, of course, could not have struggled successfully and then maintained itself in power if it had not to some extent or other made its banner the banner of the lower strata of the populace, i.e., of the artisans, peasants, and workers. In the struggle against the nobility, the bourgeoisie bound the lower strata firmly to itself with the Protestant religion.

Of course, the Scottish woodcutter did not put into his psalms the same subjective content as the respectable Mr. Dombey or his honorable great-grandson sitting in the House of Commons on the right or left of Mr. MacDonald. But the same applies equally to Liberalism. The worker Liberals, not the trade union bureaucrats, but the proletarians, interpreted the Liberal program quite differently from Gladstone. They brought into their Liberalism a class instinct, though a feeble one. Will Brailsford, however, be so bold as to deny on this account that Liberalism is a program of the rising middle and small commercial and industrial bourgeoisie and the bourgeois intellectuals?

It is true—and Brailsford wants to rest on this—that many petty-bourgeois radicals, opponents of the class struggle, lean toward atheism, whereas the pioneers of trade unionism stood equally for Christianity and the class struggle. But here is no contradiction whatsoever with what was said above. Marxism does not at all teach that each man gets his ration of religion and philosophical beliefs according to the size of his income or wages. The question is far more complex. Rising out of the material conditions of life, i.e., above all out of the class contradictions, religious ideas, like other ideas, make their way only slowly, outlive, from conservatism, those needs which engendered them, and disappear under the effects of serious shocks and stimuli.

The petty-bourgeois Radicals of the utilitarian or Owenite schools could remain militant atheists as long as they seriously believed that they possessed painless means of solving all social questions. But as the class contradictions intensified, militant Radicalism disappeared or moved into the Labour Party, taking into it its own shabby, idealistic arrogance and its own political impotence. The organizers of the trade unions, thrown up by the workers' strikes, could not renounce the basis of their work and the source of their authority, the class struggle. But because of this, they remain within the organizational limits of trade unionism, and do not carry the struggle through to its necessary revolutionary conclusions; and it is this which allowed and allows them to reconcile trade unionism with Christianity, i.e., with a discipline that the dogma and ethics of another class have imposed on the proletariat.

It is quite irrefutable that the revolution will find a good part of the Welsh miners ridden by religious prejudices. It is possible not to doubt that despite this, the miners will carry out their task. They will free themselves from some prejudices in the fire of the struggle, and from others, only after victory. But we categorically deny that the correct road can be pointed out to the Welsh miners, and in general to the British proletariat, by those people who themselves have not thrown off childish nonsense, who do not know the structure of human society, who do not size up its dynamics, who do not understand the role of religion in it, and who are prepared to some extent or other to subordinate their own actions to the dictates of a clerical ethic which unites oppressors and oppressed. Such leaders are unreliable. At the most crucial hour, the working class can always expect capitulation or direct betrayal on their part, based, of course, on the Sermon on the Mount.

The traditional forces of British Protestantism are clear to us, and Brailsford tries in vain to make out that we judge Protestantism according to Orthodoxy. Nonsense! We Marxists are accustomed to taking historical phenomena in their social context, in their concreteness, to judging them not by their names but according to that content which breathes life into them, i.e., a society divided into classes.

The traditional power of Protestantism is great but not without limits. By its very essence, i.e., as a religion and not as a political doctrine, Protestantism is no more elastic than Liberalism, its younger brother. But the elasticity of Protestantism has its own limits. A deep change in the fortunes of Britain will define them. All the national traditions will be put to the test. What took shape over centuries will be destroyed in the course of years. The revolutionary verification, proceeding from implacable facts, will reach into those last refuges of consciousness where the inherited prejudices hide. Our task is to help with this work of purification, and not to stand in its way as do the equivocal agnostics, hinting at their atheism in order to defend religion.

Thus we see that on the most fundamental questions, on which the historical life and death of the proletariat hinges, we and Brailsford stand on opposite sides of the ideological barricade. That is why our appearance with Brailsford before the British reader under one cover represents the greatest misunderstanding. As far as I can, I am correcting this misunderstanding by the present article.

Once more on pacifism and revolution

A reply to Bertrand Russell
May 3, 1926

The majority of the British critics of my book see its main defect in the fact that the author is not English and therefore cannot understand English psychology, English traditions, and so on. However, it might be said that the more the English Fabians persist with this argument the less English they themselves seem; in the end, they add very little to those arguments of which we have heard not a little from the Russian Mensheviks, and earlier, from the Narodniks.[18]

Now, after we have triumphed, the English, and in general the European socialists, are disposed to allow us to be left by ourselves—in accordance with the peculiarities of our country and national culture. In this way, they wish basically to raise an ideological fence along those very frontiers where Lloyd George, Churchill, Clemenceau,[19] and the others tried to erect the material barbed wire of a blockade. "Perhaps it is a good thing for the Russians," declare the "leftists" in conciliatory manner, "but don't let the Russians dare to cross the Russian borders with their experience and their conclusions." The peculiarities of the English national character are enlisted as the philosophical basis of the theory of Bolshevik "nonintervention."

The Fabians and other critics do not know that we have been very well hardened against arguments of this kind by our entire past. But there is irony here: the Fabians now agree—i.e., after our victory—to recognize Bolshevism, i.e., Marxism in action, as appropriate to the national peculiarities of Russia; but the old traditional Russian ideology—moreover, not just the ideology of the rulers but also that of the opposition—invariably considered Marxism as begotten by Western culture, and they proclaimed its complete incompatibility with the peculiarities of Russian national development. Even within living memory, the overwhelming majority of the Russian press proclaimed that the Russian Marxists were ideological foreigners vainly endeavoring to transpose the historical experience of England onto Russian soil. On every occasion, we were reminded that Marx originated his theory of economic development in the British Museum while observing English capitalism and its contradictions. Could the lessons of British capitalism have any meaning for Russia, with its outstanding "peculiarities," with its predominantly peasant population, with its patriarchal traditions, with its commune and its orthodoxy?

Thus spoke the Russian reactionaries and the Russian Narodniks, with the necessary variations to right and left. Not only up to and during the war, but even after the February revolution of 1917, when Mr. Henderson came to Russia to persuade the Russian workers to continue the war against Germany, there was scarcely a socialist in the world, right or left, who thought that Bolshevism was the answer to the national peculiarities of Russia. No, at that time they considered us maniacs at best.

Our own Fabians, the Russian Mensheviks and so-called Social Revolutionaries, brought against us all the same arguments which we hear today from Lansbury, Brailsford, Russell,[20] and their more right-wing colleagues, as revelations of true-British philosophy. After all, allusion to national peculiarities is the last tool of every ideological reaction defending itself against the revolutionary issues of the time. By this we do not at all want to say that national peculiarities do not exist, or that they are immaterial. The accumulations of the past in institutions and customs are a great conservative force. But it is the living forces of the present, in the final analysis, which are decisive.

It is impossible to improve the position of the British coal industry on the world market by any references to national traditions. Meanwhile, the role of the coal industry in the fortunes of Great Britain is immeasurably more important than all the devices and ceremonial rites of parliamentarism. The House of Commons is supported by coal, not the other way round. The conservatism of English forms of property and modes of production is just such a national "peculiarity," which is capable only of deepening the social crisis with all the revolutionary contradictions resulting therefrom.

Mr. Bertrand Russell, a philosopher in mathematics, a mathematician in philosophy, an aristocrat in democracy, and a dilettante in socialism, considered it his duty, and not indeed for the first time, to put his hand to the task of destroying the noxious ideas issuing from Moscow and hostile to the Anglo-Saxon spirit.

On the question of religion, Russell goes a step further than Brailsford. He recognizes that in the modern world, every organized religion, i.e., church, must be a reactionary force (this does not prevent Russell from leaving a loophole in this matter, too: personal religion is a private matter, says he). Russell approves of our arguments concerning the fact that even the most thrifty of kings cannot become a constituent part of a socialist society. Russell refuses to consider the parliamentary road as the sure road to socialism. But all these acknowledgments, and not a few others besides, are made by Russell only to reveal the more vividly the anti-revolutionary character of his thinking on the question of the paths of the English working class.

Russell declares the proletarian revolution in Britain to be not only dangerous but also disastrous. England is too dependent on transoceanic countries and above all on the United States of North America. Cut off from the outside world by a blockade, the British Isles would be able to feed not more than 20 million of the population. Under these conditions, says Russell ironically, Trotsky's sympathies will not afford us great comfort. "Until Soviet Russia can place a fleet in the Atlantic stronger than that of America, it is not clear what we should gain by sympathy, however enthusiastic."

These strategical considerations are very interesting, coming from the lips of a pacifist. We learn first of all that the fate of British pacifism, as far as it attempts to link itself with the working class, is dependent on the strength of the American fleet. We learn secondly that it would not be a bad thing for British pacifism to be guarded against its foes by a Soviet fleet of appropriate strength. Our honorable idealist contemptuously waves aside any ideological sympathy not backed up with a sufficient quantity of shells and mines. Here, however, he is evidently going too far.

Russell's own sympathy for the October Revolution (a sympathy, however, more resembling antipathy) did not afford us much "comfort" during the last years. But it was the sympathies of the British and generally speaking of the European working masses that saved us. Of course, Churchill did us as much damage as he was able. Chamberlain did everything that he could. But we would have been overwhelmed long ago had not the ruling class of Great Britain feared to move their armed forces against us. Of course, this guarantee was not absolute. But it did prove sufficient—alongside the antagonisms among the capitalist states—to protect us from large-scale intervention in the most critical years.

Meanwhile, right up to and after October, our own Russells were trying to convince us that we would be overwhelmed by the troops of either the Hohenzollerns or the Entente. They told us that the Russian proletariat, being most backward and numerically small, could take power into its own hands only in the case of the victory of world revolution.

References to the international revolution as a precondition for the overthrow of the bourgeois state in one's own country represent nothing but the renunciation of revolution. For what is the international revolution? It is a chain—and moreover not a continuous one—of national revolutions, each of which nourishes the others with its successes and in turn suffers from their failures.

In 1923, when the revolutionary situation in Germany reached its most acute point, the left Social Democrats alluded, in their fight against the Communists, to the danger of military intervention by France and Poland. The German left Mensheviks would have been quite prepared in words at least to seize power in Germany provided there was a prior victory of the proletariat in France. This Menshevik propaganda was one of the elements that paralyzed the revolutionary activity of the German working class.

In the case of a decisive intensification of the political situation in France—and it is coming to that—the French socialists will doubtless intimidate the French workers with the danger of German revenge on the one hand and a British naval blockade on the other. But who dares to doubt that Leon Blum, Jean Longuet, and other heroes would consent to the conquest of power, provided there was a prior and moreover total victory of the working class in Germany and Great Britain![21] The socialists in the small states consider it doubly impossible to begin their revolution while the bourgeoisie holds power in the big states. Performing seals in a circus toss the burning torch back and forth with approximately the same skill as is shown by the Mensheviks of different countries in tossing the right of revolutionary initiative back and forth.

The pacifist Russell thinks it is impossible to start the revolution in Britain as long as the United States maintains a mighty fleet. It would not be a bad thing, of course, for the American proletariat to take power into its own hands in the near future, and with it the navy. But won't the American Russells tell us that the combined fleets of Great Britain and Japan would inevitably threaten the proletarian power in the United States?

It is true that one could disregard this argument if the proletarian revolution actually were to break out next in the United States. Unfortunately, there is as yet no sign of this. Great Britain, in its total situation, is immeasurably nearer to revolution than North America. Consequently, we must reckon on the struggle of the proletariat for power in Britain taking place with the rule of the American bourgeoisie still unshaken.

What is to be done? Russell—rather ironically, it is true—shows us a way out of the situation: he suggests that the Soviet Union should establish a navy capable of securing the free approaches to proletarian Britain. Unfortunately, the poverty of our land and its technical backwardness do not allow us to fulfill this program for the time being. Of course, it would be more advantageous, simpler and more economical, if the proletarian revolution were to begin in the United States and to extend via Britain from West to East, through Europe and Asia. But the real course of development is not like that: the worldwide chain of capitalist rule will break, like every chain, at its weakest link. After czarist Russia, Austro-Hungary, Germany, and Italy came nearest of all to the proletarian revolution. Atonement for the war is still ahead for France and Britain. Europe as a whole is immeasurably nearer to revolutionary upsurge than the United States. It is this that we have to take into account.

Of course, in view of its fundamental dependence on imports and exports, the situation of a blockaded Britain would be more serious than the situation in any other European country. However, the resources of revolutionary Britain in the struggle to overcome obstacles would be extremely great, too.

In referring to the American fleet, Russell for some reason or other forgets about the fleet of Great Britain. In whose hands will it be? If in the hands of the bourgeoisie, then a nearer and more acute danger will threaten the proletarian revolution, from the direction not of the American but of the British fleet. But if the fleet is in the hands of the proletariat, then the situation immediately becomes immeasurably more favorable than Russell depicts it. Our critic has not a word to say on this matter of no small importance. We must dwell on the question in some detail.

The greatest peculiarities in the development of Britain are determined by its insular position. The role of the British fleet in the fortunes of the country expresses these peculiarities most vividly. The British socialists reproach us with ignorance or lack of understanding of the hidden or imponderable peculiarities of the British spirit, yet at the same time forget completely, in a discussion on the problem of the proletarian revolution, such a highly ponderable quantity as the British fleet. Russell, ironically summoning the Soviet fleet to his assistance, says nothing about that fleet which was still being strengthened with light cruisers when the party of MacDonald, Brailsford, and Lansbury was in power.

It is a question here of seizing power in a country where the proletariat makes up the overwhelming majority of the population. The political precondition for success must be the aspiration of the proletariat itself to seize power at any price, i.e., at the cost of heavy sacrifice. Only a revolution-ary party is capable of uniting the working masses in this aspiration.

The second precondition for success is a clear understand-ing of the roads and methods of the struggle. Only a labor party whose eyes are cleared of the pacifist cataract can itself see and explain to the proletariat that the real transfer of power from the hands of one class to the hands of another depends to an immeasurably greater degree on the British army and navy than on Parliament. The struggle of the pro-letariat for power must therefore be a struggle for the navy. The seamen—not, of course the admirals, but the stokers, the electrical workers, the sailors—must be taught to under-stand the tasks and aims of the working class. A way to them must be found despite all obstacles. Only through systematic, stubborn, persistent preparatory work is it possible to create a situation such that the bourgeoisie cannot rely on the navy in the struggle against the proletariat. And if the situation is otherwise, it is meaningless to talk of victory.

Of course, it cannot be conceived that in the very first pe-riod of the revolution the whole navy, moreover in full com-bat order, would go over to the side of the proletariat. This will not happen without deep internal convulsions within the navy itself. The history of all revolutions testifies to this. Convulsions in the navy connected with drastic alterations in the command structure mean inevitably a general weaken-ing of the navy for a comparatively prolonged period. And again, we cannot close our eyes to this. But the period of crisis and internal weakness will be over that much more quickly the more decisively the leading party of the prole-tariat acts, the more it has established links in the navy in the preparatory period, the more daring it is in the period of the struggle, the more clearly it shows all the oppressed that it is capable of seizing power and holding on to it.

Pacifism only affects the war machine of the ruling class

to a very insignificant degree. The best possible proof of this is Russell's own courageous but somewhat futile experience during the war. This was limited to a few thousand young men who, pleading "conscience," were thrown into prison. In the old czarist army, the members of sects, especially the followers of Tolstoy, suffered persecution not infrequently for this sort of pacifist antimilitarism. But it was not they who accomplished the task of overthrowing czarism. And in Britain, they did not prevent and could not have prevented the war being carried on to the end.

Pacifism addresses itself not so much to the military organization of the bourgeois state as to the working masses. Here its influence is absolutely pernicious. It paralyzes the will of those who in any case do not suffer from a surplus of will. It preaches the harmfulness of arms to those who are in any case unarmed and victims of class violence. In present conditions of British life, when the problem of power is posed point-blank, Russell's pacifism is reactionary through and through.

Not so long ago, the papers reported that Lansbury called on the British soldiers not to fire on strikers. Thousands of working men and women present at the meeting raised their fists as a sign of solidarity with this call, which is indeed ill-reconciled with MacDonald's policy, but which in turn represents an important step on the road to revolution. One would have to be very naive indeed to imagine that Lansbury's appeal opens up the possibility of a peaceful, bloodless, pacifist solution to the problem of power. On the contrary, this appeal, insofar as it elicits a response in practice, will inevitably promote the sharpest military clashes.

We cannot think that all the soldiers and all the sailors will refuse to fire on the workers at the same time. In fact, the revolution will drive a wedge into the army and the navy, the split will run through every company, through the crew of every battleship. One soldier will have firmly resolved already not to shoot, though it cost him his life. Another will hesitate. A third will be prepared to shoot anyone who refuses to fire. In the initial period, those who hesitate will be the greatest number. What happened with us in 1905 and 1917? A soldier or sailor who in practice showed his solidarity with the workers came under the fire of the officers. In the next stage, the officer was shot by the soldiers who were carried away by the heroic example of their more advanced comrades. Such conflicts spread. A regiment in which the revolutionary elements were predominant resisted a regiment in which the old command structure still retained power. At the same time, the workers were arming themselves with the support of the revolutionary regiments. In the navy it was no different.

We would strongly advise Russell and his cothinkers to see the Soviet-produced film *Potemkin* which shows clearly enough the mechanics of revolution within an armed mass of people. It would be even more important to show this film to the British workers and sailors. Let us hope that the Labour Party will do this when it comes to power.

The congenital bourgeois hypocrites and the civilized cannibals will, of course, speak with the utmost indignation of how we are seeking to set brother against brother, private against officer, and so on. The pacifists will echo them. Once more they will not fail to recall that we see everything in terms of bloodshed because we are not aware of the peculiarities of Great Britain, and underestimate the beneficial influence of Christian morality on naval officers, policemen, and Joynson-Hicks. But this cannot stop us. Revolutionary politics first and foremost must look the facts straight in the face in order to foresee the line of further development. A revolutionary policy seems fantastic to the philistines only because it foresees the day after tomorrow whereas they dare not even think about the morrow.

In conditions where the national organism as a whole cannot be saved by conservative therapeutics but only by surgical intervention, by the removal of the malignant organ—i.e., of the class which has outlived itself—pacifist sermons have their origins in an essentially egotistical indifference. In such conditions the most "merciful" thing is to be as firmly resolute as possible so that the period of struggle is shortened and the torment lessened. The more decisively the British proletariat expropriates all the means and instruments of the British bourgeoisie, the less the American bourgeoisie will be tempted to interfere in the fight. The sooner and more completely proletarian power in Britain takes control of the British navy, the less able will the American navy be to smash that power. By this I do not at all mean to say that military intervention on the part of the transatlantic republic is excluded. On the contrary, it is very probable, and within certain limits frankly inevitable. But the results of this intervention depend to an enormous extent on our own policy up to and during the revolution.

The behavior of the French navy will have no small importance as regards a general blockade of the British Isles and above all their isolation from the European continent. Will the French bourgeoisie be able to send their ships against a proletarian revolution in Britain? We have already had some experience on that score. In 1918, Millerand[22] sent French battleships against the Black Sea ports of the Soviet Republic. The result is well known. The cruiser *Waldeck-Rousseau* raised the flag of rebellion. Neither did all go well with the English in Northern Russia. Revolution is very catching. And naval seamen are more susceptible to revolutionary infection than anyone else.

At the time when the French sailors Marty and Badin mutinied,[23] unwilling to oppose the proletarian revolution in Russia, France was at the very zenith of her power. Now the epoch of atonement for the war has begun for France no less than for Britain. To think that the French bourgeoisie could still play the role of gendarme in the Atlantic, or even only in the English Channel, in a situation where the monarchy, the landlords, the bankers, and the industrialists have been thrown overboard in Britain, is to reveal an appalling optimism as regards the bourgeoisie and a shameful pessimism as regards the proletariat.

Britain, i.e., its bourgeoisie, was not queen of the seas for nothing. The British revolution will send great ripples rolling across all the oceans. Its first result will be to undermine discipline in all the navies. Who knows whether under these conditions the American command might not renounce all thought of a strict naval blockade, withdrawing their ships as far as possible from the European infection.

Finally, even in America itself, the navy is not the final arbiter. The capitalist regime in the United States is more powerful than it has ever been elsewhere. We are no worse acquainted than Russell is with the counterrevolutionary character of the American Federation of Labor,[24] about which he reminds us. Just as the bourgeoisie of the United States has raised the power of capital to an unprecedented height, so the American Federation of Labor has carried the methods of conciliation to the very limit.

But this does not at all mean that the American bourgeoisie is all-powerful. It is immeasurably stronger against the European bourgeoisie than it is against the European proletariat. The revolutionary instincts and sentiments of the different races which make up the working masses of North America are slumbering and fermenting beneath the surface of the American aristocracy of labor, the most privileged of all the labor aristocracies in the world.

Revolution in the Anglo-Saxon country on the other side of the Atlantic will have a greater effect on the proletariat of the United States than any other revolution. This does not yet mean that the rule of the American bourgeoisie will be overthrown the very next day after the conquest of power by the British proletariat. A series of economic, military, and political convulsions will be necessary before the rule of the dollar can be overthrown. The American bourgeoisie is itself paving the way for these convulsions by investing its capital all over the world and thereby linking its rule to the chaos of Europe and the powder magazine of the East. But the revolution in Britain will inevitably waken a powerful echo on the other side of the "herring pond," both in the New York Stock Exchange and in the working-class quarters of Chicago.

An immediate change will occur in the consciousness of both the bourgeoisie and of the proletariat in the United States: the bourgeoisie will feel weaker, the working class— stronger. Class consciousness, however, is a most important constituent element in the so-called relation of forces. This again does not mean that the American bankers and trust magnates will be unable to make attempts to stifle the revolution of the British proletariat economically, with the help of their navy. But such an attempt would in itself mean a further shock to the internal regime in the United States. Finally, not only the revolutionary events in Great Britain but also the new attitudes engendered by them in the proletariat of the United States will have an effect on the very heart of every American battleship, its engine room.

The sum total of all this does not mean that the proletarian revolution in Britain is not fraught with difficulties and dangers. On the contrary, the dangers and difficulties are enormous. But they exist on both sides. This, in fact, is the essence of revolution. The greater the place occupied by a given nation in the world, the mightier will be the forces of action and reaction which will be aroused and developed by the revolution. Our "sympathies" can in these conditions be of some use.

Revolutions do not happen in accordance with the most advantageous sequence. Revolutions in general do not happen arbitrarily. If it were possible to plan a revolutionary line of march rationally, then it would probably be possible to avoid revolution altogether. But the point is precisely this: revolution is the expression of the impossibility of transforming class society by rational methods. Logical arguments, even if carried by Russell to the status of mathematical formulas, are powerless against material interests. The ruling classes will condemn the whole of civilization to destruction—together with its mathematics—sooner than renounce their privileges. The coming revolution is already contained in embryo in the struggle between the miners and the coal magnates of Great Britain—just as the future stalk and ear of corn are already contained in the seed.

The irrational factors in human history operate most harshly of all through class contradictions. These irrational factors cannot be ignored. Just as mathematics, using irrational quantities, arrives at perfectly realistic conclusions, so politics can rationalize the social system, i.e., put rational order into it, only by clearly taking into account the irrational contradictions of society in order to overcome them once and for all: not by avoiding revolution, but with its help.

＊

Practically speaking, we could end on this. The objections raised by Russell gave us the opportunity of examining in addition those aspects of the problem which our small book left in the background. But it would be useful perhaps to dwell on our pacifist critic's last and strongest argument. Russell declares that our attitude to the British revolution is dictated by . . . our Russian patriotism. He says: "I am afraid that, like the rest of us, he [Trotsky] is a patriot when it comes to the pinch: a Communist revolution in England would be advantageous to Russia, and therefore he advises it without considering impartially whether it would be advantageous to us."

This argument has every advantage except novelty. For a long time now the press of Chamberlain and Joynson-Hicks—and also the *Morning Post*, which has pursued this line with the utmost fervor—have been arguing that the international Communist movement serves the interests of Soviet imperialism, which in turn is continuing the traditions of czarist policy. Accusations of this sort began as soon as the bourgeoisie became convinced of the fact that our party had seized power in earnest and did not intend to give it up.

In the period before and immediately after the seizure of power, the nature of the accusations against us was completely the opposite, as is well known. They accused the Bolsheviks of being devoid of any national feelings, and the Bolshevik leaders of pursuing the Hohenzollern's policy with respect to Russia. This was not so long ago either. Arthur Henderson, Emile Vandervelde, Albert Thomas, and others[25] came to Russia to convince the Russian workers that the Bolsheviks were ready to betray Russia's fundamental interests for the sake of their own international chimera (or, in other versions, for the German kaiser's gold). And again, the *Morning Post* developed this theme more vividly and more vigorously than anyone else. Just as Russell accuses us now of being prepared to reduce the population of Great Britain to twenty millions in the interests of Soviet imperialism, so they accused us nine years ago of callously being prepared to reduce the population of Russia to a half or a third in the name of our antinational objectives.

Our party, as is well known, took the view that a defeat of czarist Russia in the war would be as much an advantage to the Russian as to the international working class. The socialist lackeys of the Entente could not budge us from this position. At the time of the Peace of Brest-Litovsk,[26] the accusations of following an antinational policy (in the other version, of collaborating with the Hohenzollerns) reached the level of frenzy. Nonetheless, our party did not allow itself to be inveigled into the war in the interests of American capital. The Hohenzollern regime fell, and the October Revolution played no less a role in its overthrow than did the arms of the Entente. The antagonism between the Soviet Republic and the governments of the victorious Entente came to the fore.

The most reactionary world role is played by the rulers of Britain: in Europe, Egypt, Turkey, Persia, India, and China. Every change in the world situation in economics and politics is a blow to British rule. For this reason the decaying British bourgeoisie will fight tooth and nail against each and every change, in order to stave off the erosion of its might. The American bourgeoisie is more powerful. Its struggle against the revolution will be on a grander scale. But at the present time America still stands in the second rank. In Europe, in Asia, in Africa, the most active and the most vicious enemy of the revolutionary movement is the ruling class of Great Britain.

For a socialist, this fact would seem to be more than enough to explain the antagonism between the Soviet Union and the British Empire. Are we "patriots"? In the same measure as we were "antipatriots" during the imperialist war. With the methods of state power we are defending the same interests as we fought for with the methods of insurrection: the interests of the world proletariat.

When Russell says that we are prepared to sacrifice the interests of the British working class in the interests of the Soviet state, this is not only false but foolish. Any weakening of the British proletariat, and particularly its defeat in an open struggle, must inevitably strike a heavy blow against both the international and the internal position of the Soviet Union.

When in March 1921, the German Communists tried to force the proletarian revolution artificially, they were severely criticized at the Third Congress of the Comintern. To justify themselves, they referred to the difficult situation of the Soviet Republic and to the necessity of coming to her aid. Together, Lenin and I told them: neither heroic outbursts nor still less revolutionary adventures will be able to help the Soviet Republic; we need the same thing as the German proletariat, i.e., a victorious revolution. It would be a fundamental mistake to think that the proletariat of any country should, in the interests of the Soviet state, take any steps whatsoever that do not flow from its own interests as a class fighting for its complete liberation. This point of view, which is rooted in our flesh and blood, is alien to those socialists who—if not always, then at least at the decisive moment—invariably turn out to be on the side of their own bourgeoisie. And Russell is no exception.

It is true that during the war he did oppose his own government rather courageously, although politically his opposition was hopeless enough. That was an individual demonstration, a sop to his conscience—the fate of the regime was never even slightly in jeopardy. But when it comes to the matter of the revolution of the proletariat, Russell finds in his intellectual armory no other arguments than those which relate him to the *Morning Post* and all the Churchills of his country.

The greatest peculiarity in British politics—the past history of the country is summed up in this—is the glaring contradiction between the revolutionary maturity of the objective economic factors and the exceptional backwardness of the ideological forms, particularly in the ranks of the working class. This fundamental peculiarity is understood least of all precisely by those people who are the most striking manifestation of it: the bourgeois humanists, the latter-day enlighteners, and the pacifists. Side-by-side with the reactionary petty-bourgeois reformists, they consider themselves called upon to lead the proletariat.

Bertrand Russell is not the worst of them. But his writings on social and political themes, his appeals against the war, his polemic with Scott Nearing[27] apropos the Soviet regime, all characterize unmistakably his superficial dilettantism, his political blindness, his complete lack of understanding of the fundamental mechanics of historical development, i.e., the struggle of living classes arising from the basis of production. He opposes to history the propaganda of various pacifist slogans which he himself wretchedly formulates. In so doing, he forgets to explain to us why pacifist enlightenment did not save us from wars and revolutions, despite the fact that such eminent people interested themselves in it as Robert Owen in the first half of the nineteenth century, the French enlighteners in the eighteenth century, the Quakers since the seventeenth century, and many others besides.

Russell is a latter-day enlightener, who has inherited from the old enlightenment not its enthusiasm but its ideological prejudices. Russell is a skeptic through and through. He apparently counterposes the peaceful, gradual methods of science and technology to the violent methods of revolution. But he has as little faith in the saving power of scientific thought as he has in the power of revolutionary action.

In his polemic against Nearing, he tries, under the cover of pseudosocialist phraseology, to disparage, discredit, and compromise the revolutionary initiative of the Russian proletariat. In his polemic against the biologist Haldane,[28] he scoffs at the optimism of the technical sciences. In his little book *Icarus*, he openly expresses his conviction that the best outcome would be the destruction of our whole civilization. And this man, utterly corroded by the wormholes of his egoistic, self-centered, aristocratic skepticism, thinks he is called upon to give advice to the British proletariat and to warn it against our Communist machinations!

The British working class is entering an epoch in which it will need to have the firmest belief in its own mission and in its own strength. For this there is no need of any artificial stimulants such as religion or an idealist morality. It is necessary and sufficient that the British proletariat understand that the situation in their own country is linked with the situation in the whole world, that it understand the rottenness of the ruling classes and throw aside the careerists, the charlatans, and the bourgeois skeptics who imagine themselves to be socialists only because from time to time they are nauseated by the stench of decaying bourgeois society.

CRIMEA, ENROUTE.

P.S. These lines were written during the days when the question of the miners' strike and the general strike hung by a thin thread. At the present time there is still no final decision; at least news of it has not reached us. But whatever the direction taken by the events in Britain in the coming days and weeks, the problems with which the present article is particularly concerned will never again come off the agenda of British political life.

Appendixes to Part 2

Introduction to the English edition

by H.N. Brailsford

At the close of the Communist trial, the judge at the Old Bailey summoned seven of his prisoners to choose between a six months' sentence and the opinions expressed in this book. They are, if we must read this summons in its literal meaning, prohibited opinions on which the law has put its ban. If this were really our case, then the thesis which Trotsky maintains in these pages is established already. For we should have to admit that even before violence had been attempted, the mere appearance in our politics of a tiny revolutionary party has sufficed to frighten the ruling class out of its respect for the liberty of opinion on which democracy is founded. It needs no energetic exercise of the imagination to predict from this episode what would happen if the challenge grew to a formidable threat.

But the battle for freedom is not yet lost. It is precisely those of us who differ from Trotsky's reading of our inevitable destiny who are bound in duty to welcome the appearance of this book. If it may come freely from the press, if it may be discussed, as it deserves to be, with equal freedom for assent or dissent, then, for the moment at least, the nightmare of this trial is dissipated. Of all parties in Great Britain, the Labour Party has the chief interest in demand-

273

ing for this ruthless attack upon itself both liberty and attention. We can hold our faith in the democratic approach to Socialism as a reasoned conviction only if the opposite opinion may be argued in perfect liberty, and only then if it finds worthy and capable advocates. If the law forbids a man to draw from the study of history and the survey of contemporary politics the conclusion that force is the only adequate instrument for social change, in that moment our contrary opinion ceases to be a reasoned conviction and becomes an imposed dogma.

The opinion which Trotsky maintains has never been more brilliantly argued. Behind its wit and its logic there is the prestige of experience. The pamphleteer who tells us that if we mean to achieve Socialism we cannot escape civil war has himself conducted a civil war against terrific odds to a triumphant conclusion. It is obvious, moreover, that he has taken pains to equip himself for his task and has applied his versatile intellect to the study of our history and our contemporary life. He makes some mistakes,* it is true, in his facts, but none of these really invalidate his argument.

His book is a slashing attack on our whole movement. We shall make a grave mistake if we allow its manner to blind us to the fact that he has a strong case to argue. He assails Left and Right with equal vehemence. Sometimes in his criticisms of persons he is arrogant and offensive; sometimes his wit is irresistible; sometimes (it seems to me) he assails things in our record and muddles in our thinking which deserve to be assailed. But the odds are that with these ruthless Russian methods he will produce in the minds of most English

---

* He evidently misunderstands our electoral system. Again the life of the Independent Labour Party has been much longer than he supposes, and its membership is twice what he attributes to it. He seems at times to identify it with the Fabian Society. But such slips are of no importance.—H.N.B.

readers an effect which is far from his intention.

Trotsky is far too able a man not to realize that there are differences in the English and Russian national characters. He emphasizes again and again the lesson that history has made each of us what we are. Yet the more he displays his acquaintance with the external facts of our history, the less does he seem to understand us. His attitude to the religious beliefs of most of our readers is for me the test of his failure to understand us—and this I may say calmly, since I am myself an agnostic. No Russian that I ever met, even when he had been long in England, ever grasped the fact that English religion with its long tradition of open discussion, the democratic form of its "free" churches, its emphasis on conduct rather than ritual or belief, and its relative freedom from otherworldliness, has literally nothing in common with the Eastern Church. I wonder, would Trotsky's conviction that Protestant religion is necessarily a "bourgeois" creed which no worker can honestly profess survive a visit to a Dissenting chapel in a mining district? Has he ever read Bunyan, or glanced at the revolutionary history of Anabaptists and Fifth Monarchy men? What would he make of the queer disputes between the middle-class Freethinker Robert Owen (who hated class war) and the pioneers of English Trade Unionism, who clung with equal obstinacy to their Christianity and their belief in the class war?

One feels the same failure of a man from another world to understand us when Trotsky laughs at the idea that a Labour majority in Parliament will ever be allowed to do anything fundamental. Assuredly it will be a tremendous adventure; certainly it will want will and courage. No sane man will deny the risks to which Trotsky points. But equally, I think, every man who realizes how deeply the Parliamentary tradition and the instinct of obedience to the majority are graven on the English mind will admit that the adventure is worth attempting. Not only in Parliament, but in churches, Trade

Unions, and even clubs, this respect for the majority has been inculcated on generations of Englishmen. What can a Russian know of that? What estimate can he make of the power of tradition in our older civilization? We should answer, in the last resort, that if he is right, if the propertied class will in the end defend its privileges by force, then we prefer to fight, as Cromwell fought, with the Parliament behind us, and the rights of a majority on our side.

But it is not the business of an introducer to enter into controversy with the author. The book with all its vitality and assurance is doubly valuable—as a revelation of the Russian mind, and a criticism of our English ways. It is the work of a shrewd and realistic intellect. It will not convert many of us to the Russian standpoint. But we shall fail to use it to the full unless we take it as a challenge that forces us to think out our position anew. Trotsky sees, as some of us do not, the difficulty of our unparalleled enterprise. He realizes that the tactics which will avail to transform an old society cannot be the tactics of an opportunist Liberalism. The book may confirm us in our resolve by all means to avoid civil war, but it is a formidable challenge to us to test our own sincerity, and to ask ourselves whether, with a will and a courage that equal the audacity of these Russian pioneers, we are moving with single minds towards the achievement of our goal. ∎

Trotsky on our sins

by Bertrand Russell

Trotsky's new book is one of the most interesting that I have read for a long time, and up to a certain point, extraordinarily penetrating. There are certain errors of fact, but they are not important—e.g., that Joseph Chamberlain left Gladstone on the Protectionist issue, and that the present Parliamentary constituencies are gerrymandered so as to give a great advantage to the Conservatives.

On the politics of the British Labour Movement, Trotsky is remarkably well informed. A great deal of his criticism is, to my mind, quite convincing. I leave on one side his personalities about leaders, which will be liked or disliked according as the reader dislikes or likes the leader in question. What is more important is his complaint that the Labour Party lacks a coherent theoretical outlook. Take, for example, the question of Republicanism. He quotes British Labour pronouncements to the effect that the royal authority does no harm, and that a king is cheaper than a president. He argues that in a time of critical conflict

> the bourgeoisie can make use of the royal authority with great success, as the concentration point for all the extraparliamentary, that is to say, the real forces directed against the working class. . . . To proclaim a socialist program, and at the same time declare that the royal authority "does not hinder" and works out cheaper, is absolutely the same as, for example, acknowledging materialistic science and making use of the incantation of a sorcerer for toothache, on the ground that the sorcerer is cheaper.

278 / LEON TROTSKY ON BRITAIN

To hope to achieve Socialism without Republicanism is the sort of thing that could only occur among English-speaking people; it would hardly be possible for men with any profound knowledge of history, or any understanding of the economic and psychological links between different institutions. In spite of Mr. Brailsford's remark to the contrary in the introduction, I should agree with Trotsky in saying the same of the Churches. Personal religion is a private matter; but organized religion, in the modern world, must be a reactionary force, even when its adherents ardently desire the opposite.

"But," I shall be told, "how many Labour members would you get into Parliament if you attacked the monarchy and antagonized the Churches?" Here we come up against a most disastrous fallacy. It is thought that the important thing is to get Socialists elected to Parliament by hook or by crook, even if, in order to get elected, they have had to let it be understood that they will refrain from carrying out large parts of the Socialist programme. To secure a Government composed of professing Socialists is not the same thing as to secure Socialism; this has been proved in many European countries since the war. Socialism will never be actually established until the leaders are in earnest in desiring it; by this I mean not merely that they should favour it in the abstract, but that they should be willing, for its sake, to forego the amenities of bourgeois success, which are enjoyed by successful Labour politicians so long as they refrain from abolishing bourgeois privileges.

Another important point is illustrated by the analogy of Cromwell, upon which Trotsky dwells at some length. Cromwell, unlike most of the Parliament men, expressed a preference for soldiers convinced of the justice of the cause rather than "gentlemen," and only by this means succeeded in achieving victory in spite of the opposition of his superior officers. In our day, in England, there seems to be hardly anyone whose belief in anything is sufficient to make him indifferent to "gentlemanliness"; certain Labour leaders are constantly led into weaknesses by the desire to have their opponents consider them "gentlemen." They do not seem to realize that the ideal of a "gentleman" is one of the weapons of the propertied classes; it precludes dirty tricks against the rich and powerful, but not against the poor and oppressed. This weakness is peculiarly British. We shall achieve nothing until we desire Socialism more than the approval of our enemies, which is only to be won by treachery, conscious or unconscious.

Our British passion for inconsistency and lack of philosophy is leading the Labour Movement astray. Cromwell had a complete philosophy, however absurd it may seem to us; so had the Benthamites[29] who created the Liberal Party and the whole democratic movement of the nineteenth century. The Russian Communists have achieved what could never have been achieved by men who were content with a hotch-potch of amiable sentiments. It is useless to pretend, for instance, that Socialism is merely Christianity consistently carried out. Christianity is an agricultural religion, Socialism is industrial; it is not so much an affair of sentiment as of economic organization. And we British, like the young man who had great possessions, are prevented from thinking clearly by the vague realization that, if we did, we should have to abandon our imperialism; it is only by a skillful muddle-headedness that the Labour Party can inveigh against imperialists while taking care to retain the Empire and to carry on the tradition of oppression, as the late Government did in practice.

Let us, at least for the sake of argument, admit the whole of Trotsky's indictment of our movement; what, then, shall we say of his own programme for Britain? I say it is a programme which could only be advocated by an enemy or a fool; and Trotsky is not a fool. His view is that when we at last have a Labour Government with a clear parliamentary majority, the present leaders, both of the Right and the Left, will be as helpless as Kerensky, and will be swept away by resolute men of action.

> The police, judiciary, army, and militia will be on the side of the disorganizers, saboteurs, and fascists. The bureaucratic apparatus must be destroyed, replacing the reactionaries by members of the Labour Party. [But such meager measures] will extraordinarily sharpen the legal and illegal opposition of the united bourgeois reaction. In other words: this is also the way of civil war. . . . In the event of the victory of the proletariat, there will ensue the shattering of the opposition of the exploiters by means of revolutionary dictatorship.

It is odd how Trotsky's realism fails him at this point. Much of his book is taken up in proving how our economic position has deteriorated, and how we have become dependent upon the United States. Yet when he speaks of a Communist revolution, he always argues as though we were economically self-subsistent. It is obvious that French (if not British) aeroplanes and American (if not British) warships would soon put an end to the Communist regime; or, at the lowest, an economic blockade would destroy our export trade and therefore deprive us of our food supply.

There are some bombastic sentences about the sympathy to be expected from Soviet Russia. But until Soviet Russia can place a fleet in the Atlantic stronger than that of America, it is not clear what we should gain by sympathy, however enthusiastic. To secure economic independence without naval supremacy, we should have to reduce our population to about twenty millions. While this was being effected by starvation, no doubt Trotsky's sympathy would be a great comfort; but, on the whole, most of us would rather remain alive without it than die with it.

The fact is that Trotsky hates Britain and British imperialism, not without good reason, and is therefore not to be trusted when he gives advice. We have become, through our dependence upon foreign food, so hopelessly entangled in world politics that it is impossible for us to advance at a pace which America will not tolerate.

Trotsky himself says: "In the decisive struggle against the proletariat the British bourgeoisie will avail themselves of the most powerful support of the bourgeoisie of the United States, while the working class will base itself mainly on the working class of Europe and the oppressed peoples of the British colonies." It is scarcely credible that he should suppose our food supply would continue under such circumstances. I am afraid that, like the rest of us, he is a patriot when it comes to the pinch: a Communist revolution in England would be advantageous to Russia, and therefore he advises it without considering impartially whether it would be advantageous to us. The arguments against it, so far from being sentimental or visionary, are strategical and economic. The Pacifism which he dislikes in the British Labour Movement is forced upon it by the dependence upon America which has resulted from our participation in the Great War. If he really desires the spread of Communism, and not merely the collapse of England, it is time for him to turn his attention to the American Federation of Labour.

From *The New Leader*, February 26, 1926. ■

Trotsky on Great Britain

by J. Ramsay MacDonald

Trotsky is a pamphleteer not an historian, a devotee of theories not a slave to facts. In this lively little book, so delightfully sprightly that its most wicked darts will cause no annoyance to those at whom they are flung, no one will find the truth either about Agadir or Black Friday, the British Communists or the Labor Ministry. An Oriental riot of fancy regarding facts and events and an impish delight in impudence and expletives, combined with a resourceful art in a swashbuckling and a shrewd dialectic, make the book always entertaining and sometimes serious.

His thesis is that England, no longer the economic mistress of the world, is going down to decay through political and economic distress, and that everyone who places any social value in the Christian faith or in evolutionary processes controlled by reason and right is an enemy of mankind—especially of the British working classes. He sees no hope for anyone except through revolution, and where he has to admit reluctantly that the Russian Revolution has not been so successful as it might have been, he explains that that was owing to the backwardness of the country. The truth is that only the backwardness of the country allowed the Bolshevist Revolution. A nation organized industrially as ours is, with a society leaning at every point on international trade and contact, would be lying dead at the dike side after a year of a Soviet administration and a Cheka. Russia alone of European nations, because of its backwardness and the surrender of its government to the peasants, could show some years of Bolshevist rule.

The substantial part of the book is a study of force as the means of social change, and in this Trotsky returns again and again to two tunes. One he plays with a jazz gleefulness. "We do not believe in force," the British Independent Labor Party has said, and Trotsky with many playful variations and much impertinent comment reminds it of the policeman and of previous revolutions (which he admits did little but rivet on the nation the tyranny of the victors). The I.L.P., however, is perfectly right in rejecting the doctrine of force. It may be, as Trotsky dogmatizes, that when we have a Labor majority carrying out in Parliament a Labor program the classes that are assailed will fight. That is an interesting subject for prophetic speculation, and whoever begins with the assumption that the British Tory Party is peculiarly devoid of respect for any law and order but its own, and is not likely to show any obedience to constitutional methods except those it manipulates, may not be far wrong. The Bolshevist and the British Tory may be found to belong to the same political family. That, however, has been discussed in Labor Party literature and finds a place in Labor Party considerations, and regarding it Trotsky has nothing to warn nor to teach us. But it is beside the mark. Unblushingly and unapologetically the Labor Party rejects revolution as the way of salvation, believes in political action, and in the event of coming into power will protect that action against either the plots of Communists or the mutinies of Tories.

The other tune, played in more sober tempo, is that the evolutionary process is marked by moments of sudden outward change, and that the years of "gradualness" are only valuable in so far as they accumulate power to effect that change. Here again Trotsky is only reiterating what British Socialists have been saying and writing for over a quarter of a century. The rise of the Labor Party to being the second party in the state is a case in point; when it is enabled to give form in the state to its constructive proposals, that will be the revolution. Russian apologists are curiously blind on this point, and one of the blindest is Trotsky himself— when he is not incurring the suspicion of his colleagues for seeing their follies. They think that resolutions, manifestos, speeches, words, imprisonment, the suppression of liberty to write and speak, the subordination by their Red Army of peoples like the Georgians make up the revolution. There they are mistaken. They may yet effect their revolution, however, and I wish they would. They have so modified their policy that they encourage us to hope that they will succeed, though every new Trotsky pamphlet shows how far they have yet to go. We did our best to help them on to right ways in London, and if they were ungrateful and continued to fulminate their vain nonsense from Moscow, we did not trouble much. We were interested in the restoration of Russia and its return, under any government it cared to tolerate, to the cooperation of European nations. Trotsky's exposition of revolution within the evolutionary process indeed cuts the ground from under his feet as a politician, at the same time that it contributes to his vim as a pamphleteer.

Whither England? must indeed be read as an indication of the chagrin of Bolshevist leaders against the "stupid" British working classes. For years they have supplied their tools here with money and instructions. They have not been good tools, but they have been active ones. Under our prejudices in favor of liberty they have had plenty of rope. We have not adopted the policy of imprisonment or suppression (until the present Government, to advance its own political interests far more than to protect their country, put a dozen of them in the dock). We knew our people better than that. Even when every newspaper in the country was predicting the downfall of the Moderates (as some of us are called), when the press of the world was summoned to Liverpool last September to record the triumph of the Left (as others are called), and when Moscow was awaiting the glad tidings that its money had at long last borne fruit, the Labor Party Conference inflicted upon them a defeat more humiliating than they had received at the hands of the working classes of any country in the world.

Great Britain is facing tremendous difficulties—imperial, economic, social; the old times have, indeed, gone; rivals surround us on sea and land, in east and west; the relations between capital and labor have been such as to destroy confidence and good will, and the system of capitalism has almost swept away the pride and moral obligation in industry. Against this we have the hard and furious reaction of revolution which, were there any hope of a dawn in it, would soon come upon us. No humane man would then lift up his little finger to stave it off. But it has no such hope. The Labor movement here strives to strengthen the other reaction of social constructive transformation by the only power that we know giving prospects of success—political power used to effect economic change, to establish control over the industrial life of the nation, and to protect and promote communal well-being in a cooperative state.

From *The Nation*, March 10, 1926. ∎

Trotsky

by George Lansbury

In my unregenerate days, I occasionally went to the theater to see musical comedy. I am reminded of this when I read books such as that written by Comrade Trotsky. There was a song in the "Belle of New York" which had this refrain: "You can't expect to be like us, but be as like us as you are able to be." The air of downright superiority and dogmatic cocksureness with which our comrades abroad write about us is very flattering to themselves, and assures us of the fact that none of them need offer up the Scotsman's prayer—that God will give them a good conceit of themselves.

That this book is brilliantly written and theoretically sound is, I suppose, a fact that we must take for granted, because if anyone accepts Trotsky's starting point, they must agree that everything that follows is clearcut and logical; but where we poor frail mortals come in, I cannot understand. We are apparently all fatalistically on the road either to destruction or Socialism. Trotsky is at great pains to prove how much he dislikes all of us. What exactly he knows about us, except what he has read or been told, it is impossible to say.

When in Brixton prison a friend of mine, a pretty hefty chap, a blacksmith who weighs about seventeen stone, became rather sick, or thought he was. The doctor, who was a tiny little man, when visiting him, said, "I do not like the look of you." Whereupon our comrade answered, rather fiercely, "And I don't like the look of you, either." When asked to explain what he meant, he simply replied: "Well, you said you did not like the look of me. Why should I like the look of you?" I have that sort of feeling when I read the continual criticisms, not of one or two of us, but of everybody in the British Labour Movement who happens to refuse to accept all the theories according to men like Trotsky. And I cannot help feeling that if those of us whom he criticizes were put into the mirror of truth, we should be in effect saying to him: "Yes, and we do not like the look of you, either."

In spite of all the criticism of our faults, and in spite of all our weaknesses, Great Britain is the one country in the world where the opportunity of workers' control of every department of life is more possible of achievement than anywhere else.

It may be quite true that we are dependent upon the maintenance of the Empire in an imperial sense if we are to continue our present way of living; but already, there are signs that the Labour Movement, understanding this, is also understanding that it must set about reorganizing the agricultural life of this country and reverse the procedure of the past century and a half, and instead of living parasitically on other people for its food, must provide food within its own shores.

This, however, [is] by the way. The main contention of Trotsky is that unless there is a Communist revolution in this country, Socialism will not be accomplished. Many of us believe that Socialism can no more be fully applied here than it can be in Russia until other nations are converted. This is also part of the Bolshevik theory. Therefore we British Socialists shall, using the means and the methods that we have at our disposal, continue to build up, continue to create and maintain a Socialist movement, doing whatever we are able along Socialist lines until the world revolution takes place.

Our working class is learning the great art of administration—something which the Russian workers are only just beginning to learn. We have been getting ourselves educated for nearly a century through our co-operative societies, trade unions, friendly societies, municipal and other administrative bodies. Slowly but surely we are getting into the position that we shall not only legislate, but administer also.

On the two questions in the book in which I come in for the most attack, namely, my pacifism and religion, it is only necessary to say this: I do not deny a single word that Trotsky says or that anybody else says about the causes of war and the fact that wars have taken place and will continue in the future; but he must please remember, and all critics

must please remember, that millions of men throughout
Europe who professed to hold the Marxian creed plunged
themselves into the late war as pure and simple national-
ists. In this country the men who founded the Marxian Social Democratic Federation were the leaders, and the most
Jingo leaders, on behalf of the late war. How this happened
I do not know, but it did happen and nearly always has happened that way.

Our governing class has always been able to divide and
conquer mainly because it has taken good care to feed, clothe,
and pay its fighting forces better than any other country,
and also because it has never allowed large masses to starve
absolutely. In modern times our masters issue just sufficient
to keep them alive. We who have had to do with the business
of dealing with unemployment and the poor generally have
been doing our best to use this power of keeping people alive
and in health in order to make Socialists of them—and to
a large extent have succeeded. In any case, when the workers in Britain are sufficiently united and class-conscious to
want the revolution there is nobody here strong enough to
deny them.

The final word, though, about violence is that this has
been the weapon used all through the ages, and we are as
we were.

As to religion: Trotsky's error is not due to arrogance but
entirely to the fact that he only knows the old Greek Church
of the czars, which was almost wholly an instrument of repression, and did force its devotees to be anti-Socialist. As
Brailsford says, if he could visit England, he would discover
that some of the best and truest of our comrades are to be
found amongst those who profess and call themselves Christians; but their Christianity is of a different variety from
that which has prevailed in Russia. There is nothing novel
in there being various degrees of religious thought and the
expression of religion, any more than it is extraordinary

that there should be varying degrees of Socialist thought in what is known as the Socialist movement. But after all, I should like to ask this simple question: What earthly reason is there for Trotsky to set himself up as a kind of Pope over other people's thoughts and actions in connection with religion? It is a purely personal matter, and something which neither he nor anyone else has the right to interfere with. The British movement has not been injured, but has rather been helped by the men and women who have come out of the churches and the chapels and proclaimed their faith in the oneness of life.

As I understand our comrade, he bases his whole philosophy of life on materialism. Well: he may be right, but my experience is that when men or women join our movement purely and simply because they think it is going to bring them individually a better life, they very soon find their way into the other camp. I think the fact that the rebel of to-day becomes the orthodox person of to-morrow is due to this, and it is because I think that people must have something in life other than individual interests that I am what I am.

But how does it help our movement for Comrade Trotsky to deliver this kind of judgment on people like myself? What does he really know about the matter? I judge him not by his opinions, but by what he has done, and I admire him not because of what he says, but for what he is. And why should not people like myself and others be judged by what we are and what we do?

This book and the introduction is well worth reading, if only—and here I repeat Brailsford's words—because it is a challenge to us to make our movement more effective. I am convinced of one thing. The British people have the finest opportunity ever given to a nation to lead the world. I still believe we shall do it. We may make many mistakes during the next few years, but I feel confident that our working class will come together and by unity and comradeship, and by what is of much more importance, thoroughly understanding whither they want to go, will join with comrades in other parts of the world in building the International Commonwealth of Nations.

From *Lansbury's Labour Weekly*, February 27, 1926. ∎

The gospel according to Trotsky

by Robert Williams

This book is more epithetic than epoch-making. Its liveliness is undeniable, and the author's command of vituperative adjectives is tremendous. It moves in a swift survey of English political history—as Trotsky sees it; but what Trotsky sees is as nothing beside what he ignores, cannot see, will not see, and doesn't understand. British psychology baffles him, as it has baffled many another Continental student of British affairs. Twice he raises his hands in horror at the fact that when Curzon died the Leader of the Opposition should have added his tribute to the memory of the dead Statesman.

What he *wishes* to see is also a tremendous factor in his book. Who, except Trotsky, or someone who just as ardently wished to see it, could have seen what Trotsky sees when he says: "As a result of the General Election of 1906 the Labour Party for the first time formed a large fraction with 42 members. *Without doubt the influence of the 1905 revolution is manifest in this.*"

Naturally, the book challenges most of our preconceptions

regarding the development of the Labour and Socialist Movement. Its challenge is vitiated because, as I have indicated, Trotsky, like most other "foreigners" (I use the word in its friendliest sense), is incapable of understanding the British temperament, not merely on its political and industrial side, but on its general or racial side.

He starts out with a chapter headed "The Decline of Britain," and winds up with a series of "Prospects" in which he says: "The Communist Party will take that place in relation to the Labour Party which at present is occupied by the I.L.P."

One may be pardoned for wondering why Trotsky wrote the book, now first published. Those of us who are more or less conversant with Russian affairs will know that for over a year Trotsky was attacked, misrepresented, and vilified by the dictators of the Russian Communist Party just as much as he now condemns, misrepresents, and vilifies the leaders of the British Labour and Socialist Movement. After Lenin's death, as Max Eastman has shown us in his book, *Since Lenin Died*, Trotsky made a superhuman effort to democratise the Russian Communist Party; but he was broken by the machine, forced into retirement, and came back to the forefront of Russian politics upon the terms of the Triumvirate, which had compelled him, in the guise of illness, to go into what was then thought to be permanent retirement.

The party machine, in the hands of Stalin, Zinoviev, and Kamenev,[30] was powerful enough not only to suppress the forceful criticisms of Trotsky, but to suppress the last will and testament of Lenin himself. This is a matter which illuminates the distinction between Russian methods and British methods. Just before his death Lenin wrote a remarkable article calling for the democratization of the Russian Communist Party. He sent this to Bukharin, the editor of *Pravda*, the official organ, for publication. Lenin's wife, while Lenin was very ill though mentally efficient, urged and implored, with Trotsky, that one of Lenin's last messages should be published; but those in charge of the machine were so afraid of the criticism of one who had rendered more service to the revolution than all of them combined that they deliberately suppressed it.

Trotsky's book, however, not only has free circulation in Britain, but contains an admirably written preface by H.N. Brailsford, one of the literary leaders of the I.L.P., which as an organisation comes in for a large share of Trotsky's vituperative wit. Not only are Messrs. MacDonald, Clynes, Henderson, Thomas, and a host of others of the Right subjected to Trotsky's attacks, but a special chapter is devoted to George Lansbury because of his objection to the use of force in bringing about social and economic changes. Wheatley, Kirkwood, and others described as the Left Wingers of the Labour Party, are caricatured, condemned, and despised as much as those who held high office in the Labour Government. The present writer comes in for his share of Trotsky's censure. Trotsky says: "The mighty apparatus of the Liberal and Conservative newspapers and publishing houses can be utilised for the education of the working class. 'Give me a dictatorship over Fleet Street for only a month and I will abolish the hypnotism,' exclaimed Robert Williams in 1920. Williams himself has ratted, but Fleet Street still awaits the proletarian hand as before."

If it pleases Trotsky to say that "Williams has ratted," well and good. But two years ago the whole Russian Communist Party under the tutelage of the bureaucratic machine said exactly the same thing of Trotsky, who was broken by that machine and came back to a certain measure of popularity only upon its terms. Not only is Williams open to the charge of "ratting"—Philips Price, Walton Newbold, Ellen Wilkinson, and a host of others in Britain are subject to the same gibes. Paul Levi in Germany, Jean Longuet in France, Balabanov, of the Russian Communist

Party (now working in Vienna), and even Serrati, the Italian Keir Hardie, are all directly or indirectly anathematised by the outpourings of the Great Panjandrums of the Third International with their innumerable theses of the gospel according to Moscow.

The remarkable feature about international politics as seen by Moscow is that while they are willing to accept the statements regarding working-class development from a handful of obscure Communists, whenever something essential is required they invariably come to those who are the subject of their widespread denunciations for help in Russia's hour of need.

MacDonald is condemned for wearing Court dress when Foreign Minister, but not a word of denunciation for our old-time friend Chicherin[31] for being received by the Pope and King [Victor] Emmanuel of Italy. Ridicule and condemnation for those who act in accordance with the traditions of the British Labour Movement, but a blind eye to Kamenev, Krassin, and Rakovsky, who wear the most immaculate clothes at the receptions given at Claridge's or Chesham House. Practically every one we meet of the men of affairs connected with Russian foreign policy will admit privately and personally the need for getting down to realism in international matters: one might mention a dozen names but for fear of causing embarrassment.

People like Trotsky find it impossible to understand us— sometimes we find it impossible to understand ourselves. A well known continental Socialist said to me on one recent occasion: "You people are absolutely incomprehensible—in international Trade Union affairs you send Thomas to-day to preside over the I.F.T.U., and he is followed by Mr. A.A. Purcell. Their divergent policies appear to us like oil and water. In the Miners' International you have Hodges to-day and Cook to-morrow. In September of 1925 your Scarborough Trades Union Congress avows its undiluted militancy, its adhesion to confiscation, direct action, and the general strike; and less than a month afterwards it is followed by your Liverpool Conference of the Labour Party, at which you arrange with overwhelming majorities to expel the Communists who fostered and fathered the militant resolutions carried at Scarborough!"

Failing to understand us, Trotsky ignores most of the considerations that arise from British conditions and British temperament, and takes refuge in wide generalities based upon what he would wish to see happen. Conceive of anyone with a real understanding of British conditions committing himself to the statement that "if a real Labour Government came to power even in the most ultrademocratic manner, a civil war would be revealed as inevitable." Or, "without the application of revolutionary force it will be hardly possible to achieve even an honest distribution of the electoral regions in Britain."

That is the Trotsky method of stating a case. Willful misreading or blindness to the facts of history, stubborn incomprehension of the British temperament, sweeping generalities backed up by a torrent of invective, the play of wit, and the skillful suppression of anything that tends to discredit his theories: all this makes the book very lively, and indeed, it is a tonic. It is like a violent massage after a Turkish bath: unpleasant at first, but reinvigorating afterwards. I would commend Trotsky's book to all those who wish to see themselves as others see them. Trotsky himself is a great organizer; at one time one of the best known pacifists in the international Socialist movement, and later (1917–20) organizer and improviser of one of the finest pieces of military machinery in the world—Russia's Red Army.

We say to our Russian friends: Tell us what you think of us, be as candid as you care, make all the contribution you can to the international movement, but don't expect us to act blindly under your tutelage. British democratic and working-class forces were making their contribution to world development when Russia was in a most hopeless stage of illiteracy and backwardness. Each country must follow the line laid down by its own historical development, and, for the time being at least, British Trade Unionists and Socialists will adhere to the methods of political and social democracy.

There is no indication as to who acted as the translator of this book, but its English is decidedly forceful.

From *Labour Magazine*, March 1926. ∎

The world press looks at Trotsky's book

. . . What Trotsky forgets is that England has had bitter experience of revolution, and the fallacy in his latest arguments is that he considers the Great Rebellion to be a symptom of the Englishman's mentality, whereas, historically speaking, he really ought to look upon it as a miserable experience which the Englishman will not readily forget. . . .

The strikes and other measures of violence which have rent our economic life have further reinforced the truth that violence never reaches its professed end. And that is the explanation of the rage of Trotsky against Mr. Baldwin, who has been swift to take advantage of the reaction of his fellow countrymen against industrial terrorism and who is now leading a crusade against Bolshevism which in our opinion will inevitably spell its doom. . . .

We trust that the Government will refuse to be intimidated by the malevolence of Moscow, of which Trotsky's book is the latest manifestation. The Bolsheviks are dangerous only when the anti-Bolsheviks surrender to them. Hitherto our policy towards Moscow has consisted too often of a series of ignoble capitulations—and we might contrast in this respect the indifference with which more than one British Government has accepted the sequestration of the property of British nationals in Russia with the stern demands which Mr. Kellogg is making on the Mexican Government with reference to the "nationalisation" of the property of American citizens.[32] We should like to stand up to Moscow in the same way that the State Department is standing up to General Calles. And a beginning might be made with this absurd Trade Agreement which is simply a cover under which the Bolsheviks preach sedition within our gates. . . .

From an editorial entitled "Trotsky's Outburst,"
in The Morning Post, June 18, 1925.

✳

According to Trotsky, "England is heading rapidly towards an era of great revolutionary upheavals." Since the Russians, perhaps, blunder even more often than the Germans in their estimates of foreign nations, this diagnosis is not necessarily correct. But there are people in this country who, after reading the reports of the last Trade Unions Congress, may be inclined to believe that there is more in it than there is in most Russian predictions of inevitable and automatic revolution. The difference between this Trade Unions Congress and all others was not so much in its programme as in its method and temper. . . . The impression which one gets is that the Congress, as a whole, has drifted a long way towards acceptance of the Communist point of view. . . . The spirit is closely akin. It is the spirit of class, the belief that democratic government is a sham and that a better order of society can only be won by the exercise of economic pressure. . . .

But although the resolutions and speeches at the Congress bore unmistakable evidence of the drift towards the Communist point of view, it is no less clear that the speakers bothered little with philosophic theories about the State and the principles of government. . . . It is only another way of stating the well-known fact that, while the Communist party in Great Britain is negligible in numbers and influence, the Minority Movement within the trade unions is strong and becoming stronger.[33] The Minority Movement is led by men who are indistinguishable from Communists. . . . Most of the declared and undeclared Communists have been drawn from the trade unions rather than from the Independent Labour Party. . . . The I.L.P., and Socialists in general, abhor class government as stoutly as any—perhaps more stoutly, since it was the inequalities of class that gave birth to Socialism. The latest Trade Unions Congress, therefore, while it may mark the growth of a movement hostile to Parliamentary and democratic government in general, marks much more definitely a division within the Labour Party on the fundamental conceptions of politics. . . . The time seems to be coming when these instincts may lead to a breach between the political and industrial wings of the Labour movement. . . . When that time comes the great mass of the trade unionists will have to make up their minds whether to follow . . . the Minority Movement or . . . Labour. . . . The Minority Movement will have to capture the party before it can capture the State. It may fail in the first; it will certainly fail in the second.

From "Communism and Labour," in *The Manchester Guardian*,
September 15, 1925.

✳

The latest Englishman to have suffered from Russian aggressiveness is Mr. Brailsford, who wrote the preface to Trotsky's remarkable book *Where Is Britain Going?* in which the leaders of the British Labour Party are most severely castigated. The Russian revolutionary leader wrote an article in *Izvestia,* in which he angrily criticised Mr. Brailsford's observations about the Soviet Government's attitude to religion. "The power of Protestantism is great, but not infinite. Our task—is to help to destroy in the course of a few years the religion which has been formed over centuries." As you can see, it is clear and simple. You cannot misinterpret Trotsky's statements in any way any more. The communists who have seized power in Russia at any rate act more openly than the English socialists who, although the majority of them are members of Christian churches, at the same time defend the Soviet system and accuse their political opponents of an unjust attitude towards it. Trotsky and his co-thinkers openly express their hostility to the Christian religion in all its forms and their firm intention of destroying it—just as openly as they attack the existing economic order or the British empire. Atheism forms an important constituent part of their terrible credo; without atheism, Bolshevism would cease to be Bolshevism, and the whole Soviet regime would assume another aspect.

From *The Northern Whig*, March 19, 1926.
This article has been retranslated from the Russian.

＊

It is a curious thing that although Trotsky is diametrically opposed to Lansbury on almost every conceivable point, he is still hailed as "Comrade." It is the same with our own Labour Party, which contains men differing from each other more than they differ from members of other parties, and yet they are bound to work together for the same political objects. There are large numbers of working men who have not an atom of faith in Socialism, but they are tied to the

Socialist chariot, and do not seem to possess the strength and the courage to break their bonds.

From "Occasional Notes," by Alpha, in *The Luton News and Bedfordshire Advertiser*, March 4, 1926.

＊

One of the undoubted facts of our times is the improvement in the internal and international position of British capitalism; but Trotsky is sure that it will not improve but worsen; that the difficulties with which Britain is struggling today will sharpen and become deeper, hastening the approach of revolution. For "the wolf"—which Trotsky emphasizes approvingly—is the revolution, and he welcomes its coming with great joy. . . .

In the program of the Fabians, of course, the absence of violence fills Trotsky with disgust, because violence plays as important a role for him as the head of King Charles did for Mr. Dick. He returns incessantly to the problem of violence. His whole book is nothing but a glorification of revolutionary violence which he naturally considers the fount of origin of the Soviet Republic. And to the question posed in the title of the book *Whither England?* Trotsky replies, "Towards revolution."

From *The Japan Chronicle*, October 25, 1925. This article has been retranslated from the Russian.

＊

We print this week on the opposite page a summary with full quotations of Trotsky's latest book, *Where Is England Going?* Our purpose in so doing is to make clear, as no other method could, the abyss dug by history which separates these people from us. It is the work of a very clever man, who has taken some pains to inform himself about English life and history. But our ways repel him, as his ways repel us. . . .

[Trotsky] insists that these "oddities" of ours are "a deposit from history." And yet he argues that a nation shaped through centuries by a democratic and idealist tradition can be degraded in five years to the desired level of "material-ism. . . ."

From "Labour at Liverpool: The Communists and the Conference," by H.N. Brailsford, in *The New Leader*, October 2, 1925.

*

The Western proletariat looks without any special grief on the slow disappearance of Trotsky's impotent theories. But it is extremely interested in the living real fact of socialist Russia. Is Russia in a condition to assume the productive power of Western Europe and at the same time to avoid the evils of Western European capitalism? To this end the efforts of Trotsky and his comrades are directed. We long to hear good news about these achievements. The rest is immaterial.

From *The New Leader*, April 10, 1926.
Retranslated from the Russian.

*

Whither England?, purporting to be a learned dissertation on the industrial and financial disintegration of England due to Wall Street's supremacy, is only a thin cloak for spreading a Red call to arms by revolutionists to overthrow the American and British governments. . . .

Trotsky suggests a Bolshevist organization to overthrow England. . . . And so, under the cloak of writing a book on economics, he resorts to the only logic that he and his ilk understand—revolution!

Trotsky gives detailed information how to overthrow a government. . . .

Whither England?—one of the rankest and reddest revolutionary propagandas ever let loose on Christian civilization, is being distributed, broadcast in England and America today!

Secretary of State Kellogg has just barred the British Communist Shapurji Saklatvala from this country as a member of the British delegation to the Interparliamentary Conference in Washington because of his revolutionary views and expressions.[34]

What is the United States government going to do with this Bolshevist book of the Red revolutionist Trotsky, giving detailed instructions how to overthrow England and America?

From a review of *Whither England?*, by Frederick Boyd Stevenson, in *The Brooklyn Daily Eagle*, September 20, 1925.

＊

. . . In picturing the two leading capitalistic countries of the world as hastening toward the proletarian upheaval, Trotsky is evidently seeking to cheer the spirits of his followers who have found the spread of communism outside Russia disappointingly slow. There are a few fundamental facts, however, which seem to have escaped his attention. For instance, in recent years from 50 to 60 percent of the exports of the United States have gone to Europe. To maintain that the United States can develop a greater export outlet only through the impoverishment of its best customers is obviously absurd. Again, the ability of America to capture foreign markets in the face of European competition is still to be demonstrated. European iron and steel products have been delivered to our own seaboard cities during the past year at a price under domestic quotations and in spite of the tariff. The same thing has recently happened in the case of plate glass, and British competition is cited as one of the chief causes of depression in the New England cotton-textile industry.

Such facts do not conform to Trotsky's thesis; incidentally, they seem to give Wall Street a good alibi when he undertakes to claim partnership. As to England, that country

probably faces many social and economic changes, but the
outcome will hardly be what Moscow expects.

From "As Trotsky Sees Wall Street," in *The New York World*,
September 16, 1925.

✳

Whither England? is one of the cleverest and most dia-
bolical products of dialectical sophistry which we have ever
read. In it Trotsky predicts social revolution in Britain. . . .
The dictatorship of the proletariat is not a British concept,
and Trotsky's way of thinking cannot turn it into such. . . .

On the whole Russian reality is far from being so bad as
the perspectives which Trotsky paints for Britain. . . .

If Trotsky thinks that Britain would submit to even half
of the despotic constraints which the regime he advocates
would apply—be it even for the attainment of such a splendid objective as the dictatorship of the proletariat—then he
is mistaken.

From *The Hartford* (Connecticut) *Daily Times*, October 24, 1925.
Retranslated from the Russian.

✳

. . . Everywhere outside of Russia, it is a commonplace
that the most dangerous enemy of the proletariat is the
"yellow" socialist. That point of view is developed in Leon
Trotsky's *Whither England?* which pours scorn and venom
on Ramsay MacDonald and his kind. That kind, incidentally,
embraces everybody in the British labor movement who is
not openly and wholeheartedly Communist. Men like Kirkwood, Wheatley, and Lansbury, making up the left wing of
the British movement, are consigned to the same limbo with
MacDonald, Thomas, Clynes, Webb, Bernard Shaw, H.G.
Wells—the entire troop of "bourgeois-minded" pacifists,
religionists, and plain ignoramuses and cowards who labor
under the delusion that the victory of labor can be won by

any other instrument than force and by any other tactics than a dictatorship of the proletariat.

To bring about that longed-for consummation, Trotsky foresees for Great Britain a future directly opposite to the one for which British labor has been working. He pictures Britain losing her international status and sinking under the burden of increased unemployment and poverty. He makes no concealment of the fact that this is the necessary condition for a communist victory. He admits that if Great Britain should achieve the impossible and recover her prosperity, the British masses might once more succumb to the pleasant opiate of the bourgeoisie. Obviously there can be no cooperation between such a philosophy and tactics and the things for which the immense majority of the British Labour Party stands. . . .

From "British Labor and Communism," in *The New York Times*, September 26, 1925.

※

In his book Whither England? *Leon Trotsky supplies a special "Preface for America," in which he says in part:*

> *By exerting pressure on its debtors or giving them an extension, by granting or refusing credit to European countries, the United States is placing them in a gradually tightening economic dependence, in the last analysis an ineluctable situation, which is the necessary condition for inevitable social and revolutionary disturbance. The Communist International, viewed in the light of this knowledge, may be considered an almost conservative institution as compared with Wall Street. Morgan, Dawes, Julius Barnes—these are among the artificers of the approaching European revolution.*

Which led Mr. Barnes to answer:

Sick Russia prescribes its patent nostrums for robust America.

An ancient civilization one hundred million strong, living today just above the verge of utter barbarism, attempts to instruct orderly America, busy with its expanded economic life and social opportunities, typified by its eighteen million automobiles and its towering skyscrapers.

Tyrannized Russia, barred from free speech and free press, its ignorance of world progress typified by its scanty six pounds per capita newsprint consumption per year, preaches to America where 150 pounds newsprint consumption per capita makes the printed page the universal medium of information, where current world events show nightly on the screens of thousands of motion-picture theaters, where music and uttered thoughts enter every home through the universal radio.

Bankrupt Russia, pleading for foreign credits, seizing the product of its wooden-plow farms at government-dictated prices—only thus acquiring the means for overseas purchase of scanty necessities—instructs America in the errors of a policy which in twelve years has raised the savings account of America from six billion to twenty billion dollars.

Communistic Russia, destroying the individual productive impulse until this great agricultural country recently escaped millions of famine-deaths only by the bounty of capitalistic America, prescribes its futile rules for America, where individual opportunity and fair play have raised the common standard of living to be the admiration and despair of other peoples. . . .

Yet, when America proposes to develop thus in the far corners of the world, among other less fortunate peoples, old and new, the same magical process of production and transportation, which means individual opportunity and individual content and happiness—this mind of Trotsky's can see nothing but a selfish effort to preserve American industry against the competition of rival countries.

The great menace to this social progress is such tyranny as that in Russia today, where great treasures of coal, iron, copper, oil, timber, and idle labor lie useless because of the economic and political fallacies which maintain one hundred million people in dense ignorance and which play on their credulity with such cheap cries as "exploitation" and "world revolution."

From "The Facts That Answer Trotsky," by Julius Barnes,
in Nation's Business, November 11, 1925.

✳

. . . Apparently, Trotsky does not refuse collaboration with the revolutionaries of Wall Street. At least his new book is designed to deepen the gulf between the right and left wing of the British Labour Party, to discredit the present labor leaders, and to justify the methods of communism. . . .

And it must be said that not since Luther's pamphlets has there appeared more burning and evil invective. All the labor leaders are dealt with in turn: from Lansbury, who was "aided" by a church hymn, to MacDonald and Henderson, who "enslaved the working class to bourgeois society." And meanwhile the British masses consider the Labour Party their own party. . . .

The predominance of America has been a well-known fact for a long time already, and Britain's current difficulties are confessed even in the House of Commons. If a proletarian dictatorship were to be established in Westminster, America would retain, and probably would strengthen, its control of world trade and finance, whereas Britain would remain as before—overpopulated, hard up for capital, and searching for markets. Even Trotsky's promise that "workers' and peasants'" Russia will render warmhearted support to revolutionary Britain will hardly induce the British worker to forsake his bottle of beer and move on to fulfill his "predestined mission." Britain will probably "pull through somehow" on this occasion too, with the help of constitutional methods. . . .

From *The Baltimore* (Maryland) *Sun*, November 21, 1925.
Retranslated from the Russian.

❋

. . . Trotsky's detailed directions on how the proletarian revolution can and must be carried through terrified Frederick Boyd Stevenson of the *Brooklyn Daily Eagle*, who burst into a whole deluge of pathetic phrases and exclamations. Stevenson, in whose opinion Kellogg was absolutely correct to bar Saklatvala from our country, wants to know whether Trotsky's book will actually be allowed to circulate in America. . . .

But of course these fears are groundless. Trotsky could only stir up America if by chance several groups of Americans were already inwardly disposed to follow his leadership. *Uncle Tom's Cabin* did not make any special impression except on those who were abolitionists. . . .

Americans do not object to violence. But they are not about to use it, under Trotsky's leadership, to destroy peace, prosperity, and their greatest opportunities. Are the pamphlets written by an outsider so frightening? . . .

From *The Louisville* (Kentucky) *Times*, October 14, 1925.
Retranslated from the Russian.

❋

Chicherin will have to reckon with the impression produced in England by Trotsky's philosophy of history. At any rate, this philosophy makes propaganda against Soviet Russia much easier for the extreme English conservatives. It hampers a settlement of the present crisis in Anglo-Russian relations. . . .

And indeed, the present tension in Anglo-Russian relations has been caused not by the threat of social revolution on the part of the Comintern, but by the old antagonism of both countries in the sphere of world politics—an antagonism which was not liquidated by the world war because there it was a matter of European problems. Russia has rehabilitated itself, it carries on an active policy, and as a result the old conflicts are reviving along the entire line which divides the spheres of influence of both states in Asia. The means of struggle have changed, but the goals have remained the same.

The contents of Trotsky's latest book represent rather a musical accompaniment to this struggle. England is allegedly preparing to turn it into a general struggle against the world revolution. At any rate, this is how they look at it here in Moscow. They picture England at the head of a new anti-Soviet coalition, which does not confine itself to a single blockade. They also read anti-Russian intentions into the Guarantee Pact policy, which is explained by England's desire to estrange Germany from Russia. The thought is even expressed that England would allow France hegemony in Europe, if she were to receive in return the backing of France against Soviet Russia. . . .

From *Frankfurter Zeitung*, July 19, 1925.
Retranslated from the Russian.

✳

. . . Trotsky's new book sets itself the task of predicting the road along which Britain will develop. But he speaks not so much about Britain as a whole, nor even about its working class, as about the Labour Party and, in the main, its leaders. It is true of course that the future of Britain is the future of its working class, and the future of the working class is determined by the character of the Labour Party. Nevertheless, the author appears to give not more but less than his title promises; he seems to narrow his theme, giving more consideration to the details than to the whole. . . .

Trotsky displays a startling familiarity with everything the trade union leaders have said and written. In his criticism of these leaders he is unrivalled. But we do not perceive from his book, and he does not help us to foresee, the simple fact that a real revolution is *already* taking place in the British trade union movement, which will soon become apparent in the Scarborough resolutions and in the alliance of the six most important British trade unions. . . .

From an article by M.S. Olgin, in *Freiheit*, November 15, 1925.
Retranslated from the Russian.

*

. . . The reader time and again is treated to the hackneyed prattle of the innate virtues of the Anglo-Saxons in settling, at least all their domestic, if not all their foreign problems, peacefully. . . .

After one has waded through such balderdash, Comrade Trotsky's book is a relief. With all his skill for literary presentation and keen ability for political analysis, Comrade Trotsky shatters these illusions of Anglo-American harmony and Anglo-Saxon innate peacefulness in the development of social movements, the relationship of classes. . . .

From *"Whither England?: A Review,"* by Jay Lovestone, in *Workers' Monthly*, November 1925.

*

Trotsky's book is a challenge. And it is not surprising that the challenge has stung those at whom it was aimed.

It challenges, firstly, the assumption that . . . a return of "good times" is inevitable, if only the workers are content to await in patience their forthcoming.

This is, necessarily, the basic assumption of all orthodox Conservatism—Liberal and Tory alike. On any other view they must cease to be Conservative. If Capitalism is (as they assume) the only durable system of social-economics conceivable, it must have within itself the power of readjustment to altered circumstances and of surmounting sooner or later all . . . the difficulties left over from its settlement. . . .

Trotsky's second challenge . . . is to the theoreticians and doctrinaire Parliamentarians, who, for the time being, lead the Leaders of the Labour Party—whom he quite rightly lumps together as generically "Fabians". He challenges them to deny that . . . a fundamental identity of standpoint unites Baldwinites with MacDonaldites and the dwindling Liberal band between them.

And the specific point . . . which they unite to defend is precisely this "Inevitability of Gradualness," which they all maintain as their chief charge against Trotsky.

The practical importance of this to the British workers is immense. If they are ever to escape from the thralldom of capitalism they must make themselves the ruling-class and their instrument for this end must be their Political Party—which can win only by the total defeat of its opponents. Yet on the critical issues that such a struggle must raise—for example, the right of massed industrial struggle, the perpetuation of Monarchism and aristocracy, Soviet Russia and Communism—MacDonaldism (now dominant in Labour's counsels) is, if anything, the most hostile to a militant working-class point of view.

Hence follows Trotsky's third challenge:

Given the fact (if it be a fact) of the progressive perfectability of Capitalism, what need is there of a *Labour* Party—except perhaps as a "ginger group" [pressure group] to the Capitalist Parties? . . .

It is significant that while on details they tend to cancel each other completely they are at one . . . from the Tory Sir Sidney Low to Bertrand Russell on the I.L.P. left—in contending (for different reasons) that a Proletarian Revolution in Britain is an eventuality to be guarded against by every endeavour. . . .

The Labour Party was formed (as its name implies) to fight a class battle. Late converts and recruits from Liberalism may not be aware of that fact—others may wish to forget it. In the eagerness to escape trouble (and risk?) or the itch to pluck Parliamentary prizes at any price, some may . . . [assert] that "Labour will rule in the interests of all classes alike." But reality will have her way, and the grim logic of facts will sooner or later force the Labour Party to choose on which side of the class war it will fight.

And then Trotsky's prediction will be fulfilled.

From "The Retreat Before Moscow," by T.A. Jackson,
The Workers' Weekly, March 5, 1926.

❋

No one would guess from reading the reviews of Trotsky's book that it is a serious piece of work. However, it is. From the reviews the book might be considered to consist mainly of brilliant wit, revolutionary romance from a Russian who has never ventured beyond the borders of Russia, and malicious personalities. Actually the book is an objective estimate of the English situation, rapid, but carried out with a sure hand; and the polemic is strictly subordinate to the objective argument.

A word must be said at the outset on the common plea that Trotsky "knows nothing of England." . . . It would be more true to say that his critics know nothing of England—a charge that could be substantiated by every single statement of the reformist school for the past fifty years. . . . In fact, Trotsky is able justly to claim and substantiate that "we Marxians understand the tempo of development of the British Labour Movement and foresee its morrow much better than do the present 'theoreticians' of the Labour Party. . . ."

The notion that Trotsky is unfit to write on England because he is not an Englishman is a piece of abysmal national ignorance and self-conceit. It would be as sensible to argue that Marx could not write on "Capital" because he was not a capitalist. . . . When the critics proudly put Trotsky right on some irrelevant point of detail (and in nine cases of ten they are wrong even in their facts, and merely misunderstanding Trotsky's point) they are only giving a measure of their own smallness. . . . Certainly the scientific handling needs, when we are concerned with the living problems of the class struggle, to be carried beyond a treatment of principles, and to be realized, elaborated and worked out in closest relation to the fullest living information, experience, and action. But to imagine that the important thing is the possession of details of local information (which fifty million Englishmen have had for a generation without being any the wiser), and not the scientific handling, is childishness. . . .

A revolution that involves an actual transference of class power cannot be carried out by the working class without absolute clearness and determination of leadership, freedom from dependence on bourgeois ideology, and strong central organisation—in other words, a revolutionary mass party, leading the workers to the struggle for proletarian dictatorship. These conditions do not yet exist in the English working class, and this weakness in the subjective readiness of the workers is the retarding fact in the development of the English situation. What is the explanation of this, and what is the line of development? What are the traditions and forces that stand in the way? Here Trotsky brings to bear all his wealth of polemical power and analysis to shatter the existing confusion, cant and humbug of the ruling leadership and ideology in the existing Labour Movement, and to show the workers the plain path forward. . . .

This struggle for emancipation demands a break with the old traditions that still tie the workers to the leading strings of the bourgeoisie. Therefore Trotsky delivers the full force of his assault on these traditions; and this assault is an essential part of the attack on capitalism in England. These traditions or conceptions to which Trotsky returns again and again, may be summed up under four heads: (1) Religion, (2) Pacifism, (3) Parliamentary Democracy, and (4) Gradualism. All these, when analysed, reduce in the end to one thing: submission to the ruling class. . . .

Nothing more completely exposes the mental stage of development of the Fabian Socialists than the universal disapproval and disagreement that Trotsky's attack on Religion . . . has aroused. It is not merely that such an attack is repudiated by every reformist critic. . . . Trotsky's attack has actually to be "explained away" by the solemn statement that he, Trotsky (with his abundant West European and American experience), can only be thinking of—the Old Russian Orthodox Eastern Church! This is a truly comic failure of Malvolio to recognize himself. Every page of Trotsky's book shows that he is thinking precisely of that ethical Protestant, Puritan, musty, dusty hymn-singing Christianity which was the basis of the old Liberal Party yesterday and of the upper sections of the Labour Movement to-day, and which, despite all its sham "democratic" pretensions, has always been the sheet-anchor of the Lloyd Georges and MacDonalds and all that is canting and reactionary in politics for the degradation of the workers and their enslavement.

Nevertheless Brailsford . . . goes on to talk of Trotsky's failure to understand the "free" and "democratic" traditions of "English religion": "Would Trotsky's conviction that Protestant religion is necessarily a 'bourgeois' creed which no worker can honestly profess . . . survive a visit to a Dissenting chapel in a mining district?" To which the answer is that precisely in the mining districts the principal battle has notoriously been in case after case between Religious Revivalism with its ally Spiritualism on the one hand and the Revolution and Communism on the other.

[The slogans] "Pacifism" and "Capitalist Democracy" [and] . . . "Gradualism" [are] subjected to a no less severe analysis. It is not difficult to see that "gradualism," as soon as it is examined, disappears into a phrase meaning nothing at all save that progress must be slow. . . . It is an arbitrary and illegitimate jump from the conception of Evolution, *i.e.,* of development, which is the basis of scientific thinking, to the conception that Evolution contains no leaps or conflicts, which is contrary to all the facts of nature and experience. The whole opposition of "Evolution" and "Revolution" is childish and meaningless. "Evolution" leads to "Revolution," and "Revolution" is a part of "Evolution." . . .

The treatment of this question of revolutionary and bourgeois force by the reviewers is deeply significant. Every reviewer combines to oppose Trotsky's argument: that is, to advocate unchallenged submission to the supremacy of bourgeois force and acceptance of only such methods of agitation as are permitted by the bourgeoisie. But the arguments of every reviewer are different, contradictory, and in reality nothing but a catchword repetition of exactly the threadbare formulas Trotsky has been patiently pulling to pieces, without the slightest attempt to meet Trotsky's argument.

The arguments (if they can be so called) need only to be set out together to see their general character.

(a) Force is useless. "In the long run force accomplishes nothing" (Hunter). "The final word about violence is that this has been the weapon all through the ages, and we are as we were" (Lansbury). These confused "Tolstoyan" arguments bear no relation to the policy of the leadership of the Labour Party, who believe in and use imperialist force, and are therefore irrelevant. . . .

(b) Force is nasty. This is the argument of the Editor of the *Daily Herald* [Hamilton Fyfe]. Under the title "Two Views of Life in Conflict" he quotes a phrase of Trotsky concerning Cromwell, about the right of a historic mission to cut through all obstacles and triumphantly affirms the "break-down" of this argument because Mussolini and British Imperialism also believe in their "historic mission." Certainly they do, and this is precisely why their force can only be met by force. . . . Fyfe rejects this as a "gloomy view." He prefers to set against it the "hope of persuading people that Force is futile," etc. In other words, he puts his "hopes," wishes, personal feelings in front of the facts that he himself admits, because the latter are "gloomy." This is Illusionism. . . .

(c) Force is unnecessary. "The battle for freedom is not yet lost . . ." (Brailsford). "Our traditions and training in majority rule" (Johnston). Here the wish is father to the thought. This is nowhere more curiously illustrated than in Brailsford's own introduction, where . . . he actually declares that if Trotsky's book is successfully issued in England and permitted to be discussed, "then for the moment at least the nightmare of this trial [of the Communists] is dissipated." Unfortunately the twelve remain in prison; Hicks remains Home Secretary; the O.M.S. and Special Police recruiting go on;[35] the intentions of the Conservatives are open. But for Brailsford all these mere facts are "dissipated," because a book is issued and he has written an introduction. . . . Once again, in all this "democratic" view, "hopes" are put forward instead of facing facts.

(d) We will fight if . . . etc. These are the "heroic promises" dealt with by Trotsky in the quotation already given, as "not worth a brass farthing." These promises are actually trotted out again by Brailsford, Johnston and others in exactly the same form as before without the slightest attempt to meet Trotsky's destructive arguments: that such promises are practically valueless without previous preparation, that the bourgeoisie will not necessarily allow the proletariat free choice of a strategic ground before attacking, etc.

(e) We can't fight because . . . etc. This is an alternative line of argument favoured by Johnston, Russell and others.

The "because" always brings up some purely technical reason for inability to face the ruling class. Before the war the favourite argument was modern artillery. After the Russian Revolution had disposed of that technical argument, the modern favourite argument follows the line of chemical warfare, the air force or—in England—the food supply. . . .

Now these arguments, if placed together, are all mutually contradictory. . . . The argument that all force is wrong is in complete contradiction to the practice of the official Labour leadership. The argument that all force is useless is in complete contradiction to the argument that we will use force if necessary. The argument that we will use force if necessary is in complete contradiction to the argument that we could not fight if we would. And so on endlessly. . . . But all these contradictory arguments agree in one thing, and in one thing only, and that is the practical conclusion: that we need do nothing now to face the question of bourgeois force and the working class struggle.

The bankruptcy of the answers published in the official Labour press is very striking. There is no attempt . . . to meet Trotsky's objective argument. There is no attempt to consider the objective situation in England, the line of development, the policy of the bourgeoisie, . . . the next problems of the British working class struggle. These questions, which are of very serious importance . . . do not exist for the light and airy writers of the official Labour press. For them everything is turned into the personal. Trotsky is "brilliant," "witty," but "arrogant," "offensive," with "execrable taste." Trotsky has "attacked" the Labour leaders, and the natural desire is to attack him back: it is felt as a personal quarrel. . . .

Trotsky is a "Russian"; his standpoint—familiar enough in every country since the *Communist Manifesto* of 1847— is "the Russian standpoint" (Brailsford—perhaps Brailsford thinks the *Communist Manifesto* a "Russian" document?); he sees everything through "Russian spectacles" and imagines every country must imitate Russia . . . his real aim in advocating revolution in England is because it would be "advantageous to Russia" (Russell). . . .

When finally an attempt is made to touch on any of the central themes and issues raised by Trotsky . . . the critic at once falls back on personal feelings, emotions, opinions, hopes, aspirations; dismisses Trotsky's view as "a gloomy view," and expresses warmly, as if they were arguments, his private hopes and faiths, without even attempting to consider the alternative if his faiths should prove unfounded.

This bankruptcy is of course not accidental, but is simply the expression of the ideological bankruptcy of the whole school of Fabian Socialism and the Independent Labour Party. To-day it is becoming more and more widely clear that the only coherent view of actual problems possible is the Communist view. Marxism is conquering in England also by the power of facts. Just as thirty years ago the Independent Labour Party was permeating and capturing the trade union bureaucracy, so to-day the younger trade union masses are advancing to Communism. The contrast and conflict between Trotsky's book, with its objective firmness and militant confidence, and his reviewers, with their vague confusion and shoddy sentiment in place of argument, is the contrast between two worlds and the conflict between two classes. Between these two worlds there can be no real contact. The older school of leaders who were bred up in the Liberal tradition . . . will never understand, but will go on repeating their catchphrases and empty sentiments until they pass away or are pushed aside. But the younger workers, who have been bred up in the conditions of the war and after . . . are learning very fast: and Trotsky's book will help them to learn. . . .

The English working class has cause to be grateful to Trotsky for his book; and to hope that he will not stay his hand at this short sketch, but will carry forward his work of interpretation, polemic and elucidation, and elaborate his analysis further, which is so much needed in England. For despite all the national philistines, the problems of England, more than of any country, will only be solved by the united force of the whole international movement.

From "Trotsky and His English Critics," by R. Palme Dutt, *The Labour Monthly*, April 1926. ∎

Part 3

After the general strike

Editorial note

None of Part 3 was published in the Soviet Union, although typewritten copies were circulated by hand in the late twenties in the same way that *samizdat* (self-publication) material is circulated today.

"The Future of the British Communist Party" was translated by C.S. Checkley and printed as an appendix in *The British Communist Party*, by L.J. Macfarlane (New York and London), and is reprinted here with the permission of Humanities Press and MacGibbon & Kee.

"Resolution on the General Strike in Britain" was written by Trotsky and submitted to the plenum of the Central Committee of the Communist Party of the Soviet Union, which met July 14–23, 1926, by Zinoviev, Kamenev, Piatakov, and Krupskaya, as well as by Trotsky. The first English translation was made for this volume by George Saunders, with the permission of the Harvard College Library, where the original is held under the code number T881.

"Amendments to the Resolution on the Situation in Britain," and "Resolution on the Anglo-Russian Committee" were translated for this volume by Julia Drayton from a German book published in October 1927, *Der Kampf um die Kommunistische Internationale.* But the editors were unable to learn the occasions or dates when these two documents were written. Louis Sinclair's *Leon Trotsky: A Bibliography* (Hoover Institution Press, 1972) lists them as having been published in periodicals bearing the date of March 1927.

"The Struggle for Peace and the Anglo-Russian Committee" was first translated into English in *The New International,* October 1935. Section 15, which was inadvertently omitted there, has been translated for this volume by Iain Fraser from the 1927 Dutch pamphlet, *Verkeerde Eenheidsfronttaktiek,* published by

321

the Nationaal Arbeids-Secretariaat.

"What We Gave and What We Got" was first translated into English by John G. Wright in *The New International,* September–October 1934.

"A Balance Sheet of the Anglo-Russian Committee" is excerpted from John G. Wright's translation of *The Third International After Lenin* (Pathfinder Press, 1970).

The future of the British Communist Party

June 3, 1926

In our party life legends are playing an ever-increasing part.
One such legend is the absurd rumor, which is being spread
systematically, concerning my "fear" of the harvest. On the
same ideopolitical level is based a new legend to the effect
that I regard the British Communist Party as a reactionary
organization, an obstacle in the path of the working class.
Anyone who has merely glanced at my little book *Where
Is Britain Going?* will easily understand how foolish, how
absurd are these assertions, the object of which is not to
elucidate the essence of the question, but to put me at odds
with the British Communist Party.

On the eve of great events in England, in a letter to
the Politburo, I expressed the fear that the British Communist Party, like the Bulgarian, in a critical moment of
mass activity, might adopt too passive or temporizing an
attitude—the more so because against it would be ranged
the immense pressure of a bourgeois state, of bourgeois social opinion, and of all the officialism of the working class.

What conclusion did I draw from this? Well, here it is. "One of the most important problems is to assist the British Communist Party to thoroughly understand and examine this prospect." We must help it to select and group around itself those elements "which are capable of understanding the inevitability of great mass struggles, of going fearlessly to meet them." This is the conclusion which I drew from my own doubts and misgivings. Can this really be said to be directed against the British Communist Party? Since when has uttering a caution, before great struggles, against the dangers of passivity, recommending a choice of more active elements, implied speaking against the Communist Party? And this in Lenin's party.

At an extended plenary session of the Executive Committee some British comrades warned against overestimating the critical state of British capitalism. By this they revealed they underestimate the depth of the crisis and the imminence of social clashes. An incomparably less significant fact, namely the publication of my book with a preface by Brailsford, was for me a further symptom of a willingness to compromise by an important section of the British Communists. They have not yet had experience of leadership by mass action. Taken together, all this aroused quite reasonable fears of excessive caution, lack of decision, and even passivity on the part of the powerful bureaucratic opposition in all the old administrative organizations of the working class.

Does not fundamental revolutionary teaching suggest that in these circumstances it was indeed necessary to stress, to repeat, to emphasize the danger that in all the old organizational superstructure, the imminent strike would meet counteractivity, resistance, sabotage, and from the side of the Communist Party, a lack of decision? I consider that the main task of our party in the International consists in warning before the action and not in punishing by bureaucratic means after the action. In a letter reporting on the British party, we read:

> Unfortunately, in some of our regional organizations, it could be noted that there still remained in the party sectarian survivals; these organizations have not taken root sufficiently deeply in the trade unions; by which is also explained the fact that, during the strike, they lagged behind the masses. [letter from T. Stewart[1] to the secretary of the Comintern of May 21, 1926]

Thus, from the words of the British Communists themselves it is apparent that shortcomings of this kind had emerged, shortcomings which could and must be feared. Fortunately, the revolutionary activity of the party was, on the whole, at a reasonably high level. This is our general achievement, which, however, does not minimize the necessity for issuing a warning. Without criticism of certain British comrades on the Executive Committee of the Comintern, without friendly cautions and warnings, the elements of passivity and indecision might have proved more influential than, fortunately, they were found to be.

Yet it is criminal to portray the matter in this way, as if the British Communist Party had coped with all its problems. The discrepancy between its strength, its resources, its means, and those objective tasks which are becoming increasingly imminent, is gigantic; and about this we must speak openly, not replacing revolutionary policy by party legends and formulas.

But meanwhile, in view of the monstrous conservatism of British social life, the young British Communist Party needs to increase tenfold its implacability, its criticism, its counteractivity, to the pressure of bourgeois social opinion and its "worker" organization.

Resolution on the general strike in Britain

July 1926

In view of the completely indisputable fact that the General Council, having betrayed the coalminers on May 12 by viciously breaking the general strike, is now preparing for the final betrayal of the miners' strike, already isolated by the Council's action;

In view of the fact that the General Council, in this work of betrayal, is trying to gain time and apparently wants to conceal its traitorous work from the eyes of the masses, at least for a certain time longer, by maintaining the formality of the Anglo-Russian Committee;[2]

In view of the fact that it is for these and only these purposes that the traitors of the General Council have need of the Paris conference of the Anglo-Russian Committee;

The plenum instructs the Politburo:

To hasten the convening of the Anglo-Russian Committee in every way, not allowing the Paris conference to be put off for a single day.

To pose all questions at the Paris conference with full

bluntness and sharpness, denying the traitors any opportunity to dodge or evade the question and to once again
deceive the workers;

And having exposed the traitors' intents in all respects,
since we may not either directly or indirectly conceal or go
along with the betrayers of the miners' continuing struggle,
to immediately break off the Anglo-Russian Committee. At
the same time, to intensify every effort to strengthen the
united front,[3] from below, relying above all on the ties that
have been established with the mine workers' union.

In addition, the plenum declares that the Politburo majority has pursued a profoundly incorrect policy on the question of the Anglo-Russian Committee. The point at which
the working masses of Britain exerted the greatest opposing
force to the General Council was when the general strike
was being broken. What was necessary was to keep step with
the most active forces of the British proletariat and to break
at that moment with the General Council as the betrayer of
the general strike. For many decades the bourgeois Labour
politicians of Great Britain have periodically deceived the
working masses, each time arousing the workers' indignation. But the absence of a genuinely revolutionary party has
always allowed them to let some time pass for the anger of
the masses to cool down and then to resume their traitorous
work once again. Therefore, it was necessary to break with
the General Council without hesitation over the question of
the betrayal of the strike at the moment of the betrayal and
before the eyes of the masses. The traitors should not have
been allowed to appear as our "allies" for a single hour after the breaking of the strike. Only the British workers can
throw out the present General Council, but they should be
supported in this work by our example, and not hindered,
even by indirect support to the General Council through
the maintenance of organizational ties.

It would be an impermissible error, bordering on the

criminal, if we allowed the General Council in the future to move this question back, step by step, and to gradually and imperceptibly reduce the Anglo-Russian Committee to nothing or to break with it themselves over some second-rate question, as over the statutes of the committee or the like. Every conscious British worker would then ask us why we did not break with the General Council when it betrayed the general strike or later, when on top of that, it betrayed the coalminers' strike, but rather broke with it on this or that second-rate question after the miners' strike had been liquidated. For all the efforts of the General Council are aimed in that direction. A passive, wait-and-see policy on our part would contribute to the success of this policy of the General Council chiefs, a policy that counts on the Anglo-Russian Committee being buried unobtrusively with the minimum of losses for the British traitors.

To defend the maintenance of the Anglo-Russian Committee with the argument that we cannot leap over the organizations of the proletariat that are "historically given" is to engage in crude sophistry, which will invariably lead to opportunist conclusions. We cannot leap over the trade unions, since they are "historically given" organizations of the proletariat. But the Anglo-Russian Committee is a temporary formation, brought into existence by a temporary situation.

We were absolutely correct to conclude this alliance when we did, but in order to turn it against the opportunists; in order to push vacillating leaders forward as far as possible; and in order to expose them and break with them in the event of their betrayal. But to break with the betrayers of the general strike in the way that we have done by our example and our actions is to say to the British masses: "Curse your leaders as traitors but let them stay in their posts; that is, do as we have done in relation to the Anglo-Russian Committee."

All the arguments about the impermissibility of "leaping over" the traitorous General Council can and should be applied with tenfold force to the question of entering the Amsterdam International. From this point of view the very existence of the Profintern could be declared an attempt to "leap over" Amsterdam. . . . The most consistent advocates of maintaining the Anglo-Russian Committee, no matter what, are in fact gradually sliding over to support for entry into the Amsterdam International.

The attempt to justify the existence of the present Anglo-Russian Committee is fundamentally wrong. True, Baldwin is fighting against the General Council just as Hindenburg fought against the German Social Democrats. It does not follow from either of these facts that it is necessary or permissible for us to bloc with Purcell or Scheidemann.

The tactic of the united front still retains all its power as the most important method in the struggle for the masses. A basic principle of this tactic is: "With the masses—always; with the vacillating leaders—sometimes, but only so long as they stand at the head of the masses." It is necessary to make use of vacillating leaders while the masses are pushing them ahead, without for a moment abandoning criticism of these leaders. And it is necessary to break with them at the right time when they turn from vacillation to hostile action and betrayal. It is necessary to use the occasion of the break to expose the traitorous leaders and to contrast their position to that of the masses. It is precisely in this that the revolutionary essence of the united front policy consists. Without this, the struggle for the masses always threatens to turn into an opportunist kowtowing to spontaneity covered up by an in-no-way-binding criticism of opportunism in words alone. The line of the Politburo majority on the question of the Anglo-Russian Committee was clearly a transgression in terms of the *revolutionary essence* of the united front policy.

The trade unions are the main mass organizations in

Britain. But the struggle for influence with the masses organized in these unions should in no case lead to bowing down before the conservative forms of trade unionism in the spirit of completely opportunistic tail-ending formations. The more rapid the revolutionary development in Britain and the more sharply new organizational forms (shop stewards, action committees) are counterposed to the old ones, not in circumvention of the trade unions but based on them—the more attention the British Communists should pay to the formation and development of new organizational forms based on the mass movement.

The plenum emphatically rejects the attempt to use Lenin's teaching on the need for constant, untiring, and stubborn struggle within every kind of workers' organization as a justification for a passive, conciliatory, wait-and-see attitude toward the traitorous leaders on the pretext that they reflect the present stage of development of the working class, that "they are the best there is," that "there is no one yet ready to replace them," and so forth. Lenin allowed the possibility of a temporary bloc even with opportunist leaders under the condition that there would be a sharp and audacious turn and a break based on the actions of the masses when these leaders began to pull back, oppose, or betray. An attempt to abandon this truly intransigent aspect of Lenin's teaching on taking the offensive, which is in the sharpest contrast with Menshevik passivity and watchful waiting, would signify nothing less than the devitalization of the revolutionary doctrine of Leninism.

The plenum expresses its unshakable conviction that the international interests of the USSR, as the first state in the world consisting of a proletarian dictatorship, coincide totally and completely with those of the workers of the world and with those of the oppressed peoples. The development of the revolutionary movement on the basis of fraternal solidarity remains as before the main guarantee of the USSR's inviolability and the possibility for us of world socialist development.

At the same time the plenum declares with all its energy that the crudely erroneous policy stands exposed, which aroused hopes that the present General Council headed by Thomas, MacDonald, and Purcell would be ready and able to conduct a struggle against imperialism, military intervention, etc. These compromising leaders who so basely betrayed their own workers during the strike will all the more inevitably and shamefully betray the British proletariat, and the Soviet Union, and the cause of peace along with them, at the moment of the danger of war. Only an unrelenting exposure of the traitors in the eyes of the masses, only their removal from their posts, will prevent the bourgeoisie from catching the workers unprepared when it decides to try to start a war. Linking up with the British working masses on the basis of an effective unmasking of their present treacherous general staff, the General Council, will be the firmest guarantee against a war. The Thomases, MacDonalds, and Purcells are as little able to prevent an imperialist attack as the Tseretellis, Dans, and Kerenskys were to stop the imperialist slaughter.[4] It would be a great crime toward the peoples of the USSR and the world proletariat to sow any kind of illusions whatsoever on that score.

The Comintern's tactics, which were worked out in all essentials under Vladimir Ilyich [Lenin]'s leadership, ought to remain hard and fast. The following elements of these tactics are of special importance: (1) the necessity for Communists to work in the most reactionary trade unions in order to fight to win over the masses under conditions of all kinds; (2) the necessity for British Communists to enter the Labour Party and to fight against being expelled from that organization, since the experience of the past five years fully confirms what Lenin said on this question at the Second World Congress of the Comintern and in his *Left-wing*

Communism, an Infantile Disorder, and (3) the necessity for a struggle against the right opportunist deviation as well as against the ultraleft.

"Anarchism," Lenin wrote, "has often enough served as a kind of punishment for the opportunist sins of the labor movement. The two types of deformity mutually reinforce one another."

The plenum regards as totally impermissible the ever more obvious course of the Politburo majority toward the replacement of Lenin's statement of the question by a struggle (sometimes an entirely principled one) against the ultraleft alone and by a glossing over of the right opportunist dangers (Poland, England, Germany). The situation is especially dangerous since the more people warn against the growing rightward danger, the more they are accused of being ultraleft.

The plenum calls attention to the changes introduced into the statutes of most of our trade unions by the leading clique in the All-Union Central Council of Trade Unions [AUCCTU] without the knowledge of the party or of the mass membership of these unions. Whereas before the end of last year the trade union statutes spoke of their adherence to the Red International of Labor Unions, through the AUCCTU, at the end of last year and early this year, the Red International of Labor Unions was replaced by the International Federation of Trade Unions. A change of such importance in principle cannot be understood as anything but the setting up of preconditions for entering the Amsterdam International.

The plenum categorically condemns these efforts and proposes that the fraction in the AUCCTU take steps to see that all union statutes indicate clearly and precisely that our unions, in full agreement with the opinions and wishes of the working masses, belong to the Red International of Labor Unions.

The plenum regards as totally unjustified the action of a number of comrades in carrying disputes within the Politburo on the question of the Anglo-Russian Committee into the press and into meetings outside the Politburo, spreading the crudest distortions of the views of the members of the Politburo minority, making crude personal attacks, etc.

Politburo members who are in the minority on this question, which was by no means decided in advance (or even discussed) at the Fourteenth Party Congress, were not given the opportunity to state their actual views on this question. As a result a distorted and one-sided "discussion," poisoning the atmosphere in the party, has developed.

In the Moscow party organization and in those of other cities, reports were given and theses introduced with the aim of exacerbating the differences in the Politburo and of carrying the one-sided "discussion" into the Comintern.

This kind of activity brings very serious injury to the cause of party unity in the All-Union Communist Party and can substantially damage the Comintern.

The plenum rejects the motion for approval of the tactics of the Politburo, since that would mean the following:

(a) to maintain the bloc with the strikebreakers and traitors of the General Council as long as possible;

(b) to leave uncriticized and uncondemned the plainly erroneous shift to the right in the politics of the Politburo majority;

(c) to leave uncriticized as well the corresponding changes in trade union statutes, pointing toward entry into the Amsterdam International;

(d) to leave the trend toward entering the Amsterdam International itself uncriticized; and

(e) to strike a blow at those members of the party who have criticized the above-listed errors and have demanded their correction. To do this would inevitably result in a deepening of the opportunist deviation and would not only strengthen

Purcell but would also give preponderance to the rightward tendencies in the British Communist Party, which are already significant enough without that.

Zinoviev, Trotsky,
L. Kamenev, Piatakov,
Krupskaya

Amendments to the resolution on the situation in Britain

Published 1927

1. The plenum states that for the whole direction of our work in the English workers' movement, especially for the correct understanding and carrying out of the tactic of the united front, the question of the Anglo-Russian Committee at the present moment has a decisive significance. Without a clear principled attitude to this question, the Comintern and above all the British Communist Party will be condemned to ever newer mistakes and vacillations. In the struggle against the war danger, the resolution of the question of the Anglo-Russian Committee is the basic prerequisite for resolving all other questions, just as (by way of example) in the year 1914, no step forward could be made without first resolving the question whether Social Democratic deputies could vote for the war budget.

2. In the English trade union movement, just as in the Labour Party, the leading role is played by reformists of different varieties, *the majority of whom are liberal Labour politicians.* In view of the profound leftward development of

the working masses, it must be acknowledged that the most dangerous variety of the liberal Labour politicians are politicians of the type of Purcell, Hicks, Brailsford, and Company. The tottering structure of English imperialism is being supported at present not so much on Thomas and MacDonald as on Purcell, Brailsford, and the like, without whom politicians such as Thomas and MacDonald, despite the fact that they are supported by the bourgeoisie, would no longer be able to maintain their leading position in the workers' movement. The irreconcilable and relentless struggle against the left lackeys of imperialism, both in the trade unions and in the Labour Party, is becoming especially urgent now, when the sharpening international and domestic situation will strike mercilessly at every indecision and hypocrisy.

3. The trade unions and the party have without doubt their special characteristics, their special methods of work, in particular their special methods of carrying out the united front. But it is precisely on the question of the political bloc with the reformist leaders that the distinction between the trade unions and the party is completely effaced. In all important and critical cases, the General Council proceeds hand-in-hand with the Executive Committee of the Labour Party and the parliamentary fraction. In calling off the great strike, the leading politicians and trade unionists went hand-in-hand. In such conditions, not a single honest worker will understand why Purcell is said to be politically *a left lackey of the bourgeoisie*, while on the other hand with respect to the trade unions we stand in "cordial relations," "mutual understanding," and "unanimity" with him.

4. In particular cases, the tactic of the united front can lead to temporary agreements with this or that left group of reformists against the right wing. But such agreements must not in any circumstance be transformed into a lasting political bloc. Whatever concessions of principle we make for the purpose of artificially preserving such a political bloc

must be recognized to be contrary to the basic aim of the united front and to be extremely harmful for the revolutionary development of the proletariat. During the last year the Anglo-Russian Committee has become just such an extremely harmful, thoroughly conservative factor.

5. The creation of the Anglo-Russian Committee was at a certain juncture an absolutely correct step. Under the leftward development of the working masses, the liberal Labour politicians, just like the bourgeois liberals at the start of a revolutionary movement, made a step to the left in order to maintain their influence among the masses. To reach out to them at that time was absolutely correct. However, it had to be clearly kept in mind that, just like all liberals, the English reformists would inevitably make a leap backwards to the side of opportunism, as the mass movement openly assumed revolutionary forms. This is just what happened at the moment of the general strike. From the time of this gigantic event, the temporary agreement with the leaders had to be broken, and the break with the compromising of the "left" leaders used to advantage among the broad proletarian masses. The attempt to cling to the bloc with the General Council after the open betrayal of the general strike, and even after the betrayal of the miners' strike, was one of the greatest mistakes in the history of the workers' movement. The Berlin capitulation is a black stain in the history of the Comintern and represents the inevitable consequence of this false line.[5]

6. One must be blind or a hypocrite to see the "main defect" of the Berlin decisions in the fact that they narrowed the competence of the Anglo-Russian Committee instead of broadening it. The "competence" of the Anglo-Russian Committee during the last year consisted of this: that the All-Union Central Council of Trade Unions [AUCCTU] was trying to support the general strike, while the General Council was breaking it. The AUCCTU was helping the miners' strike

on a broad scale, while the General Council was betraying it. If one talks about the broadening of the activity of the Anglo-Russian Committee (cf. no. 29 of the Resolution of the Commission), one is hypocritically pretending that this activity served some real interest of the workers, while in reality the Anglo-Russian Committee merely shielded and covered over the base and treacherous work of the General Council. To broaden this "activity" contradicts the basic interests of the working class. Ridiculous and disgraceful is the attempt to get free from the Berlin decisions simply by appealing to the fact that the General Council bears responsibility for them (cf. again no. 29 of the draft Resolution). That strikebreakers, who descend lower and lower, seek to protect their strikebreaking work from outside intervention; that strikebreakers take pains to cover over their strikebreaking with the capitulation of the All-Union Central Council of Trade Unions; all that is quite in the order of things. But all that does not justify our capitulation one iota.

7. The plenum indignantly rejects the vulgar, philistine, thoroughly Menshevik argument that Chamberlain "also" wants the break-up of the Anglo-Russian Committee. The very attempt to determine our revolutionary line according to the arbitrary guidance of the enigma of what at every given moment Chamberlain wants or doesn't want is nonsensical. His task consists in getting the left lackeys, as far as possible, into his hands. For this purpose he squeezes them, unmasks them, blackmails them, and demands they break with the Bolsheviks. Under the influence of this pressure and this blackmail, the General Council blackmails the All-Union Council of Trade Unions and, for its part, threatens it with a split. Under the pressure of the General Council, the AUCCTU agrees to capitulate. In this devious way Chamberlain's task has been completed, for his blackmail has led to the capitulation of the AUCCTU.

8. If we were to break with the General Council in order

to discontinue all intervention in the affairs of the English working class; if, after the break, we were to confine ourselves to our internal affairs, while the British Communist Party was not developing with redoubled energy its campaign against the General Council; then Chamberlain would have every cause to be satisfied with this state of affairs. But the break-up of the Anglo-Russian Committee ought to mean the very opposite. Since we flatly reject the Berlin principle of nonintervention as the principle of chauvinism and not of internationalism, we must support with redoubled energy the British Communist Party and the Minority Movement in their redoubled struggle against the left lackeys of Chamberlain. In the presence of such a policy, Chamberlain will very soon be convinced that the revolutionary wing of the movement grew stronger after it shed the reactionary connection with the General Council.

9. The plenum therefore considers it absolutely necessary to break up in the shortest space of time the political bloc, which carries a disastrous ambiguity into our whole policy towards English reformism. The plenum is of the opinion that the English Communist Party must at once openly pose the question of the mutual relationship between the AUCCTU and the General Council. The English Communist Party, as well as the left-wing trade union Minority Movement, must demand the immediate summoning of the Anglo-Russian Committee in order to develop, in the name of the AUCCTU, a clear revolutionary program of struggle against war and the offensive of the bourgeoisie against the proletariat. The program must be so formulated that it provides no scope to the charlatan trickery of Baldwin's pacifist party. Refusal of the General Council to summon the Anglo-Russian Committee, or refusal of its delegation to accept the program of struggle, is to lead to immediate breaking up of the bloc from our side and to a broad campaign against the reformists, especially the left variety who, better and on a wider

scale than all the rest at the present moment, are helping the English Conservatives drag the English working class into war, without themselves being aware of it.

10. While giving all-round support to the movement of the truly revolutionary minority and particularly while giving support to acceptable candidacies of representatives of this minority for this or that position in the trade union movement (always on the basis of a specific practical program), the British Communist Party must not in any circumstances or under any conditions identify itself with the Minority Movement or merge the organizations. The British Communist Party must maintain full freedom of criticism with respect to the Minority Movement as a whole as well as with respect to its individual leaders, their mistakes and vacillations.

11. The sharpening class struggle in England and the approaching danger of war are creating conditions under which the policy of the particular "labor" parties, organizations, groups, and "leaders" will quickly be put to the test by the course of events.

The inconsistency of word and deed should manifest itself in the shortest space of time. In such a period the Communist Party can rapidly enhance its revolutionary authority, its numbers, and especially its influence, provided that it conducts a clear, firm, bold, revolutionary policy, calls everything by its right name, makes no concessions of principle, keeps a sharp eye on its temporary alliance partners and fellow travellers and their vacillations, and mercilessly exposes trickery and above all direct treachery.

Resolution of the Opposition on the Anglo-Russian Committee

Published 1927

After the betrayal of the English general strike by the right and "left" trade union leaders, the Anglo-Russian Committee has not only lost all meaning, but has become simply the source of deception of the English and of the international working class.

All the more incomprehensible, then, is the official report on the last Berlin conference of this committee. Therein was announced, without even a single resolution being referred to, "complete unanimity" and "cordial understanding" between the Russian and the English delegates. Present among the English delegates was one of the most typical, most right-wing English social-imperialists, the notorious Citrine,[6] so that even the former threadbare excuse for maintaining this committee, namely, that behind the left reformists stand workers who consider them revolutionary, is unmasked as a conscious lie.

The Conference of Party Workers condemns most resolutely:

- the methods of secret diplomacy which were employed at the conference of the Anglo-Russian Committee
- the complete inactivity of this committee with regard to all questions of pressing importance at the present time (war-transport to China, imperialist war preparations, the fascist putsch in Latvia)[7]
- the "cordial understanding" with right-reformist leaders, which by its very nature can only occur upon a reformist, never on a communist basis.

and demands the immediate break-up of this committee by putting forward feasible demands for action, which are obviously rejected by the reformists:

- boycott of the murderously fascist country of Latvia
- prevention of all further troop-transport to China
- revolutionary propaganda among the troops already sent there
- international conferences of transport workers, seamen, arms, munitions, and chemical workers for the preparation in a revolutionary manner of real resistance to every imperialist war.

The struggle for peace and the Anglo-Russian Committee

May 16, 1927

The whole international situation and all the tendencies of its development make the struggle against war and for the defense of the USSR as the first workers' state the central task of the international proletariat. But it is just the tension of the situation that demands clarity, a precisely political line and firm correction of the errors made. . . .

1. War is the continuation of politics by other means. The struggle against war is a continuation of revolutionary policy against the capitalist regime. To grasp this idea means to find the key to all opportunist errors in questions relating to war. Imperialism is no external factor existing by itself; it is the highest expression of the basic tendencies of capitalism. War is the highest method of imperialist policy. The struggle against imperialist war can and must be the highest expression of the international policy of the proletariat.

Opportunism, or radicalism that is turning to opportunism, always inclines to estimate war as such an *exceptional* phenomenon that it requires the annulment of revolutionary policy and its basic principles. Centrism reconciles itself to revolutionary methods but does not believe in them. That is why it is always inclined, at critical moments, to refer to the *peculiarity* of the situation, to *exceptional* circumstances, and so on, in order to substitute opportunist methods for revolutionary ones. Such a shift in the policy of centrism or pseudoradicalism is of course acutely provoked by the war danger. With all the greater intransigence must this touchstone be applied to the main tendencies of the Communist International.

2. It is already clear to everybody that the Anglo-Russian Committee must not be regarded as a trade union organization into which the Communists enter to fight for influence over the masses, but as a "peculiar" political bloc with well-defined aims, directing its activities primarily against the war danger. With tenfold attention to the experience and the example of the Anglo-Russian Committee, the methods of struggle against the war danger must be closely reexamined so as to be able to tell the revolutionary proletariat openly and precisely *what must not be done* if the Comintern is not to be destroyed and the bloody work of imperialism against the international proletariat and the USSR facilitated.

3. In the presidium of the ECCI [Executive Committee of the Comintern] on May 11, Comrade Bukharin advanced a new interpretation of our capitulation to the General Council in Berlin.[8] He declared that the capitulation must not be considered from the standpoint of the international revolutionary struggle of the proletariat, but from the standpoint of a "diplomatic" counteraction to the offensive of imperialism against the USSR.

Various weapons of international action are at our disposal: the party (Comintern), the trade unions, diplomacy, the press, etc. Our activities in the trade union field are dictated to us by the tasks of the class struggle. But only "as a general rule." In certain cases, as exceptions, we must—according to

Bukharin—utilize the organs of the trade union movement as instruments of diplomatic action. This is what happened with the Anglo-Russian Committee. We capitulated to the General Council not as the General Council, but as the agent of the English government. We obligated ourselves not to interfere not out of party reasons, but for reasons of state. That is the substance of the new interpretation of the Berlin capitulation which, as we will soon show, only makes it still more dangerous.

4. The Berlin agreement of the Central Council of the Soviet Union with the General Council was discussed a short time ago at the April plenum of the Central Committee of our party. The decisions of the Berlin Conference were defended by Comrades Tomsky, Andreyev, and Melnichansky,[9] that is, our outstanding trade unionists, but not our diplomats. All these comrades, in defending the Berlin capitulation, accused the Opposition of not understanding the role and methods of the trade union movement, and declared that the masses of trade unionists cannot be influenced by breaking with the apparatus, that the apparatus cannot be influenced by breaking with its upper sections, and that these were just the considerations that dictated the attitude of our trade unionists in Berlin.

Now Comrade Bukharin explains that the decisions of the Berlin Conference constitute, on the contrary, an exceptional case, an exception from the principled Bolshevist method of influencing the trade unions, an exception in the name of temporary, but acute, diplomatic tasks. Why did not Comrade Bukharin, and Comrade Tomsky with him, explain this to us at the last plenary session of our Central Committee? . . .

5. Where did such an appalling contradiction come from in the course of a few weeks? It grew out of the impossibility of standing, if even for a single month, on the April position. When our delegation left for Berlin, it did not have

Bukharin's subsequent explanation of the position it was to take. Did Comrade Bukharin himself have this explanation at that time? At all events, it was nowhere expressed by anybody. . . . It is quite clear that this explanation was thought up after the event.

6. It becomes still clearer when we go back further, that is, to the origin of the question. After the criminal calling off of the general strike by the General Council, the "left" vying with the right for the palm, the Opposition in the CPSU demanded an immediate break with the General Council so as to make easier and accelerate the liberation of the proletarian vanguard from the influence of the traitors. The majority of the Central Committee opposed to this their viewpoint that the retention of the Anglo-Russian Committee was allegedly required in the interests of our revolutionary influence on the English proletariat, despite the counterrevolutionary policy of the General Council during the strike.

It was precisely at this moment that Comrade Stalin advanced his theory of stages that cannot be skipped over. By the word "stage," in this case, must not be understood the political level of the masses, which varies with different strata, but of the conservative leaders who reflect the pressure of the bourgeoisie on the proletariat and conduct an irreconcilable struggle against the advanced sections of the proletariat.

In contradiction to this, the Opposition contended that the maintenance of the Anglo-Russian Committee after its open and obvious betrayal, which closed the preceding period of "left development," would have as its inevitable conclusion an impermissible weakening of our criticism of the leaders of the General Council, at least of its "left" wing. We were answered, primarily by this same Bukharin, that this is a revolting slander; that the organizational alliance does not hinder our revolutionary criticism in the slightest degree; that we would not permit any kind of principled concessions;

that the Anglo-Russian Committee would only be an organizational bridge to the masses for us. It occurred to nobody at that time to justify the maintenance of the Anglo-Russian Committee by referring to grounds of a diplomatic character which necessitate a temporary abandonment of the revolutionary line. . . .

7. The Opposition foretold in its writings that the maintenance of the Anglo-Russian Committee would steadily strengthen the political position of the General Council, and that it would inevitably be converted from defendant to prosecutor. This prediction was explained as the fruit of our "ultraleftism." Incidentally, an especially ridiculous theory was created, namely, that the demand for the dissolution of the Anglo-Russian Committee was equivalent to the demand for the workers to leave the trade unions. By that alone, the policy of maintaining the Anglo-Russian Committee was invested with the character of an exceptionally important question of principle.

8. Nevertheless, it was very quickly proved that the choice must be made between maintaining organizational connections with the General Council or calling the traitors by their name. The majority of the Political Bureau inclined more and more to maintain the organizational connections at any cost. To achieve this aim, no "skipping over stages" was required, it is true; but it did require sinking politically one degree after another. This can most distinctly be followed in the three conferences of the Anglo-Russian Committee: in Paris (July 1926), in Berlin (August 1926), and most recently in Berlin (April 1927). Each time our criticism of the General Council became more cautious, and completely avoided touching on the "left," that is, on the most dangerous betrayers of the working class.

9. The General Council felt all along, by its consistent pressure, that it held the representatives of the All-Union Central Council of Trade Unions in its hand. From the defendant it

became the prosecutor. It understood that if the Bolsheviks did not break on the question of the general strike, which had such a tremendous international importance, they would not break later on, no matter what demands were placed before them. We see how the General Council, under the pressure of the English bourgeoisie, conducted its offensive against the All-Union Central Council of Trade Unions with ever greater energy. The Central Council retreated and yielded. These retreats were explained on the grounds of revolutionary strategy in the trade union movement, but by no means for diplomatic motives. . . .

The line of the Political Bureau ended naturally and inevitably with the Berlin conference of the Anglo-Russian Committee at the beginning of April. The capitulation of the All-Union Central Council of Trade Unions on the basic questions of the international working class movement was neither an unexpected side-leap nor an abrupt maneuver. No, it was the inevitable crowning, predicted by us long before, of the whole line followed in this question.

10. At the beginning of June of last year [1926], Comrade Bukharin, as we said, was the creator of a theory according to which the necessity of working in reactionary trade unions allegedly brought with it the maintenance of the Anglo-Russian Committee under all circumstances. In the face of all the evidence, Bukharin at that time flatly denied that the Anglo-Russian Committee was a political bloc and called it a "trade union organization."

Now Bukharin creates a new theory, according to which our remaining in the Anglo-Russian Committee, bought at the price of an absolutely unprincipled capitulation, was not called forth by the needs of a "trade union organization," but by the necessity of maintaining a *political bloc* with the General Council in the name of diplomatic aims.

Bukharin's theory of today is in direct contradiction to his theory of yesterday. They have only this in common, that they are both 100 percent deceitful, that they were both dragged in by the hair in order to justify after the fact, at two different stages, the sliding down from a Bolshevist to a compromising line.

11. That the right will betray us in the event of war, is recognized as indisputable even by Bukharin. So far as the "left" is concerned, it will "probably" betray us. But if it betrays us, it will do it, according to Bukharin, "in its own way," by not supporting us but by playing the role of ballast for the English government. Pitiful as these considerations may be, they must nevertheless be demolished.

Let us assume for a moment that all of this is really so. But if the "left" betrays us "in its own way," that is, less actively, in a more veiled manner than the right, it will surely not be because of the lovely eyes of the delegation of the All-Union Central Council of Trade Unions, but because of the English workers. That is the general line of policy of the "left" in all questions, internal as well as external: to betray, but "in its own way." This policy is profitable for it. Then why are we obliged to pay the "left" with the abandonment of *our* policy, for a policy which they are forced in any case to carry out in their own interests?

12. But in what sense will the "left" be a ballast for the English government? Obviously, in the same sense that they were "ballast" during the imperialist war, or are now, during the war of England against revolutionary China, and during the campaign of the Conservatives against the trade unions. The "left" criticizes the government within such limits as do not interfere with its role as exploiter and robber. The "left" gives expression to the dissatisfaction of the masses within these limits, so as to restrain them from revolutionary action.

In case the dissatisfaction of the masses breaks through to the outside, the "left" seeks to dominate the movement in order to strangle it. Were the "left" not to criticize it, not to expose, not to attack the bourgeoisie, it would be unable to serve it "in its own way."

If it is admitted that the "left" is a ballast, then it is admitted that it is the useful, appropriate, necessary, succoring ballast without which the ship of British imperialism would long ago have gone down.

To be sure, the [Tory] diehards are fulminating against the "left." But this is done to keep the fear of God in it, so that it will not overstep the bounds prescribed for it, so that no unnecessary expense be incurred for their "ballast." The diehards are just as necessary an ingredient in the imperialist mechanism as the "left."

13. But under the pressure of the masses cannot even the "left" overstep the bounds prescribed for it by the bourgeois regime? This unexpected argument is also launched.

That the revolutionary pressure of the masses can undo the game of Chamberlain-Thomas-Purcell is incontestable. But the dispute does not hinge on whether the international revolutionary movement of the proletariat is advantageous for a workers' state, but rather whether we are helping or obstructing it by our policy.

The pressure of the masses, all other conditions being equal, will be all the stronger the more the masses are alarmed by the perspective of war, the less they rely upon the General Council, and the less confidence they have in the "left" traitors (traitors "in their own way"). If we sign "unanimously" a pitiful, lying, hypocritical declaration on the war together with the General Council, we thereby pacify the masses, appease their restlessness, lull them to sleep, and consequently reduce their pressure on the "left."

14. The Berlin conference can be justified by the "international interests of the USSR!" Here the mistake of Bukharin becomes especially atrocious. Precisely the interests of the USSR will suffer chiefly and most directly as a result of the false policy of the Political Bureau towards the General

Council. Nothing can cause us such harm as mistakes and hypocrisy in the revolutionary camp of the proletariat. We will not deceive our enemies, the experienced and shrewd imperialists. Hypocrisy will help the vacillating pacifists to vacillate in the future. And our real friends, the revolutionary workers, can only be deceived and weakened by the policy of illusions and hypocrisy.

15. Bukharin will reply to this: "The Berlin decisions would be inadmissible if we worked only in the trade union movement. However, everything we have done in Berlin can be extended and improved with the means that the party has. Just look: we even criticize the General Council in *Pravda*, in speeches by English Communists, etc."

This argument amounts to poisoning of the revolutionary consciousness. Bukharin's words mean only that we support the General Council "in our fashion" while it in turn "in its fashion" supports the imperialist state. If we criticize the General Council, then under the present circumstances, that is only to cover our political support of it and our political alliance with it.

The articles in *Pravda* (which are extremely foolish in regard to Purcell and Co.) are not read by the English workers. But the decisions of the Berlin conference are distributed through the press over the whole world. For the moment only a small minority of the English proletariat knows anything of the articles by the English Communists. But all the English workers know one thing: that Purcell and Tomsky maintain "friendly relations" with each other, "understand each other," and "are in agreement with each other." The attitude of the Russian trade union delegation, which represents the victorious proletariat of the Soviet Republic, is much more decisive than the speeches of the English Communists and thus belies their criticism, *which—by the way—is inadequate, since their freedom is limited by the Anglo-Russian Committee.*

In short: the capitulation of the Russian trade union movement in the name of the alliance with Purcell is one of the most important facts in the international workers' movement at the present moment. The "critical" articles in *Pravda* and Bukharin's ever-new theories are only the sauce on it.

That is just why Lenin wrote in his instructions for our delegation to the pacifist congress at the Hague,[10] where we had to deal with the same trade unionists, cooperators, and so forth:

> I think that if we have several people at the Hague Conference who are capable of delivering speeches against war in various languages, the most important thing would be to refute the opinion that the delegates at the Conference are opponents of war, that they understand how war may and will come upon them at the most unexpected moment, that they to any extent understand what methods should be adopted to combat war, that they are to any extent in a position to adopt reasonable and effective measures to combat war. [Lenin, *Collected Works*, Vol. 33 (Moscow, Progress Publishers, 1966), p. 479]

What interests did Lenin have in mind in writing these words: the international interests of the USSR or the revolutionary interests of the international proletariat? In such a basic question Lenin did not and could not set the one against the other. Lenin was of the opinion that the slightest yielding to the pacifist illusions of the trade unionists would render more difficult the real struggle against the war danger and injure the international proletariat as much as the USSR.

Lenin had conscientious pacifists in mind here, and not branded strikebreakers who are condemned by their whole position after May 1926 to a further chain of betrayals. . . .

16. In what manner can the thoroughly rotten, pseudo-pacifist agreement with traitors, whom we have already de-

clared by common accord to be the "only representatives" of
the English proletariat, strengthen our international position?
How? The Berlin conference took place in the period of the
opening of hostilities by the English government against
China and the preparation of similar hostilities against us.
The interests of our international position demanded above
all that these facts be openly called by their proper name.
Instead, we passed them over in silence.

Chamberlain knows these facts and is obliged to conceal
them. The English masses do not correctly know these facts
and are obliged to learn them from us. Honest pacifists among
the workers can go over to a revolutionary line in the face
of these facts. The base merchants of pacifism in the General Council cannot speak aloud about facts which would, at
best and without doubt, expose their silent conspiracy with
Chamberlain against the English workers, against China,
against the USSR, and against the world proletariat.

Now what did we do in Berlin? With all the authority of
a workers' state, we helped the "pacifist" lackeys of imperialism to preserve their thieves' secret. Worse yet, we assumed
responsibility for this secret. We proclaimed before the whole
world that we are "in unanimous accord" with the agents
of Chamberlain in the General Council in the cause of the
struggle against war. We thereby weakened the resistance
power of the English workers against the war. We thereby
increased Chamberlain's freedom of action. We thereby injured the international position of the USSR.

It must be said more concretely: the Berlin capitulation of
the All-Union Central Council of Trade Unions to the General Council extraordinarily facilitated Chamberlain's attack
on the Soviet institutions in London, with all the possible
consequences of this act.

17. It must not be forgotten that thanks especially to the
insular position of England and the absence of a direct threat
to its borders, the English reformists, during the war, allowed

themselves a somewhat greater "freedom" of words than their brothers-in-treason on the Continent. But in general they played the same role. Now, with the experiences of the imperialist war, the reformists, especially of the "left," will endeavor in the event of a new war to throw even more sand in the eyes of the workers than in the years 1914–18.

It is entirely probable that as a result of the attack on the Soviet institutions in London, which was prepared by the whole policy of the "left," they will protest in a little louder tone than the liberals. But if the Anglo-Russian Committee were in any way capable of helping, not Chamberlain, but us, then would not both sides have come to an agreement in the first twenty-four hours, sounded the alarm, and spoken to the masses in a language corresponding to the seriousness of the circumstances? But nothing of the sort occurred, and nothing will.

The Anglo-Russian Committee did not exist during the general strike when the General Council refused to accept the "damned gold" of the All-Union Central Council of Trade Unions; the Anglo-Russian Committee did not exist during the miners' strike; the Anglo-Russian Committee did not exist during the bombardment of Nanking; and the Anglo-Russian Committee will not exist in the event of the breaking of diplomatic relations between England and the USSR. These harsh truths must be told the workers. They must be honestly warned. *That* will strengthen the USSR!

18. It may be replied: But concessions on our part to the bourgeoisie are permissible, and if the present General Council is considered an agent of the bourgeoisie within the working-class movement, why should we not make concessions to the General Council out of the same considerations that we make concessions to imperialism? Certain comrades are beginning to play with this formula which is a classic example of the falsification and overthrow of Leninism for opportunist political aims.

If we are forced to make concessions to our class enemy, we make them to the master himself, but not to his Menshevik clerk. We never mask and never embellish our concessions. When we resigned ourselves to Curzon's ultimatum,[11] we explained to the English workers that at the present moment we, together with them, are not yet strong enough to take up the challenge of Curzon immediately. We bought ourselves off from the ultimatum to avert a diplomatic break, but we laid bare the real relations of classes by a clear presentation of the question; by that, we weakened the reformists and strengthened our international position as well as the position of the international proletariat.

In Berlin, however, we got absolutely nothing from Chamberlain. The concessions we made to the interests of English capitalism (new crowning of the General Council, principle of "noninterference," and so forth), were not exchanged for any concession at all on their part (no breaking-off of relations, no war). And at the same time we camouflaged everything by depicting our concessions to capitalism as a triumph of the unity of the working class. Chamberlain received a great deal gratis. The traitors of the General Council received a great deal. We received—a compromise. The international proletariat received—confusion and disorder. English imperialism came out of the Berlin conference stronger. We came out weaker.

19. But, it is said, to break with the General Council at such a critical moment would mean that we could not so much as live in peace with the organized workers of England; it would give the imperialists a trump card, and so on and so forth.

This argument is false to its very roots. Of course it would have been incomparably more advantageous had we broken with the General Council immediately after its betrayal of the general strike, as the Opposition demanded. The year would then not have been frittered away with doleful gallantries towards the traitors, but would have been used for their merciless exposure. The past year was not lacking in occasions for this.

Such a policy would have forced the "left" capitulators of the General Council to fight for remnants of their reputation, to separate themselves from the right, to half-expose Chamberlain, in a word, to show the workers that they, the "left," are not half as bad as the Moscow people present them. This would have deepened the split in the General Council. And when the swindlers of reformism come to blows, many secrets come to light, and the workers can only gain by it. Such a struggle against the General Council would have been the sharpest form of struggle against the policy of Chamberlain in the labor movement. In this struggle, the revolutionary working class cadres in England would have learned in a year more skillfully to catch the sharpers of the General Council at their swindles and to expose the policy of Chamberlain. English imperialism would have had to face much greater difficulties today. In other words: *Had the policy proposed by the Opposition been adopted in June of last year, the international position of the USSR would now be stronger.*

Even if belatedly, the break should have been made at least during the miners' strike, which would have been quite clear to the million miners, as well as the millions of workers betrayed in the general strike. But our proposals in this respect were rejected as incompatible with the interests of the international trade union movement. The consequences are well known. They were registered in Berlin. Today it is declared that the radically false line that already caused so much harm must be maintained in the future as well because of the difficulties of the international situation, which means in essence that the international position of the USSR is being sacrificed in order to conceal the errors of the leadership. All the new theories of Bukharin have no other meaning.

20. A correction of the errors now, even after a year's delay, would only be of benefit and not detriment. Chamberlain will say, of course, that the Bolsheviks are not able to maintain peace with his trade unionists. But every honest and even partly conscious English worker will say: the far-too-patient Bolsheviks, who did not even break with the General Council during our strikes, could no longer maintain any friendship with it when it refused to struggle against the suppression of the Chinese revolution and the new war that is being hatched by Chamberlain. The putrid decorations of the Berlin Anglo-Russian Committee will be cast aside. The workers will see the real facts, the real relationships. Who will lose thereby? Imperialism, which needs putrid decorations! The USSR and the international proletariat will gain.

21. But let us return again to the latest theory of Bukharin. In contradiction to Tomsky, Bukharin says, as we know, that the Berlin decisions are not the policy of the united front, but an exception to it, evoked by exceptional circumstances.

What are these circumstances? The war danger, that is, the most important question of imperialist policy and the policy of the world proletariat. This fact alone must forthwith compel the attention of every revolutionist. It would appear from this that revolutionary policy serves for more or less "normal" conditions; but when we stand before a question of life or death, the revolutionary policy must be substituted by a policy of compromise.

When Kautsky justified the iniquity of the Second International in 1914, he thought up the ex post facto theory that the International was an instrument of peace but not of war. In other words, Kautsky proclaimed that the struggle against the bourgeois state is normal, but that an exception must be made under the "exceptional conditions" of war, and a bloc made with the bourgeois government, while we continue to "criticize" it in the press.

For the international proletariat, it is now a question not only of the struggle against the bourgeois state, but of the direct defense of a workers' state. But it is precisely the interests of this defense that demand of the international proletariat not a weakening but a sharpening of the struggle against the bourgeois state. The war danger can only be averted or postponed for the proletariat by the real danger to the bourgeoisie that the imperialist war can be transformed into a civil war. In other words, the war danger does not demand a passing over from the revolutionary policy to a policy of compromise, but on the contrary, a firmer, more energetic, more irreconcilable execution of the revolutionary policy. War poses all questions forcefully. It admits of evasions and half-measures infinitely less than does a state of peace. If the bloc with the Purcells who betrayed the general strike was a hindrance in peaceful times, in times of war danger it is a millstone around the neck of the working class.

If one admits that the turning back from Bolshevism to opportunism is justified by circumstances on which the life and death of the workers' state depend, then one capitulates in principle to opportunism: for what value has a revolutionary policy that must be abandoned under the most critical circumstances?

22. In general, can the trade unions be utilized at one time in the interests of international class policy, and at another time for any sort of alleged diplomatic aims? Can such a situation be established where the same representatives of the CPSU, the Comintern, and the All-Union Central Council of Trade Unions say at one moment that the General Council is a traitor and strikebreaker, and at another time that it is a friend with whom we are in hearty accord? Is it sufficient to whisper secretly that the former must be understood in the revolutionary class sense and the latter in a diplomatic sense? Can such a policy be spoken of seri-

ously? Can one speak seriously to people who propose and defend such a policy?

After the Berlin conference, the word "traitor," as used for a Menshevik agent of the bourgeoisie, became terribly cheap. But such expressions as "hearty accord," "mutual understanding," and "unanimity" (the words of Comrade Tomsky), became equally cheap. Who benefits by this unusually artful combination of methods? It does not deceive our enemy for a moment. It only confuses our friends and reduces the weight of our own words and deeds.

23. The new theory of Bukharin is not an isolated one. On the one hand, we are told that the unprincipled agreement with the notoriously treasonable General Council allegedly facilitated the defense of the USSR. On the other hand, we hear ever more loudly that the building of workers' and peasants' soviets in China would be a threat to the defense of the USSR.[12] Doesn't this mean turning the foundations of Bolshevist policy upside down? Workers' and peasants' soviets in China would signify a magnificent extension of the soviet front and the strengthening of our world position. The agreement with the General Council signifies on the contrary a weakening of the internal contradictions in England and the greatest facility to Chamberlain in his work of brigandage against China and against us.

Once it is avowed that soviets in China are harmful to our international position, but that the General Council is useful, then the recognition of the principle of "noninterference" is essentially correct; but then supplementary conclusions must be drawn, at least with regard to Amsterdam. One can be sure that these conclusions will be drawn today or tomorrow, if not by Bukharin himself then by someone else. The new principle of opportunist exceptions "in particularly important cases" can find a broad application. The orientation of the opportunist chiefs of the labor movement will be motivated everywhere by the necessity of avoiding intervention. The possibility of building socialism in one country will serve to justify the principle of "noninterference." That is how the various ends will be knotted together into a noose that will strangle to death the revolutionary principles of Bolshevism. An end must be made to this once and for all!

We must make up for lost time. A broad and politically clear international campaign against war and imperialism is necessary. Our bloc with the General Council is now the principle obstacle in the road of this campaign, just as our bloc with Chiang Kai-shek[13] was the chief obstacle in the road of the development of the workers' and peasants' revolution in China and, because of that, was utilized by the bourgeois counterrevolution against us. The more acute the international situation becomes, the more the Anglo-Russian Committee will be transformed into an instrument of British and international imperialism against us. After all that has happened, only he can fail to understand who does not want to understand. We have already wasted far too much time. It would be a crime to lose even another day.

What we gave and what we got

September 25, 1927

In his report at the general membership meeting of the Moscow railwaymen, Comrade Andreyev made the first—and still the only—attempt to put two and two together in the question of the Anglo-Russian Committee. Comrade Andreyev did not succeed in putting two and two together, but instead—despite his own intentions—he did make a serious contribution toward explaining just where lies the difference between opportunist and Bolshevik policies.

1. Comrade Andreyev begins by very plaintively relating how the British busted up the ARC just at the time when it should have gone on living for many, many years. Imperialism has passed over to the offensive, strangling China, preparing a war against the USSR: "That is why the existence and activities of the ARC and similar organizations are most urgently needed right now." Again, further on: "It is precisely right now, at the time of this offensive of capital against the working class, that the urgent need for the existence of the ARC becomes especially clear." And so

on, in the same vein.

Concurrently, Comrade Andreyev supplies a lot of direct information about the measures that were taken to preserve the ARC (in enumerating these measures, however, he religiously avoids the Berlin conference of the ARC in April of this year). But all these exertions availed nothing: the ARC broke up just at the moment when the need for it became most acute.

As a matter of fact, this presentation as it stands is of itself a merciless condemnation of the very policy that Andreyev is defending. One may suffer defeat at the hands of an enemy despite the most correct policy, because the enemy is stronger. But when, in the course of many months, one forges a weapon against the enemy and then complains that this weapon went to pieces in one's hands on the eve of the battle—that is tantamount to self-condemnation: either the blacksmith is bad, or he forged out of worthless material.

2. After the General Council had broken the general strike in May 1926, the defenders of the official line said to us: "But didn't we know all along that the General Council is composed of reformist traitors?" Let us allow that we knew. But did we foresee that the General Council would collapse precisely when the need for it would be most urgent? Obviously this was not foreseen. Because not even the worst blacksmith would begin forging a weapon that he knew beforehand would fall apart on the eve of the battle.

Yet the controversy between the Opposition and the majority revolved precisely around this question. The Opposition said:

> The members of the General Council are liberal labor politicians of diverse shades. As is always the case with liberals, they have been plunged to the left by the first and still formless revolutionary wave. The general strike swept them to the right. They can have no independent

policy. Swept to the right, they become transformed into the active agency of the bourgeoisie. Their role will be counterrevolutionary. Since they have betrayed the general strike of their own workers, and the strike of their own coalminers, only a pathetic philistine can pin any hope on the possibility that these people would protect the Chinese revolution or the Soviet Union from the blows of British imperialism. Quite the contrary. In the critical moment they will come to the aid of imperialism against the revolution.

Such was our prognosis in this question. But after the English had broken the ARC, Comrade Andreyev comes before the Soviet workers with his pathetic lamentations: the ARC left this world just at the time when its activity was "most urgently needed."

In politics, Comrade Andreyev, this is called bankruptcy!

3. We said above: let us allow that the representatives of the official line did actually know whom they were dealing with—in which case their responsibility would be all the greater. As a matter of fact, they are vilifying themselves after the event. Their appraisal of the General Council was false, they did not understand the internal processes in the English working class, and they sowed illusions because they shared them themselves.

a) There is no need of going into the period prior to the strike: during that period Purcell, Hicks, and the others were pictured as our most trustworthy friends, almost our adherents. A veritable cloud of proof can be produced. We shall confine ourselves to a single instance. In his pamphlet, *The Practical Questions of the Trade Union Movement*, published in 1925, Comrade Tomsky said:

Those [trade unionists] who have entered into the agreement with us are maintaining themselves staunchly both against bourgeois lies and slanders, and against the former [?] leaders of the English movement: Thomas, Clynes, and MacDonald. The leaders of the British trade unions, the section that is furthest to the left—one can say with assurance, the majority—are working harmoniously with us. This gives us the assurance of and the occasion for hoping that the English, who are averse to striking quick agreements, who take a long time to think, weigh, discuss, and hesitate prior to coming to this or another decision, *will strictly fulfill the agreement;* and that we shall not have to put to ourselves the question: What will the unity of the world trade union movement give the Russian worker? [p. 48]

b) In the nature of things, matters did not improve very much after the strike was broken, either. Even after the Opposition came out with utmost decisiveness for a break with the Anglo-Russian Committee as an institution which was false and rotten to the core and which served only to befuddle the workers by its existence, the Moscow Committee lectured the party as follows in the special theses issued against the Opposition:

> The Anglo-Russian Committee can, must, and undoubtedly will play a tremendous role in the struggle against all types of intervention directed against the USSR. It will become the organizing center for the international forces of the proletariat in the struggle against all attempts of the international bourgeoisie to start up a new war. [*Materials Toward the Summary of the July* [1926] *Plenum of the CC of the CPSU,* Agit-prop Department of the Moscow Committee]

As a matter of fact, in the agitation among the rank and file, that is, in the really important agitation embracing the masses, the fundamental, chief, and pertinent argument against the Opposition was the following: We are threatened by the war danger and the General Council will help us to ward it off, but the Opposition, pursuing its "factional aims," demands that we break with the General Council. And from this sprang the stupid and base accusation of semi-defensism, defeatism, etc.

On the other hand, the Opposition maintained that the General Council would dilly-dally so long as no serious danger threatened its masters, the bourgeoisie, and then later on it would break with us at the moment when it best serves the bourgeoisie, i.e., when most dangerous to us.

Now Comrade Andreyev comes forward and tearfully laments that the General Council broke with us, you see, just at a time when the activity of the ARC was "most urgently needed." Needed by whom—us or the English bourgeoisie? For the General Council is the agency of the English bourgeoisie in the workers' movement. It is clear that it broke the bloc with us when this break happened to be "most urgently needed" by Chamberlain.

In politics, Comrade Andreyev, this is precisely what is meant by bankruptcy.

c) As for the famous argument of Comrade Rykov[14] to the effect that since Baldwin was demanding the dissolution of the ARC, therefore the Opposition was aiding Baldwin—didn't this argument in its entirety flow from the false appraisal of the General Council, from the misunderstanding of its class nature and its social role?

The General Council is the agency of the English bourgeoisie. A good master must watch his agency like a hawk. Agents have their own personal interests. The agent in his operations may go further than is profitable to the master. Baldwin watches sharply after his agency, he exerts pressure on it, frightens it, and presents it with demands for an accounting. Baldwin had to see to it that the General Council

makes no extra promises, and that it will be able to make a
timely break with us. The closer the approach of great problems the more inevitable the rupture. Among us, those who
made a false appraisal of the General Council, painted it up,
cherished illusions on this score, and hoped that in a major
and serious question the ARC would carry out a policy directed against Chamberlain—they failed to understand this.
The Opposition took its point of departure from the fact that
a break was inevitable and that this break must occur over
*such questions as would be most clear and comprehensible
to the English working masses.*

4. But even during the very last period, even after the
Berlin conference, Comrade Tomsky continued to paint up
the General Council. He rejected indignantly all references
to the fact that the ARC had become a reactionary impedi-
ment in the way of the workers' movement. He asserted that
the ARC is playing and can play a progressive role, even in
the case of war. True, in April 1927 he expressed himself
much more cautiously: 99 percent in favor of the General
Council's betraying us in case of war, as against one chance
in a hundred that it might not betray. Can we—demanded
Tomsky—reject even one chance against ninety-nine in so
great a cause?

To reason in such a manner is to turn politics into a lottery. But guaranteeing the defense of the USSR by lottery
methods is a pitiful policy indeed, all the more so since the
odds to lose are 100 percent. And when the loss became
patent, Comrade Andreyev, with many sighs, told the assembled railwaymen how fine it would have been had the
opportunists turned out to be not as they are in reality but
as Comrade Andreyev had imagined them to be.

All this, Comrade Andreyev, is precisely what is called
the opportunistic policy of illusions.

5. Today, after the event, there is no lack of volunteers
anxious to renounce the wretched crib of Comrade Uglanov[15]

upon the subject that the Anglo-Russian Committee "will become the organizing center of the international forces of the proletariat in the struggle against all attempts of the international bourgeoisie to start up a new war."

But precisely in this hope lay the crux of our entire official policy. It was precisely in this that the party was fooled. It was precisely by this that the Opposition was "beaten."

In the July 1926 joint plenum, Comrade Stalin lectured to us complacently:

> The aim of this bloc [the ARC] consists in organizing a wide working-class movement against new imperialist wars in general, and against intervention into our country on the part [especially so!] of the most powerful of the imperialist powers of Europe—on the part of England in particular. [*Minutes*, first issue, p. 71]

Instructing us Oppositionists that it is necessary to "be concerned about the defense of the first workers' republic in the world from intervention," Stalin added for good measure:

> If the trade unions of our country in this cause, meet with the support on the part of the English, even if reformist, trade unions, then this should be hailed. . . .
> voices: Correct! [Idem., p. 71]

We may be quite sure that among those shouting "correct" was also the voice of Comrade Andreyev. Yet these were the voices of blind men who were exposing the defense of the USSR to the danger of a sudden blow. It is not enough for one to "be concerned about the defense of the USSR"; one must also be concerned about the Marxist line of the policies; one must know the basic forces of the world struggle, understand class relations and the mechanics of parties; and one must be a Marxist-Leninist and not a philistine.

Stalin keeps chewing his ideas with the smugness of a provincial wiseacre. Each vulgarity is numbered: first, second, third, and fourth. First, pinning hope on Chiang Kai-shek; second, pinning hope on Wang Ching-wei; third, on Purcell; fourth on Hicks.[16] Today's hope is being pinned on the French Radicals, who, if you please, will repel the French imperialists,[17] but this falls under fifth. . . . It is not enough for one to "be concerned about the defense"; one must have some inkling as to what's what.

In the same speech Stalin goes on to sermonize:

> If the reactionary English trade unions are willing to enter into a bloc with the revolutionary trade unions of our country against the counterrevolutionary imperialists of their own country—then why not hail this bloc? [p. 71]

Stalin cannot understand that were the "reactionary trade unions" capable of waging a struggle against their own imperialists, they would not be reactionary trade unions. Falling into middle-class superficiality, Stalin loses all sight of the line of demarcation between the concepts *reactionary* and *revolutionary*. Out of sheer habit he refers to the English trade unions (i.e., obviously their leadership) as reactionary, but he really cherishes entirely Menshevist illusions about them.

Stalin sums up his philosophy as follows:

> And so, the ARC is the bloc between our trade unions and the reactionary trade unions of England . . . for the purpose of struggle against imperialist wars in general, and against intervention in particular. [p. 71]

That's just it: both in general and in particular. In general, and in particular—middle class narrowness (suggested topic for the "red" professors of the Stalinist school).

With the smugness of a provincial wiseacre, Stalin concludes his sermonizing with an attempt at irony: "Comrades Trotsky and Zinoviev should remember this, and remember it well." [p. 72]

That's just it! We have remembered everything very firmly indeed. We have remembered that our criticisms of the Stalinist hopes in Purcell as the guardian angel of the workers' state were called by Stalin a deviation from "Leninism to Trotskyism."

> VOROSHILOV: Correct!
>
> A VOICE: Voroshilov has affixed the seal!
>
> TROTSKY: Fortunately all this will appear in the minutes. [p. 71]

Yes, this is all to be found in the minutes of that very same July plenum which removed Zinoviev from the Political Bureau, which thundered against "Trotskyism," which assumed the defense of the Uglanov-Mandelstamm crib.

We now propose that the speeches of Stalin together with our speeches on the question of the ARC be published for the congress. This would provide an excellent examination as to whose views stand the test of events and of time: the views of Stalin or the views of the Opposition?

6. We shall pass over the scholastic constructions of Bukharin. Upon this question he observed seven theoretical Fridays a week. Here is the sophism that the ARC is a trade union organization and not a political bloc. Here is also the sophism that the ARC is not the union of leaders but the union of the masses. Here, too, is the defense of the April capitulation in Berlin by an argumentation of a state and diplomatic character. And many, many other things besides.

We evaluated these theories in their own time for what

they were worth. It would be a fruitless waste of time to unwind, after the event, Bukharin's talmudic knots. The course of events has swept away Bukharin's scholasticism, as so much rubbish, out of which only one fact emerges clearly: *the ideopolitical bankruptcy*. And just to think that all this put together is being served up as the general line of the Comintern!

From the moment the general strike was broken [relates Andreyev] there was begun the preparation of a plan how best to destroy the ARC, or to reduce the ARC completely to a cipher, to such a position as would keep it from being a hindrance to the General Council. . . . This is what the plan of the present leaders of the General Council amounted to. And what happened at the last congress was the fulfillment of this plan.

All of which is entirely correct. The General Council did have its own plan, and it did execute this plan methodically. "The break is the fulfillment of a carefully thought-out plan which the General Council had prepared and which it executed during the last congress." This is absolutely correct. The General Council knew what it wanted. Or rather, the masters of the General Council knew where it had to be led. But did Comrade Andreyev know where he was going? He did not. Because not only did he fail to hinder but he also assisted the General Council to fulfill its perfidious plan to the greatest benefit of the General Council itself, and its actual political principles, i.e., the British bourgeoisie.

8. If the General Council did have a plan and if it was able to execute this plan methodically, then couldn't this plan have been understood, deciphered, and foreseen? The Opposition did foresee. As early as June 2, 1926, two weeks after the general strike was broken, we wrote to the Political Bureau:

But may not the General Council itself take the initiative to break away? This is more than probable. It will issue a statement that the CEC of the Russian trade unions is striving not toward the unity of the world working class but to fan discord among trade unions, and that it, the General Council, cannot travel along the same road with the CEC of the Russian unions. Then once more we shall call after them: *Traitors!*—which will express all the realism there is in the policy that consists of supporting rotten fictions. [*Minutes of the Political Bureau,* June 8, 1926, p. 71]

Hasn't this been confirmed literally, almost letter for letter? We did not break with the General Council after it had betrayed the general strike and had aroused against itself the extreme exasperation of millions of English workers. We did not break with it under conditions already less favorable to us, after it had broken the coalminers' strike, together with the priests of the bourgeoisie. Nor did we break with it under still less favorable conditions—on the question of British intervention in China. And now the English have broken with us over the question of our interfering in their internal affairs, our striving to "give orders" to the English working class, or to turn the English trade unions into instruments of our state policies. They broke on those questions which are most favorable to them, and which are most apt to fool the English workers. Which is precisely what we had been forecasting. Whose policy, then, turns out to be correct, sober, and revolutionary? The one that penetrates the machinations of the enemy and foresees the morrow?—or the policy that blindly assists the enemy to carry its perfidious plan to completion?

9. During the July 1926 plenum, a cable was received from the General Council with its gracious consent to meet with the representatives of the CEC of the Russian unions.

At that time, this cable was played up as a victory not over the General Council but over the Opposition. What an effect there was when Comrade Lozovsky brought up this telegram![18]

> What will you do [he demanded from the Opposition] if they [the General Council] do consent; more than that, what will you do if they have already consented? We have received such a cable today.
> TROTSKY: They have consented that we shield them temporarily by our prestige, now when they are preparing a new betrayal. [*Disorder, laughter*] [p. 53]

All this is recorded in the minutes. At that time our forecasts were the subject for taunts, disorder, and laughter. Comrade Tomsky did indeed crow over the receipt of the cable.

> TOMSKY: Our little corpse is peering out of one eye. . . . [*Loud laughter*] [p. 58]

Yes, the laughter was loud. Whom were you laughing at then, Comrade Andreyev? You were laughing at yourselves.

And how Comrade Lozovsky did taunt the Opposition with the fact that its expectations had not materialized.

> What makes you so certain [he inquired] that your second supposition will materialize? Wait. . . . [p. 53]

To which we answered:

> TROTSKY: This means that for the moment the wiser and the more astute among them have gained the day, and that is why they have not broken as yet [*Disorder*] [p. 53]

Again "disorder." To Andreyev, Lozovsky, and others it was absolutely clear that the Opposition was motivated by "gross factional considerations," and not by the concern for how we should distinguish correctly friends from enemies, and allies from traitors. Hence, the laughter and the disorder in the production of which Comrade Andreyev by no means took the last place. "What makes you so certain that your second supposition will materialize?" inquired Comrade Lozovsky. "Wait. . . ." The majority was with Andreyev and Lozovsky. We had to wait. We waited more than a year. And it so happened that the Anglo-Russian Committee, which according to Rykov should have tumbled bourgeois strongholds—assisted instead its own bourgeoisie to deal us a blow, and then screened Chamberlain's blow by dealing its own supplementary blow.

When the test of great events comes, Comrade Andreyev, one must always pay heavily for the policy of opportunistic illusions.

10. We have already recalled that Andreyev in his report skipped completely over the Berlin conference of the ARC, April 1927, as if no such conference had ever been. Yet this conference marks the most important stage in the history of the ARC after the general strike was broken. At the Berlin conference, the delegation of the CEC of the Russian unions renewed its mandate of faith in the General Council. The delegation behaved as if there had been neither the betrayal of the general strike, nor the betrayal of the coalminers' strike, nor the betrayal of the Chinese revolution, nor the betrayal of the USSR. All the notes of credit were renewed and Comrade Tomsky boasted that this was done in the spirit of perfect "mutual understanding" and "heart-to-heart relations."

It is impossible to give traitors aid. What did we get for it? The disruption of the ARC within four months, at the time when our international position became worse. In the name of what did we capitulate in Berlin? Precisely upon this question, Comrade Andreyev didn't have a word to say to the membership meeting of the railwaymen.

Yet in Berlin capitulation was no accident. It flowed in its entirety from the policy of "preserving" the ARC at all costs. From the end of May 1926, the Opposition hammered away that it was impermissible to maintain a bloc with people we call traitors. Or the converse: we cannot call traitors people with whom we maintain a bloc.

We must break with the traitors at the moment of their greatest betrayal, in the eyes of loyal and indignant masses, aiding the masses to invest their indignation with the clearest possible political and organizational expression. This is what the Opposition demanded. And it also forewarned that if the bloc was not broken, the criticism of the General Council would necessarily have to be adapted to the bloc, i.e., reduced to nothing. This forecast was likewise completely verified.

The manifesto of the CEC of the Red International of Labor Unions on June 8, 1926, contained a rather sharp, although inadequate, criticism of the General Council. Subsequent manifestos and resolutions became paler and more diffuse. And on April 1, 1927, the Russian delegation capitulated completely to the General Council.

At no time was the position of the British trade union leaders so difficult as in May, June, and July 1926. The fissure between the leaders and the revolutionary vanguard of the proletariat stood revealed during that period as never before.

We had two courses open to us: to deepen this fissure or to assist the General Council to plug it up. Thanks to the assistance we gave the strikers, our prestige was very high. Our breaking relations with the General Council would have been a powerful supplementary blow to its authority and position. On the contrary, the preservation of the political and organizational bloc assisted the General Council to negotiate with least losses the frontier most dangerous to it. "Thank you," it said to those who helped keep it in the saddle. "I can go on from here myself." Incidentally, there was no gratitude expressed; the CEC of the Russian trade unions merely received a kick.

On one point Andreyev is correct: this break is the fulfillment of a carefully thought-out plan.

11. But did Andreyev have a plan himself? We have already stated that he had none whatever. Perhaps the most severe indictment of Andreyev lies in his silence about the Berlin conference of April 1927. Yet at the April plenum of the CEC, Comrade Andreyev spoke very decisively in defense of this conference. Here is what he said then:

> What did we set as our task? At this Anglo-Russian Committee [in Berlin] we set as our task to force the English to give us a direct and clear [!] answer to what their views were about continuing the existence of the Anglo-Russian Committee. And in my opinion, *we did force them to do this.* [?!] Jointly with us, they said that they were for continuing the existence of the Anglo-Russian Committee, for activizing it, and so forth. At this Anglo-Russian Committee we were to force through a definite decision upon the question of unity and to a certain degree the condemnation of the Amsterdam International for its evasion of unity proposals. . . . *We forced such a decision.* [?!] We forced through a resolution on this question. We had to force an answer from them on the question of the war danger, and imperialist mobilization. In my opinion, *in this sphere also, we forced through,* of course not a 100 percent Bolshevik decision [?!], but a maximum possible decision that could have been forced through under the given conditions. [p. 32]

Such were the victories gained by Comrade Andreyev at the Berlin conference: the English expressed themselves "directly and clearly" in favor of continuing the existence of the ARC; more than that, in favor of "activizing it." It is no laughing matter indeed! Andreyev forced a clear answer from the English on the question of trade union unity, and finally—hear! hear!—on the question of war. Small wonder that in that very same speech of his, Comrade Andreyev— poor fellow!—spoke of how the Opposition "has hopelessly sunk in the mire of its mistakes."

But what to do now? In April "we forced the General Council to give us clear and direct answers." The Opposition, sunk in the mire of its mistakes, alone failed to understand these successes. But in September, the Trades Union Congress arranged by the General Council broke with the Anglo-Russian Committee. Whence comes this contradiction between April and September? Right *now*, Andreyev admits that the collapse of the ARC is the fulfillment of a plan conceived back at the time of the general strike, that is, in May 1926. What then was the import of the "clear and direct" answers of the English in April 1927? Hence, it follows that these answers were neither clear nor direct, but swindles. The job of the General Council consisted in hoodwinking, gaining time, causing a delay, preparing the congress, and using it as a shield.

The Opposition issued timely warning on this score as well. Open the minutes of the April 1926 plenum to page 31. We said at that time:

"A particular danger to world peace is lodged in the policy of the imperialists in China." This is what they have countersigned. How come their tongues didn't turn inside out, or why didn't we pull them by the tongue and compel them to speak out precisely who the imperialists were? It is no mere coincidence that *all this*

was signed on the first day of April, this date is sym-
bolic. . . . [*Laughter*]

KAGANOVICH: You mean to say we fooled them!

As may be observed, Comrade Kaganovich hit the bull's
eye. Now it has become quite clear as to who fooled whom.
Andreyev has some cause to be plaintive over the fact that
after all his victories in April 1927 the English liquidated
the ARC at that very moment when it was most urgently
needed.

This, Comrade Andreyev, is what one would call having
hopelessly sunk in a mire!

12. But this wasn't enough; Comrade Andreyev expressed
himself even more harshly about the Opposition at the April
plenum:

> Our Opposition comes out with the demand that we
> break with the English unions. Such a position is a posi-
> tion to isolate us at the most difficult moment, when im-
> perialism is mobilizing its forces against us. You maintain
> that your position is presumably revolutionary, but you
> are giving objective aid to the Chamberlains because the
> Chamberlains want no connections whatever between
> our trade union movement and the English trade union
> movement, and they want no Anglo-Russian Commit-
> tees to hinder them. [p. 33]

The Opposition proposed that we do not seize hold of a
rotten twig while passing over a precipice. But the policies
defended by Comrade Andreyev did bring us into isolation
"at the most difficult moment, when imperialism is mobilizing its forces against us." That is the job which was literally
fulfilled by the official policies. By supporting the General
Council, we weakened the Minority Movement.

Within the minority itself, by our conciliationist line, we

supported the right elements against the left. By this policy we put a brake on the revolutionary education of the proletarian vanguard, including the Communist Party among the number. We assisted the General Council to hold its position without losses, to prepare a reactionary congress of trade union bureaucrats in Edinburgh, and to break with us against the resistance only of a small minority. We assisted the General Council to isolate us in our most difficult moment and thus to realize the plan conceived by the General Council far back during the time of the general strike.

This, Comrade Andreyev, implies giving objective aid to the Chamberlains!

13. But now, defending the policies of bankruptcy before a nonparty meeting, Comrade Andreyev says:

> A few hotheads from the Opposition in our Communist Party proposed to us during the entire period the following tactic: "Break with the English traitors, break with the General Council."

This utterly cheap, philistine phrase about "hotheads" is taken from the dictionary of middle-class reformism and opportunism, which are incapable of a long-range policy, that is to say, the policy of Marxian prescience and Bolshevik resolution. In April 1927, Andreyev reckoned that he had forced serious commitments from the English. To this we replied:

> Political swindlers in the staff of the Amsterdam agency of capitalism commonly sow pacifist bargains of this type in order to lull the workers and thus keep their own hands free *for betrayal at the critical moment.* [p. 38]

Who proved to be correct? Policies are tested by facts. We saw above what Andreyev expected in April of this year, and what he received in September. Wretched niggardliness, shameful nearsightedness! That is the name for your policy, Comrade Andreyev!

14. Andreyev has one remaining solace: "The responsibility (!) for the breaking up of this organization [the ARC] falls entirely and squarely (!!) upon the leaders of the English trade union movement." This statement proves that Andreyev has learned nothing. The "responsibility" for the breaking of the ARC! One might think that this was the most frightful of crimes against the working class. The General Council broke the general strike, assisted the coal barons to enslave the miners, screened the destruction of Nanking, supported the policies of Chamberlain against the workers' state, and will support Chamberlain in case of war. And Andreyev seeks to scare these people by "responsibility" for breaking the ARC.

What did the English workers see of the ARC, particularly from the time of the general strike: banquets, hollow resolutions, hypocritical and diplomatic speeches.

And on the other hand, since when have we become afraid of assuming the responsibility for breaking with traitors and betrayers? What sort of a pathetic, wishy-washy, rotten liberal way is this of putting the question, anyway! To prolong the life of the ARC for four months we paid by the most disgraceful capitulation at Berlin. But in return, don't you see, we have rid ourselves of the most horrendous "responsibility"—the responsibility of having broken with the betrayers of the working class. But the entire history of Bolshevism is impregnated with the determination to assume responsibility of this sort!

Comrade Andreyev, you are also one of those who babble about Trotskyism but who have yet to grasp the main thing in Bolshevism.

15. The perplexed reporter says: "Now every proletarian must give himself a clear accounting, weigh the documents,

and compare our policy with theirs" (Andreyev, *Report at the Meeting of Railwaymen*).

This is, of course, a praiseworthy manner of putting the question. One shouldn't accept anyone's say so. On this score Lenin had the following to say: "He who accepts somebody's word is a hopeless idiot." This Leninist aphorism applies to all countries, the Soviet Union among them. It is essential that our workers gain a clear conception of the policies of Comrade Andreyev, i.e., the entire official policy in the question of the Anglo-Russian Committee. To this end, all the documents must be published and made available to every worker.

We trust that Comrade Andreyev will support this proposal of ours. Otherwise he'll be in the position of one who maintains that what is good for the English is death for Russians. But this is the viewpoint of chauvinists and not internationalist revolutionists.

16. But what to do now, after the rotten stage decoration has collapsed completely? Comrade Andreyev replies: "The leaders refuse to make agreements with us—we will carry on this policy of the united front over the heads of the leaders and against their wishes, we shall carry it on from below, by means of our ties with the masses, their rank-and-file organization, and so forth."

Fine. But didn't Manuilsky[19] say more than a year ago, at the July plenum:

> Comrade Zinoviev appears here to console us that after breaking with the Anglo-Russian Committee we shall have to build new bridges to the workers' movement. But I want to ask—*have you seen these bridges?* Did Comrade Zinoviev outline new ways for realizing the idea of trade union unity? What is worst in the entire Opposition of Comrades Zinoviev and Trotsky is *this state of helplessness* (!!!). [p. 24]

Thus a year ago the proclamation read that the liquidation of the Anglo-Russian Committee must create a state of helplessness: there being no other bridges in sight. He was considered a true revolutionary optimist who believed in the Purcellian bridge. And now this bridge has collapsed. Cannot one draw the conclusion that precisely Manuilsky's position is the position of helplessness and occlusion? It may be objected that no one would take Manuilsky seriously. Agreed. But didn't all the other defenders of the official line declare that the ARC is the "incarnation" of the brotherhood between the Russian and English proletariat, the bridge to the masses, the instrument of the defense of the USSR, and so forth and so on . . . ?!

To the Opposition—such was the objection of the representatives of the official line—the Anglo-Russian Committee is the bloc between leaders, but for us it is the bloc of toiling masses, the incarnation of their union. Now, permit us to ask: Is the breaking of the ARC the breaking of the union of the toiling masses? Comrade Andreyev seems to say—no. But this very same answer goes to prove that the ARC did not represent the union of toiling masses, for it is impossible to make a union with strikers through the strikebreakers.

17. It is incontestable that we must find ways other than the General Council. Moreover, after this *reactionary partition* has been eliminated, only then do we obtain the possibility of seeking genuine connections with the genuine masses. The first condition for success on this road is the merciless condemnation of the official line toward the Anglo-Russian Committee for the entire recent period, i.e., from the beginning of the general strike.

18. The tremendous movements of the English proletariat have naturally not passed without leaving a trace. The Communist Party has become stronger—both in numbers and in influence—as a result of its participation in the mass

struggles. The processes of differentiation within the many-millioned masses continue to take place. As is always the case after major defeats, certain and rather wide circles of the working class suffer a temporary drop in activity. The reactionary bureaucracy entrenches itself, surmounting internal shadings. At the left pole a selection of revolutionary elements and the strengthening of the Communist Party takes place at a rate more rapid than prior to the strike.

All these phenomena flow with iron inevitability from the gigantic revolutionary wave which broke against the resistance not only of the bourgeoisie but also of its own official leadership. One can and must continue building on this foundation. However, the thoroughly false policy restricted to the extreme the sweep of the offensive and weakened its revolutionary consequences. With a correct policy, the Communist Party could have garnered immeasurably more abundant revolutionary fruits. By the continuation of the incorrect policies it risks losing what it has gained.

19. Comrade Andreyev points to the workers' delegations as one of the ways toward establishing connections with the English masses. Naturally, workers' delegations, well-picked and well-instructed, can also bring benefit to the cause of workers' unity. But it would be a rock-bottom mistake to push this method to the foreground. The import of workers' delegations is purely auxiliary. Our fundamental connection with the English working class is through the Communist Party.

It is possible to find the road to the toiling masses organized into trade unions not through combinations, nor through false deals at the top but through the correct revolutionary policy of the British Communist Party, the Comintern, Profintern, and the Russian unions. The masses can be won over only by a sustained revolutionary line. Once again this stands revealed in all its certainty, after the collapse of the ARC. As a matter of fact, the point of departure for the erroneous line in the question of the ARC was the straining to *supplant* the growth of the influence of the Communist Party by skilled diplomacy in relation to the leaders of the trade unions.

If anyone tried to leap over actual and necessary and inevitable stages, it was Stalin and Bukharin. It seemed to them that they would be able through cunning maneuvers and combinations to promote the British working class to the highest class without the Communist Party, or rather with some cooperation from it. This was also the initial error of Comrade Tomsky. Again, however, there is nothing original in this mistake. That is how opportunism always begins. The development of the class appears to it to be much too slow and it seeks to reap what it has not sown, or what has not ripened as yet. Such, for example, was the source of the opportunistic mistakes of Ferdinand Lassalle.[20]

But after the methods of diplomacy and combination have described a complete circle, opportunism then returns, like the fishwife in the fable, to its broken trough. Had we from the very beginning correctly understood that the ARC is a temporary bloc with reformists which can be maintained only up to their first shift to the right; had we generally understood that a united front with the "leaders" can have only an ephemeral, episodic, and subordinate significance; had we, in correspondence with all this, broken with the Anglo-Russian Committee on that very day when it refused to accept the assistance of the Russian workers to the English strikers—this entire tactical experiment would have been justified. We would have given impetus to the movement of the left minority and the British Communist Party would have received a lesson in the correct application of the tactic of the united front.

Instead of this we shifted the tactical axis over to the side of the bloc with the reformist leaders. We attempted to transform a temporary and an entirely legitimate agreement into a permanent institution. This institution was proclaimed by us to be the core of the struggle for the unity of the world proletariat, the center of the revolutionary struggle against war, and so forth and so on. Thus we created political fictions, and we preached to the workers to have faith in these fictions, i.e., we were performing work which is profoundly harmful and inimical to the revolution.

To the extent that the treacherous character of our allies became revealed—to which we tried to shut our eyes as long as possible—we proclaimed that the crux of the matter lay not in them, not in the General Council: that the ARC is not a bloc between leaders but a union of masses, that the ARC is only the "incarnation," only a "symbol," and so forth and so on. This was already the direct policy of lies, falsehoods, and rotten masquerades. This web of falseness was crumpled by great events. Instead of lisping, "the responsibility for this does not fall on us," we must say, "to our shame—we deserve no credit for it."

Andreyev says that the whole truth must be told to every English worker. Of course, everything possible must be done. But this is not at all easy. When Andreyev says: "Now no one will believe the members of the General Council any longer," that is simply a cheap phrase. As the Edinburgh congress shows, our policy strengthened the General Council. The Berlin conference alone—disregarding all the rest—did not pass scot-free for us. We shall have not only to scrub but to scrape away the ideological confusion we have spread. This primarily refers to the British Communist Party, and in the second place to the left-wing Minority Movement.

As far back as the time of the general strike, as well as the coalminers' strike, the leadership of the British Communist Party was far from always able to display initiative and resolution. One must not forget that the CEC of the British Communist Party long refused to print the July 8 manifesto of the Russian unions as too sharp toward the General Council.

For him who is able to judge symptoms, this episode must appear as extremely alarming. A young Communist Party, whose entire strength lies in criticism and irreconcilability, reveals at the decisive moment a surplus of qualities of the opposite order. At bottom of it is the false understanding and the false application of the policy of the united front.

Day in and day out the English Communist Party was taught that the union with Purcell and Hicks would aid the cause of the defense of the USSR and that the Russian Opposition, which does not believe this, was guilty of defeatism. Everything was stood on its head. This could not pass without leaving its traces upon the consciousness of the British Communist Party. . . .

This could not and it did not pass scot-free. The right-wing tendencies have become extremely strengthened among the leading circles of the British Communist Party: enough to recall the dissatisfaction of a number of the members of the English Central Committee with the Comintern theses on war as being too far "left"; enough to recall Pollitt's speech in Edinburgh, the speeches and articles of Murphy, and so on.[21]

All these symptoms indicate one and the same thing: for a young party, still lacking real Bolshevik tempering, the policies of the Anglo-Russian Committee inevitably implied the opportunistic dislocation of its entire line.

This applies even to a larger measure to the left-wing Minority Movement. The evil caused here is not so easily remedied. It is pregnant with party crises in the future. Of course these words will supply pathetic functionaries with the pretext to speak of our hostility toward the British Communist Party and so forth. We have witnessed this in the past more than once, particularly in the case of China. Up to the last moment the Chinese Communist Party was proclaimed as the exemplar of Bolshevist policies, and after the collapse—as the progeny of Menshevism. We have nothing in common with such repulsive political sliminess. It has already brought the greatest harm both to our party and to the Comintern. But this will not cause us to pause on the road of fulfilling our revolutionary duty.

Andreyev's report aims to smear over one of the greatest tactical lessons of the recent period. In this lies the most serious harmfulness of the report and of similar speeches and documents. It is possible to move forward only on the basis of an all-sided examination of the experience with the Anglo-Russian Committee. To this end all the basic documents that shed light on this question must be made available to all Communists. In order to move forward it is necessary to tell the truth, the whole truth, and nothing but the truth, both to the Russian and English workers.

A balance sheet of the Anglo-Russian Committee

June 1928

... The weaknesses of the English Communist Party gave birth at that time [1924] to the necessity of replacing it as quickly as possible with a more imposing factor. Precisely then was born the false estimate of the tendencies in English trade unionism. Zinoviev gave us to understand that he counted upon the revolution finding an entrance, not through the narrow gateway of the British Communist Party, but through the broad portals of the trade unions. The struggle to win the masses organized in the trade unions through the Communist Party was replaced by the hope for the swiftest possible utilization of the ready-made apparatus of the trade unions for the purposes of the revolution. Out of this false position sprang the later policy of the Anglo-Russian Committee which dealt a blow to the Soviet Union, as well as to the English working class; a blow surpassed only by the defeat in China.

In the *Lessons of October*, written as early as the summer of 1924, the idea of an accelerated road—accelerated through friendship with Purcell and Cook, as the further development of this idea showed—is refuted as follows:

> Without a party, apart from a party, over the head of
> a party, or with a substitute for a party, the proletarian
> revolution cannot conquer. That is the principal lesson of
> the past decade. It is true that the English trade unions
> may become a mighty lever of the proletarian revolution;
> they may, for instance, even take the place of workers'
> soviets under certain conditions and for a certain period
> of time. They can fill such a role, however, not apart
> from a Communist party, and certainly not *against* the
> party, but only on the condition that communist influ-
> ence becomes the decisive influence in the trade unions.
> We have paid far too dearly for this conclusion—with
> regard to the role and importance of a party in a prole-
> tarian revolution—to renounce it so lightly or even to
> minimize its significance. [Trotsky, *Lessons of October*,
> Pioneer Publishers, 1937, reprinted in *The Challenge of
> the Left Opposition (1923–25)*, Pathfinder, 1975]

The same problem is posed on a wider scale in my book
Whither England? This book, from beginning to end, is devoted to proving the idea that the English revolution, too,
cannot avoid the portals of communism and that with a correct, courageous, and intransigent policy that steers clear of
any illusions with regard to detours, the English Communist
Party can grow by leaps and bounds and mature so as to be
equal in the course of a few years to the tasks before it. . . .
As to the Anglo-Russian Committee, the third most
important question from the strategical experiences of the
Comintern in recent years, there only remains for us, after
all that has already been said by the Opposition in a series
of articles, speeches, and theses, to make a brief summary.
The point of departure of the Anglo-Russian Committee, as
we have already seen, was the impatient urge to leap over

the young and too slowly developing Communist Party. This invested the entire experience with a false character even prior to the general strike.

The Anglo-Russian Committee was looked upon not as an episodic bloc at the tops which would have to be broken and which would inevitably and demonstratively be broken at the very first serious test in order to compromise the General Council. No, not only Stalin, Bukharin, Tomsky, and others, but also Zinoviev saw in it a long-lasting "copartnership"—an instrument for the systematic revolutionization of the English working masses, and if not the gate, at least an approach to the gate through which would stride the revolution of the English proletariat. The further it went, the more the Anglo-Russian Committee became transformed from an episodic alliance into an inviolable principle standing above the real class struggle. This became revealed at the time of the general strike.

The transition of the mass movement into the open revolutionary stage threw back into the camp of the bourgeois reaction those liberal labor politicians who had become somewhat left. They betrayed the general strike openly and deliberately; after which they undermined and betrayed the miners' strike. The possibility of betrayal is always contained in reformism. But this does not mean to say that reformism and betrayal are one and the same thing at every moment. Not quite. Temporary agreements may be made with the reformists whenever they take a step forward. But to maintain a bloc with them when, frightened by the development of a movement, they commit treason, is equivalent to criminal toleration of traitors and a veiling of betrayal.

The general strike had the task of exerting a united pressure upon the employers and the state with the power of the five million workers, for the question of the coalmining industry had become the most important question of state policy. Thanks to the betrayal of the leadership, the strike was broken in its first stage. It was a great illusion to continue in the belief that an isolated economic strike of the mine workers would alone achieve what the general strike did not achieve. *That is precisely where the power of the General Council lay.* It aimed with cold calculation at the defeat of the mine workers, as a result of which considerable sections of the workers would be convinced of the "correctness" and the "reasonableness" of the Judas directives of the General Council.

The maintenance of the amicable bloc with the General Council, and the simultaneous support of the protracted and isolated economic strike of the mine workers, which the General Council came out against, seemed, as it were, to be calculated beforehand to allow the heads of the trade unions to emerge from this heaviest test with the least possible losses.

The role of the Russian trade unions here, from the revolutionary standpoint, turned out to be very disadvantageous and positively pitiable. Certainly, support of an economic strike, even an isolated one, was absolutely necessary. There can be no two opinions on that among revolutionists. But this support should have borne not only a financial but also a revolutionary-political character. The All-Union Central Council of Trade Unions should have declared openly to the English mine workers' union and the whole English working class that the mine workers' strike could seriously count upon success only if by its stubbornness, its tenacity, and its scope, it could prepare the way for a *new outbreak of the general strike.* That could have been achieved only by an open and direct struggle against the General Council, the agency of the government and the mine owners. The struggle to convert the economic strike into a political strike should have signified, therefore, a furious political and organizational war against the General Council. The first step to such a war had to be the break with the Anglo-Russian Committee, which had become a reactionary obstacle, a chain on the feet of the working class.

No revolutionist who weighs his words will contend that a victory *would have been guaranteed* by proceeding along this line. But a victory was *possible* only on this road. A defeat on this road was a defeat on a road that could lead *later* to victory. Such a defeat educates, that is, strengthens the revolutionary ideas in the working class. In the meantime, mere financial support of the lingering and hopeless trade union strike (trade union strike—in its methods; revolutionary-political—in its aims), only meant grist to the mill of the General Council, which was biding calmly until the strike collapsed from starvation and thereby proved its own "correctness." Of course, the General Council could not easily bide its time for several months in the role of an open strikebreaker. It was precisely during this very critical period that the General Council required the Anglo-Russian Committee as its political screen from the masses. Thus, the questions of the mortal class struggle between English capital and the proletariat, between the General Council and the mine workers, were transformed, as it were, into questions of a friendly discussion between allies in the same bloc, the English General Council and the All-Union Central Council of Trade Unions, on the subject of which of the two roads was better at that moment: the road of an agreement or the road of an isolated economic struggle. The inevitable outcome of the strike led to the agreement, that is, tragically settled the friendly "discussion" in favor of the General Council.

From beginning to end, the entire policy of the Anglo-Russian Committee, because of its false line, provided only aid to the General Council. Even the fact that the strike was long sustained financially by the great self-sacrifice on the part of the Russian working class, did not serve the mine workers or the English Communist Party, but the very same General Council. As the upshot of the greatest revolutionary movement in England since the days of Chartism, the English Communist Party has hardly grown while the General Council sits in the saddle even more firmly than before the general strike.

Such are the results of this unique "strategical maneuver."

The obstinacy evinced in retaining the bloc with the General Council, which led to downright servility at the disgraceful Berlin session in April 1927, was explained away by the ever recurring reference to the very same "stabilization." If there is a setback in the development of the revolution, then, you see, one is forced to cling to Purcell. This argument, which appeared very profound to a Soviet functionary or to a trade unionist of the type of Melnichansky, is in reality a perfect example of blind empiricism—adulterated by scholasticism at that. What was the significance of "stabilization" in relation to English economy and politics, especially in the years 1926–27? Did it signify the development of the productive forces? The improvement of the economic situation? Better hopes for the future? Not at all. The whole so-called stabilization of English capitalism is maintained only upon the conservative forces of the old labor organizations with all their currents and shadings in the face of the weakness and irresoluteness of the English Communist Party. On the field of the economic and social relations of England, the revolution has already fully matured. The question stands purely politically. The basic props of the stabilization are the heads of the Labour Party and the trade unions, which in England constitute a single unit but which operate through a division of labor.

Given such a condition of the working masses as was revealed by the general strike, the highest post in the mechanism of capitalist stabilization is no longer occupied by MacDonald and Thomas, but by Pugh,[22] Purcell, Cook, and Company. They do the work and Thomas adds the finishing touches.

Without Purcell, Thomas would be left hanging in midair and along with Thomas also Baldwin. The chief brake upon the English revolution is the false, diplomatic masquerade "leftism" of Purcell which fraternizes sometimes in rotation, sometimes simultaneously with churchmen and Bolsheviks and which is always ready not only for retreats but also for betrayal. *Stabilization is Purcellism.* From this we see what depths of theoretical absurdity and blind opportunism are expressed in the reference to the existence of "stabilization" in order to justify the political bloc with Purcell. Yet, precisely in order to shatter the "stabilization," Purcellism had first to be destroyed. In such a situation, even a shadow of solidarity with the General Council was the greatest crime and infamy against the working masses.

Even the most correct strategy cannot, by itself, always lead to victory. The correctness of a strategical plan is verified by whether it follows the line of the actual development of class forces and whether it estimates the elements of this development realistically. The gravest and most disgraceful defeat which has the most fatal consequences for the movement is the typically Menshevist defeat, due to a false estimate of the classes, an underestimation of the revolutionary factors, and an idealization of the enemy forces. Such were our defeats in China and in England.

Notes

Part 1

1. Charles Dawes (1865–1951), Republican vice-president of the United States (1925–29), developed the **Dawes Plan,** the U.S. proposal to assist the post–World War I recovery of German capitalism and avert a revolution there.

2. **Julius Barnes** was an influential financier.

3. **The Third (Communist) International** was organized under Lenin's leadership as the revolutionary successor to the Second International. In Lenin's time, the World Congress was held once a year. Trotsky regarded the theses of the Comintern's first four congresses as the programmatic cornerstone of the Left Opposition and later of the Fourth International. By 1924, Stalin's machine, in a bloc with Zinoviev and Kamenev, was already in control of the Comintern. Stalin announced the dissolution of the Comintern in 1943 as a gesture to his wartime allies.

4. **J. Pierpont Morgan** (1887–1943) was a major American finance capitalist who acted as the agent of the Allied governments in floating large loans in the United States during World War I.

5. Trotsky later revised his position somewhat. In a March 1929 letter to the American Opposition, for instance, he wrote: "... in the last historical analysis all the problems of our planet will be decided upon American soil. There is much in favor of the idea that from the standpoint of revolutionary order, Europe and the East stand ahead of the United States. But a course of events is possible in which the order might be broken in favor of the proletariat of the United States" ("Tasks of the American Opposition," in **Writings of Leon Trotsky (1929)** [Pathfinder Press, New York]).

6. **Charles I** (1600–1649) had dissolved three British parliaments

in four years for noncompliance with his demands for defense allocations and had ruled for eleven years without a parliament. Parliament created its own army, and the civil war began in 1642. It ended three years later with a rout of the royalist forces by the parliamentary army under Cromwell's command. Charles was beheaded as an enemy of the nation.

Oliver Cromwell (1599–1658), then a member of Parliament, had assumed the task of forging an antiroyalist army. After the royalist forces were defeated, the parliamentary army refused to disband, and demanded the election of a new parliament on the basis of universal manhood suffrage. Cromwell suppressed the revolutionary agitation. In 1653 he assumed the title Lord Protector of the Commonwealth.

Two years after Cromwell's death, the monarchy was restored under **Charles II** (1630–1685), son of the executed Charles I.

7. British Protestants of the sixteenth and seventeenth centuries who regarded the Elizabethan reform of the church as incomplete were called **Puritans.** Those who did not emigrate to the American colonies grew to impressive political status during the Commonwealth (1649–1659).

8. A dispute between Germany and France over "political rights" in Morocco erupted in July 1911 with a bomb explosion in **Agadir** and the appearance there of a German gunboat. War between the two countries seemed imminent, with England siding with France. In a treaty signed later that year, both sides made concessions.

9. **James Ramsay MacDonald** (1866–1937) opposed British entry into World War I and consequently lost the leadership of the Labour Party in 1914. In 1924, however, he was prime minister of Britain's first Labour government, and in 1929 of its second Labour government. In 1931 he quit the Labour Party to form the "National" government, a coalition with the Tories.

10. With the British coalminers' postwar demands for higher wages, and the reversion of the mines to private ownership, the mine owners announced a wage cut and initiated a lock-out. The miners sought help from their fellow trade unionists in the **Triple Alliance,** but when the miners refused to consider a humiliating compromise proposal, J.H. Thomas, then general secretary of the railwaymen's

union, called off the general strike begun in support of the miners. Within two months of that announcement ("Black Friday," April 15, 1921), the miners were starved into submission.

11. **The British Labour Party** was founded in 1906. It developed out of the Labour Representation Committee, which had been constituted in 1899 to secure the election of Labour members to Parliament. Individual members were not accepted until 1918.

12. **The Liberals** were a coalition of reformers that emerged from the Whigs in the mid-nineteenth century.

13. **David Lloyd George** (1863–1945) was the Liberal prime minister from 1916 to 1922. After the war, he coauthored the Versailles Treaty.

14. **Karl Marx** (1818–1883) was, with Frederick Engels, the founder of scientific socialism and a leader of the First International (1864–76).

The Conservative Party, or Tories, emerged in the eighteenth century from the old royalist party of the civil war, the Cavaliers. Formerly the party of the aristocracy, they exist in Britain today as the party of the current ruling class, the bourgeoisie.

15. **The Constitutional Democrats,** or Cadets, of Russia were a bourgeois party committed to a constitutional monarchy and moderate liberalism. It dominated the Provisional Government from February to October 1917.

16. **Chartism** (1838–50) was a movement of revolutionary agitation around "the people's charter," a six-point petition drawn up in 1837 by the London Workingmen's Association in response to the fraudulent Reform Bill of 1832, which partially extended the franchise, although it remained restricted to the middle class. The charter proposed, among other things, universal suffrage and abolition of property requirements. Despite the threat of a general strike, the House of Commons rejected the charter in 1839. Only in 1867 and 1884 was legislation finally passed meeting the Chartists' chief demands.

17. **The Reform Bill of 1832** extended the franchise and redistributed the constituencies to avoid some of the more obvious gerrymandering. However, most workers and all women remained without the vote.

The Corn Laws were protective legislation which enforced starvation on some Britons to ensure high profits for certain agricultural magnates by preventing the import of competitively priced grain.

18. **William E. Gladstone** (1809–1898) became leader of the Liberal Party in 1867 and was prime minister four times between 1868 and 1894.

Joseph Chamberlain (1836–1914), a Liberal, was in two Gladstone cabinets. He resigned as colonial secretary in 1895 over the refusal of the government to grant tariff preference to colonial grain and food.

19. **Archibald P. Primrose, Lord Rosebery** (1847–1929) was Liberal prime minister (1894–95), and advocated an imperialist policy during the Boer War.

20. **Sidney Webb** (1859–1947) was one of the founders of the Fabian Society and helped begin the **New Statesman**. He collaborated on a number of books with his wife and lifetime companion, **Beatrice Webb** (1858–1943). Both were opponents of Bolshevism, but they came to admire the Stalinized Soviet Union of the 1930s.

21. **Stanley Baldwin** (1867–1947) was Conservative prime minister (1923, 1925–29, 1935–37).

22. **Robert Owen** (1771–1858) was a Welsh philanthropist and social experimenter. He founded several utopian communities in Britain and the United States, all of which failed.

23. **Arthur J. Cook** (1885–1931) was a militant miner and secretary of the Miners' Federation in 1924. He authored the widely circulated strike pamphlet **The Nine Days,** a bitter condemnation of the General Council's betrayal of the miners.

John Wheatley (1869–1930) was minister of health in the first Labour cabinet (1924).

24. **Russia's three revolutions.** The first revolution, in 1905, grew out of discontent over the Russo-Japanese war. Although it was crushed by the czar, Trotsky called it a dress rehearsal for later events. In February 1917, the czar was overthrown and the bourgeois Provisional Government was set up. It lasted until October, when the soviets, under the leadership of the Bolsheviks, came to power.

25. **Sir George W. Buchanan** (1854–1924) was the British am-

bassador to Russia from 1910 to 1918, and encouraged British intervention against the Bolsheviks.

Grigori E. Rasputin (1871?–1916) was an illiterate peasant, mystic, and favorite of the Russian court, who gained ascendancy over Nicholas II and Alexandra. His interference in religious and secular politics generated a national uproar. He was assassinated by Russian noblemen.

26. **Robert Gascoyne-Cecil, Lord Salisbury** (1830–1903) was secretary for India (1866–67, 1874–78). He was also prime minister and foreign secretary (1885–92, 1895–1902), annexed Burma, secured an "open door" in China, and conducted the Boer War (1899–1902).

27. **General Frederick Roberts** (1832–1914) led the British to victory over the Boer guerrillas in May 1902.

28. **The Roundheads,** so called because of their close-cropped hair, were Puritans and adherents of Cromwell during the Great Rebellion. They fought as antiroyalists in the parliamentary army.

The Cavaliers were royalists who fought on the side of Charles I.

The Independents were a coalition of sects and religious dissidents in the parliamentary army during the Great Rebellion who demanded religious toleration and vigorous prosecution of the rebellion.

29. After Charles I had dissolved the Short Parliament (April–May 1640) for noncompliance with his demands for defense funds, Scotland invaded England and forced him to a humiliating armistice. The **Long Parliament** was then convened (November 1640) and compelled the king to accept its program of reform. Within two years the king and Parliament were locked in military combat. The Long Parliament was in session from 1640 to 1660.

30. **Ethel Snowden** (1881–1951) was prominent in the Independent Labour Party and a crusader for a spectrum of "good causes" ranging from a negotiated settlement to the imperialist war to the welfare of the British royal family.

Thomas B. Macaulay (1800–1859) was an English writer and a member of Parliament (1830–34, 1839–47, 1852–56); he was also secretary of war (1839–41). He is the author of **The History of**

England, covering the reigns of James II and William III.

31. **William Pitt** (1759–1806) initiated the Combinations Act, which made trade union activity illegal. The act was repealed in 1825.

32. **The July revolution of 1830** in France, against undemocratic and unconstitutional acts by the king, led to the replacement of King Charles X by Louis Philippe, a former Jacobin with a revolutionary record. He appeased the rebellious workers with an extension of the franchise.

33. **William MacKenzie** (1795–1861) was a Canadian reform leader who led a Toronto uprising in 1837 with the intention of setting up a provisional government. When that failed, he fled to the U.S., but was arrested and imprisoned until 1840.

34. **Henry J. Temple, Viscount Palmerston** (1784–1865) was prime minister from 1855 to 1865, and supported the policy of "neutrality" in the American Civil War.

35. **Philip Snowden** (1864–1937) was chairman of the Independent Labour Party (1903–06, 1917–20) and a member of Parliament (1906–18, 1922–31). He was in both MacDonald Labour governments, but he resigned from the National government because of MacDonald's protectionist measures.

36. **George Curzon** (1859–1925), a Conservative Party leader, proposed a British declaration of war on the Soviet Union in the spring and summer of 1920, as the Red Army approached Warsaw. Only the threat of a general strike prevented Britain's intervention against the USSR.

37. **James H. Thomas** (1874–1949) was general secretary of the National Union of Railwaymen. He was responsible for the Black Friday (1921) sellout of the miners and was later one of the three negotiators with Baldwin in the general strike of 1926. He deserted the Labour Party with MacDonald to form the coalition government with the Tories, and was consequently expelled from the railway union without a pension.

38. **Winston Churchill** (1874–1965) began his political career as a Tory, switched to the Liberals in 1906, and then reverted to the Tories in 1924. He was a leading advocate of intervention against Soviet Russia after the Bolshevik revolution, and a director of the

efforts to break the 1911 strike of the Liverpool dockworkers. He was prime minister from 1940 to 1945 and from 1951 to 1955.

39. In 1707 England and Scotland united under the **Act of Union** to form the Kingdom of Great Britain.

40. **George Lansbury** (1859–1940) was an early British socialist, a Labour MP, and a founder of the party's newspaper **The Daily Herald**. Throughout his life, he was a member of the Church of England.

41. **David Kirkwood** (1872–1955) was a member of the ILP and a member of Parliament from 1922 to 1952. He was a pacifist but opposed an engineers' strike during World War I on the basis of "national defense."

42. Named after its founder, the French theologian John Calvin (1509–1564), **Calvinism** was a sixteenth-century religious doctrine emphasizing predestination.

43. **George Canning** (1770–1827) was a supporter of Pitt, and feared the impact of the French Revolution on England. He edited **The Anti-Jacobin** during Pitt's administration.

44. **Arthur Henderson** (1863–1935) was instrumental in securing Labour Party support of the British war policy in World War I. He was also president of the Second (Socialist) International (1925–29).

45. **The Fabian Society** was founded in 1883 in London by George Bernard Shaw, Sidney Webb, and others. They called themselves socialists but rejected Marxism and called for achieving socialism through a gradual evolutionary reform of capitalism. In the early 1890s, Fabian branches became Independent Labour Party bodies, and were widely influential.

46. **Henry M. Hyndman** (1842–1921) was a founder of the British Social Democratic Federation in 1881. He left the British Socialist Party in 1916 and organized the National Socialist Party.

47. **William Godwin** (1756–1836) was an English philosopher, romantic, and primitive radical.

Wilhelm Weitling (1808–1871) was a German utopian and an early collaborator with Marx.

Nikolai Chernyshevsky (1828?–1889) was a Russian anarchist exiled to Siberia by Alexander II in 1864. He wrote **What Is To Be Done?,** a novel with a profound impact on the Russian populists.

48. The English text is translated from the Russian, which in turn was translated from the Prague Social Revolutionary newspaper **Volya Narodnaya** (People's Will).

49. In order to defeat MacDonald's Labour government in the general elections of 1924, the Tories forged a letter purportedly giving the British Communist Party "instructions" on taking over the Labour Party. It was supposedly signed by Grigori Zinoviev (1883–1936), in his capacity as president of the Communist International.

50. **The Independent Labour Party** was founded in 1893 by Keir Hardie and Ramsay MacDonald. The party played a major role in the founding of the Labour Party, to which it was affiliated and in which it usually held a position on the left. At the outbreak of World War I, the ILP at first adopted an antiwar position, but later supported the British war role. The ILP left the Second International when the Comintern was formed, but did not join it. When it returned to the Second International, its left wing split to join the Communist Party. Briefly attracted by the Stalinists, and then by other centrists, the ILP left the Labour Party in 1931, but later returned.

51. **The Entente,** or alliance, between France, Russia, Britain, and Serbia went to war against Austria-Hungary and Germany in August 1914, thus beginning World War I.

52. **The English Reformation** began when King Henry VIII obtained from Parliament the Act of Supremacy, creating the Anglican (English) Church with Henry as its head, and disestablishing the Roman Catholic Church. In 1535 he suppressed the monasteries in England and confiscated their properties.

53. **Vladimir Ilyich Lenin** (1870–1924) initiated the political tendency that became known as Bolshevism, which was the first to point the way on how to build the kind of party needed to lead a working class revolution. He was a main leader of the first victorious workers' revolution in Russia in 1917, and served as the first head of state of the Soviet government. He founded the Communist International and helped elaborate its principles, strategy, and tactics.

54. **John Stuart Mill** (1806–1873) was an English economist and philosopher. Among his books is **Principles of Political Economy,**

an application of economic theory to social conditions.

55. **Karl Kautsky** (1854–1938) was regarded as the outstanding Marxist theoretician until World War I, when he abandoned internationalism. He later opposed the Russian Revolution. In 1891 he had drafted the **Erfurt Program,** which was the model program for all the European Social Democratic parties, including the Russian one.

56. **George Bernard Shaw** (1856–1950), playwright and socialist, was a founder of the Fabian movement.

57. **The "enlighteners"** were members of a movement begun in the eighteenth century for the emancipation of culture and science from ignorance.

58. At the time that Trotsky wrote this book (1925), fascism had been in power in Italy only a few years, and it was difficult to distinguish between some of its essential features and others that were secondary or purely national. Later, when fascism began to have a mass following in Germany, it was easier to single out its basic characteristics. As is shown in the major collection of his writings on the subject, **The Struggle Against Fascism in Germany** (Pathfinder Press, 1971), Trotsky then began to use the term "fascism" with more precision than he had in 1925.

59. **Hohenzollern** was the name of the ruling family of Prussia and, after 1870, of Germany. They were closely related to the British royal family. The dynasty fell with the November 1918 revolution in Germany.

The German Social Democratic Party was founded in 1875 by a fusion of Marx's followers with those of the German socialist Ferdinand Lassalle. In August 1914, the German party became the first to support its government in World War I, thus violating the most elementary socialist principles.

60. **The June 3 regime** in Russia began on June 3, 1907, when Peter Stolypin (1862–1911), czarist prime minister, began a series of reforms, after a "pacification" program in which thousands were executed.

The Russian Mensheviks were moderate socialists who claimed allegiance to Karl Marx but believed that the working class must combine with the liberal bourgeoisie to overthrow czarism and establish a democratic bourgeois republic.

61. **Edward Carson** (1854–1935) was a member of Parliament who acted as a spokesman for the Irish Unionists. He organized the formation of the Unionist paramilitary force in Ulster, and the signing of the covenant to oppose self-determination for Ireland.

62. In 1920, in preparation for the Second World Congress of the Comintern, Lenin wrote **Left-Wing Communism: An Infantile Disorder,** urging the British Communists to make use of the electoral opportunities that parliamentary democracy gave them.

63. **John R. Clynes** (1869–1949) was a Labour member of Parliament for twenty-five years, and deputy leader of the House of Commons in the first British Labour cabinet.

64. **Robert Williams,** a leader of the transport workers, was expelled from the British Communist Party for violating discipline in 1921. He later became a Labourite and an advocate of class peace and collaboration. Trotsky's statement that Williams has since "changed" was given in the British translation as "Williams has since ratted."

65. **Paul Lafargue** (1842–1911) was an organizer of the early Marxist movement in France. He married Marx's daughter Laura.

66. **Louis Blanqui** (1805–1881) was a participant in several nineteenth-century uprisings and spent thirty-three of his seventy-six years in prison. His name has become associated with the theory of armed insurrection by small groups of selected and trained conspirators, as opposed to revolution based on mass action and organization.

67. **The Paris Commune** was the first example of a workers' government. It was in power from March 18 to May 28, 1871, just seventy-two days, before it was overthrown in a bloody series of battles.

68. **The Levellers** were a political party that developed from the "agitators" of the parliamentary army during the Great Rebellion. They were representatives elected from the military to oppose the Long Parliament's proposal for disbanding the army. Their demands for "parity, equality, and universal suffrage" were rejected, and the party itself was suppressed by Cromwell.

69. **Benito Mussolini** (1883–1945) was a socialist in his youth,

but organized the fascist movement in Italy, and took power in 1922 as dictator, crushing the Italian labor movement and banning opposition parties.

70. **Maximilien Robespierre** (1758–1794) became the leader of the radical popular party, the Montagnards, during the Great French Revolution, and was effective head of state from 1793 to 1794.

Alexei Arakcheyev (1769–1834) was a political advisor to the Russian czar Alexander I and was minister of war in 1806.

71. During the Great French Revolution, the counterrevolutionaries were strongest in the province of **Vendee**. Trotsky is drawing an analogy between the southeastern plains in Russia, homeland of the reactionary Cossacks, and the French province.

72. **John Hampden** (1594–1643), Cromwell's cousin, raised an infantry for Parliament after being impeached as one of the five MPs in opposition to the king.

73. **The Girondists** were moderate bourgeois republicans during the French Revolution. They wanted to overthrow the old regime but they feared the city poor and the peasant masses who were capable of overthrowing it, and they therefore wavered between the revolution and the counterrevolution, finally going over to the latter.

74. **Martin Luther** (1483–1546) was a German religious reformer who initiated the Protestant Reformation in Germany.

75. **The Barebone's Parliament,** named for one of its more obscure members, Praise-God Barebone, was summoned by Cromwell in 1653. Within a few months, the Parliament was dissolved, and Cromwell was installed as Lord Protector of the Commonwealth.

76. **Herbert Henry Asquith** (1852–1928) was Liberal prime minister of England from 1908 to 1916.

77. **Richard Cobden** (1804–1865) was an English industrialist and politician, the leader of the Free Traders (a mid-nineteenth-century group opposed to protective tariffs) and a founder of the Anti-Corn Law League (1839), which propagandized against protective tariffs on agricultural products, especially grain.

78. **Theodore Roosevelt** (1858–1919) was the twenty-sixth president of the United States, succeeding to the office on McKinley's death (1901) and holding office for an additional term (until 1909).

Because of the efforts of the "muckrakers," Roosevelt launched an aggressive-sounding campaign against American trusts and monopolies.

79. **John Burns** (1858–1943) was a labor organizer and a Left MP who became a cabinet member as president of a local government board in 1905.

80. **Robert Smillie** (1859–1940) was president of the Miners' Federation and was its representative to the General Council.

81. **Sir Edward Grey** (1862–1933) was responsible for consolidating the wartime alliance among Britain, France, and Russia. Before 1914, he had secretly committed Britain to the defense of France in case of war.

Austen Chamberlain (1863–1937) was the half-brother of Neville Chamberlain. In 1921, he helped draft the plans for decontrolling the postwar coal industry, which led to the lockout of the miners and their eventual defeat.

82. **The Second International** was established in 1889 as the organization of the Social Democratic parties. It collapsed with the outbreak of World War I, when the majority of its members chose to ally with their respective national bourgeoisies in the imperialist conflict. After the war, it was reassembled on the basis of class collaboration and reformism.

83. **August Bebel** (1840–1913) was a cofounder with Wilhelm Liebknecht of the German Social Democracy. The party became powerful under his leadership, which formally rejected revisionism but bore responsibility for the growth of the opportunist tendencies that took over the party shortly after his death.

Centrism is the term used by Trotsky for tendencies in the radical movement that stand or vacillate between reformism, which is the position of the labor bureaucracy and the labor aristocracy, and Marxism, which expresses the historic interests of the working class. Since a centrist tendency has no independent social base, it must be evaluated in terms of its origins, its internal dynamic, and the direction it is taking or being pushed in by events.

84. **Philipp Scheidemann** (1865–1939) and **Friedrich Ebert** (1870–1925) took over the leadership of the German Social Democratic Party after Bebel's death in 1913. They were supporters of

German militarism in World War I, and were instrumental in defeating the November 1918 revolution in Germany. They were responsible for the murder of German revolutionists, including Karl Liebknecht and Rosa Luxemburg. Ebert was the first president of the Weimar Republic (1919–25).

85. **Benjamin Disraeli, Lord Beaconsfield** (1804–1881) was a member of the Young England Party and a political opponent of Gladstone who supported the Corn Laws and championed protectionism. He was prime minister (1868, 1874–80).

86. This quotation has been retranslated from the Russian.

Part 2

1. The British miners' union fought a bitter strike from May 1 to November 1926. In solidarity, the British Trades Union Congress called a general strike, beginning May 3, 1926, but the reformist General Council of the Trades Union Congress called it off after nine days, with an agreement between the government and the officials of the TUC.

2. From **Communist International,** no. 22, 1926. All quotes in this article have been retranslated from the Russian.

3. **The Russian Bolsheviks** were the majority wing of the Russian Social Democracy after 1903, who believed that the workers had to unite with the poor peasants, taking the lead in a struggle against the bourgeoisie. They led the successful October Revolution in 1917.

4. Within a week of the Liverpool Conference's decision to bar Communists from membership, the annual Conservative Party convention opened a campaign against the Communists. A week later the London headquarters of the CP was raided and the dozen most prominent leaders arrested. They were convicted of seditious libel and given sentences from six to twelve months.

5. **The Independent Social Democratic Party of Germany** was a left split-off from the right-wing German Social Democracy in 1917. In 1920 the majority of the Independents voted to fuse with the Communist Party of Germany, leaving the rest to rejoin the German Social Democratic Party in 1922.

The Social Revolutionary Party (SRs), founded in 1900, soon became the political expression of the Russian populist currents; prior to the 1917 revolution, it had the largest share of influence among the peasants. In October 1917, the party split, with the left wing forming a coalition government with the Bolsheviks. The coalition broke up when the left SRs turned against the Soviet government for signing the peace of Brest-Litovsk with Germany.

6. **Wilhelm Groener** (1867–1939) was Hindenburg's chief of staff at the end of World War I. He was at the head of the German army during the November 1918 revolution.

7. **The Spartacists** (Spartacus League) was organized by Rosa Luxemburg, Karl Liebknecht, and the antiwar wing of the German Social Democracy. The name derives from Spartacus, the leader of a slave uprising at the end of the Roman Republic, which was crushed by the party of Julius Caesar.

Karl Liebknecht (1871–1919) was a prominent left-wing Social Democrat who led the opposition to World War I within the German party. He formed the Spartacus League with **Rosa Luxemburg** (1871–1919), an outstanding leader of the Marxist movement and a prominent opponent of revisionism and opportunism before World War I. They were both jailed for antiwar activity at the outbreak of the war; but they were freed by the November 1918 uprising and organized the German Communist Party. They were assassinated in January 1919 by officers of the Social Democratic government.

8. **Paul von Hindenburg** (1847–1934) had been the commander of German forces in World War I. He was elected president of the Weimar Republic in 1925, succeeding Ebert, and with Social Democratic support was reelected in 1932. He appointed Hitler chancellor in January 1933.

9. **William Joynson-Hicks** (1865–1932), as Baldwin's home secretary (1924–29), was responsible for the conviction of the twelve Communists in 1925, and for the strikebreaking during the 1926 general strike.

10. **Henry Noel Brailsford** (1873–1958), a pacifist during World War I, was the editor of the Independent Labour Party newspaper, **The New Leader,** from 1922 to 1926.

Albert A. Purcell (1872–1935), a left Labourite, was a labor leader and an MP. In 1924 he was chairman of an official Trades Union

Congress delegation to the Soviet Union, which helped pave the way for the Anglo-Russian Trade Union Unity Committee.

11. The French invasion of the Ruhr in 1923, because Germany had not paid reparations on time, triggered a revolutionary situation that rapidly turned a majority of the German working class toward support of the Communist Party. But the CP leadership wavered, missed an exceptionally favorable opportunity to conduct a struggle for power, and the German capitalists were able to recover their balance before the year was ended. The Kremlin's responsibility for this wasted opportunity was one of the factors that led Trotsky to form the Russian Left Opposition at the end of 1923.

12. **Arthur J. Cook** (1885–1931) was a militant leader of the miners, twice imprisoned for his strike activities. He became a member of the General Council of the Trades Union Congress in 1927.

Arthur Crispien (1875–1946) was a leader of the Independent Social Democratic Party of Germany who opposed affiliation with the Comintern.

Rudolph Hilferding (1877–1941) was also a member of the Independents who left the Second International but refused to join the Third. In 1923 he became minister of finance in the Weimar Republic.

13. The International Federation of Trade Unions, based in Amsterdam, included the British Trades Union Congress and was opposed to the Red International of Labor Unions, which included trade unions associated with the Third International.

14. **John Bromley** (1876–1945) was general secretary for the Association of Locomotive Engineers and Firemen. He was later elected to the General Council of the Trades Union Congress, where he and others in the left wing of the Labour Party defended the rights of the Communist Party. He caused a scandal by exposing the secret report of the General Council on the general strike, which made clear the cowardly role of the trade union leaders in negotiations with the government.

15. **The American Relief Association** (ARA) provided medicine and supplies to the famine- and disease-ridden areas of Europe at the end of World War I. It particularly served the counterrevolutionary White Guard forces during the civil war in Russia.

16. **John Bunyan** (1628–1688) defended the "Gospel truth" against the religious deviance of the Quakers. He wrote **Pilgrim's Progress**.

The Anabaptists were a religious sect that originated in Zurich, Switzerland, in 1523. They opposed infant baptism and the union of church and state, and advocated the renunciation of private possessions in a sort of religious communalism.

The Fifth Monarchy Men were a fanatical religious sect that arose in England during the Cromwell era. They believed that the Fifth Monarchy, prophesied in Daniel II as Christ's thousand-year rule on earth, was to be installed by force.

17. **Nadezhda K. Krupskaya** (1869–1939) was a leader of the Bolshevik Party and was married to Lenin. In 1926–27 she sided with the Joint Opposition of Trotsky and Zinoviev against the Stalin machine.

18. **The Narodniks** (populists) were an organized movement of Russian intellectuals who conducted activities among the peasantry from 1876 to 1879, when they split. One faction later developed into the Social Revolutionary Party.

19. **Georges Clemenceau** (1841–1929), as premier of France in 1906–09 and 1917–20, used military force to break a miners' strike. He also headed the French delegation to the Versailles conference in 1919.

20. **Bertrand Russell** (1872–1970), an English mathematician and philosopher, was a pacifist during World War I. Towards the end of his life he was a leader of the anti–Vietnam War movement, and organized a War Crimes Tribunal that found the United States government guilty of war crimes in Southeast Asia.

21. **Leon Blum** (1872–1950) was the leader of the French Socialist Party and premier of the Popular Front governments in 1936 and 1937.

Jean Longuet (1876–1938) was a right-wing French Socialist.

22. **Alexandre Millerand** (1859–1943) in 1899 became the first socialist to enter a bourgeois cabinet, and was subsequently expelled from the French Socialist Party. He held several ministerial posts, and was elected president of the French Republic in 1920. As

prime minister, he was an advocate of French intervention against Soviet Russia.

23. **Andre Marty** (1886–1956) led a mutiny on April 16, 1919, among French sailors of the Black Sea fleet, which had been sent to assist the counterrevolutionary White Guard in Russia. The fleet was withdrawn. Marty became a prominent figure in the French CP.

24. **The American Federation of Labor** was founded in 1881 as a conservative federation of skilled craft unions. In 1935, several member unions formed the Committee of Industrial Organizations, which later became a federation of industrial unions.

25. **Emile Vandervelde** (1866–1941) was a Belgian Socialist Party leader and president of the Second International (1929–36). When World War I broke out, he joined the bourgeois cabinet.

Albert Thomas (1878–1932), a member of the French Socialist Party, joined the French coalition government in 1914.

26. **Brest-Litovsk** was a town on the Russo-Polish border where a treaty ending hostilities between Russia and Germany was signed by the Soviet delegation on March 3, 1918. The terms were exceedingly unfavorable for Soviet interests, but the new Soviet government had to sign because it was unable at that time to continue fighting.

27. **Scott Nearing** (1883–1983) is an American scholar and sociologist who was dismissed from his university post for his opposition to World War I. He is the author of many books, including **Poverty and Riches, Education in Soviet Russia,** etc.

28. **John Scott Haldane** (1860–1936) was a Scottish scientist who conducted extensive research into mining and industrial diseases caused by poor ventilation.

29. **Jeremy Bentham** (1748–1832), an English jurist and philosopher, was one of the chief exponents of the utilitarian ethic that the morality of actions is determined by utility, the actions' capacity for giving pleasure or preventing pain.

30. **Joseph Stalin** (1879–1953) became general secretary of the Communist Party in 1922. Lenin called in 1923 for his removal from the post of general secretary because he was using it to bureaucratize the party and state apparatuses. After Lenin's death in

1924, Stalin gradually eliminated his major opponents, starting with Trotsky, until he became virtual dictator of the party and the Soviet Union in the 1930s. The chief concepts associated with his name are "socialism in one country," "social fascism," and "peaceful coexistence."

Gregory E. Zinoviev (1883–1936) was a top Bolshevik leader, and the first president of the Comintern. With Kamenev, he was an ally of Stalin in initiating the crusade against "Trotskyism," and then joined with Trotsky to form the Joint Opposition against Stalinism until the Opposition was defeated and the leaders expelled in 1927. He recanted in 1928, but was executed in 1936 as one of the first victims of the Moscow purge trials.

Leon Kamenev (1883–1936) was, like Zinoviev, an Old Bolshevik. With Zinoviev, he capitulated in 1927 and was reinstated in 1928; was expelled again in 1932 and capitulated again in 1933. He was also a victim of the first Moscow trial.

31. **Gregory Chicherin** (1872–1936) had been in the czarist diplomatic service until 1904, but resigned out of sympathy with revolutionary agitation. After the revolution he became People's Commissar of Foreign Affairs (1918–30).

32. **Frank B. Kellogg** (1856–1937), U.S. secretary of state from 1925 to 1929, protested the nationalization of U.S.-owned property in Mexico by the president of Mexico. He was also the author of the Kellogg Pact, an agreement signed by fifteen nations in 1928 to renounce war as an instrument of national policy. It was later ratified by a total of sixty-three countries, including the Soviet Union.

33. **The National Minority Movement,** begun in August 1924, represented some 200,000 British trade union militants organized around the formation of factory committees and in favor of industrial unionism. At its height, it commanded the loyalty of about 25 percent of the trade union movement.

34. **Shapuri Saklatvala,** an Indian, was recruited to the British Communist Party from the Independent Labour Party. He spent two months in jail for a May Day speech given in Hyde Park just before the general strike.

35. The Organization for the Maintenance of Supplies **(OMS)**

was a "volunteer" organization begun in the months preceding the general strike to systematize strikebreaking activity.

Part 3

1. The **T. Stewart** referred to here is probably R. Stewart, who was then acting secretary of the British Communist Party.—Trans.

2. British and Russian trade union leaders formed the **Anglo-Russian Trade Union Unity Committee** on May 14, 1925, for the purpose of achieving trade union unity and averting the imperialist war danger. The British section of the Committee included members of the General Council of the Trades Union Congress, the British labor federation, who used it as a device to shield themselves against criticism from the left. It was particularly useful to them in the tense situation that existed in the period before and during the general strike in 1926. The Russians clung to the committee, however, even after the General Council betrayed the general strike, and it collapsed only when the British walked out of it in September 1927.

3. The policy of forming **united fronts** with other working class tendencies was formulated by Lenin and Trotsky and endorsed by the early congresses of the Comintern. It was based on the need to win over the masses of workers to a revolutionary course of action, in situations where a majority of the workers followed reformist leaders. Trotsky's reference here to the united front "from below" should not be confused with the policy followed by the Comintern during its "third period" (1928–34), when the Stalinists opposed united front action with the leaders of Social Democratic and other non-Stalinist organizations, insisting that united fronts were permissible only when achieved "from below," that is, over the heads of the leaderships of other organizations. This policy, which Trotsky vigorously opposed, guaranteed that no real united fronts could be built, and proved disastrous especially in Germany, where it helped pave the way for Hitler's seizure of power.

4. **Iraklii Tseretelli** (1882–1959) was a Russian Menshevik who supported World War I and held ministerial positions in the Provisional Government, from March to August 1917. He opposed the Bolshevik revolution in October, and emigrated in 1919.

Feodor Dan (1871–1947), a Menshevik leader, was on the presidium of the Petrograd Soviet in 1917. He later became an active opponent of the revolution. Arrested in 1921, he was expelled from the Soviet Union in 1922, and died in the United States.

Alexander Kerensky (1882–1970) was a member of the Russian Social Revolutionary Party and was head of the Provisional Government from July to October 1917.

5. The last three conferences of the Anglo-Russian Committee were held in Paris (July 1926), and in Berlin (August 1926 and April 1927). Trotsky, Zinoviev, Kamenev, Krupskaya, and Piatakov had called for the Russian delegation to walk out of the Anglo-Russian Committee at the July 1926 conference—the first opportunity after the General Council of the British Trades Union Congress had betrayed the general strike—and renewed their arguments after the August 1926 Berlin conference. But the Russian delegation, under Stalin's orders, argued that the committee only needed to be made into a more effective body. Trotsky refers to the Berlin experience as a capitulation because the Russian delegation, which should have publicly severed its connections with the British labor leaders, chose instead to sacrifice the needs of the British workers in the hope of appeasing British imperialism.

6. **Sir Walter Citrine** (1887–1993) was general secretary of the Trades Union Congress from 1926 to 1946.

7. The British government was sending war material to China in order to aid the bourgeois nationalist government under Chiang Kai-shek to crush the revolutionary upsurge in that country.

8. **Nikolai Bukharin** (1888–1938) was an Old Bolshevik and was the second president of the Comintern (after Zinoviev), 1926–29. He joined with Stalin against the Left Opposition, but they split in 1928 and Bukharin formed a Right Opposition before he was expelled in 1929. He capitulated, but was convicted and executed in the 1938 Moscow trial.

9. **Mikhail Tomsky** (1886–1936), an Old Bolshevik, was always in the right wing of the party and opposed the Bolshevik insurrection. He was head of the Soviet trade unions and a member of the Politburo until he joined the right-wing fight against Stalin led by Bukharin. He committed suicide during the first Moscow trial in 1936.

Andrei Andreyev (1895–1971) joined the Bolsheviks in 1914. For his loyalty to the Stalinists in the trade union apparatus, he was elevated to the Organization Bureau in the 1920s and to the Politburo in the thirties.

Grigory Melnichansky (1886–1937) joined the Russian Social Democracy in 1902. After the Bolshevik Revolution, he became the chairman of the Moscow Gubernia Council of Trade Unions.

10. **The Hague International Peace Congress,** December 10–15, 1922, was convened by the Amsterdam International. The Soviet delegation was invited on the demand of revolutionary trade unionists and over the resistance of the majority. The congress rejected the program of action that the Soviet delegation proposed for the proletariat with regard to war. Lenin's remarks were written on December 4.

11. Lord Curzon threatened Soviet Russia with war in 1920, when the Red Army was advancing on Warsaw.

12. The Stalinists counterposed support to the bourgeois nationalist Chinese government, under Chiang Kai-shek, to the building of independent organs of workers' and peasants' power.

13. **Chiang Kai-shek** (1887–1975) was the military leader of the bourgeois nationalist Kuomintang (People's Party) of China during the revolution of 1925–27. He stood in the right wing of that party, which the Communists had entered on the orders of the Comintern's Executive Committee. Chiang was hailed as a great revolutionary by the Stalinists until April 1927, when he conducted a bloody massacre of the Shanghai Communists and trade unionists.

14. **Alexei Rykov** (1881–1938), an Old Bolshevik, succeeded Lenin as chairman of the Council of People's Commissars. With Bukharin he led the right-wing tendency in the party. When Stalin broke with the right wing in 1929, Rykov recanted. He was removed from the post of chairman of the Council of People's Commissars in 1930. He was a defendant in the third Moscow trial in March 1938; he "confessed" and was executed.

15. **N. Uglanov** was picked by Stalin to replace Kamenev as secretary of the Moscow Communist Party in 1924, but in 1929 was himself branded as a Bukharinist. He was executed as a saboteur.

16. **Wang Ching-wei** (1884–1944) was the leader of the Chinese

government in the industrial area of Wuhan. Wang was as disappointing as Chiang in the role of revolutionist that the Stalinists assigned to him. Only six weeks after Chiang's coup at Shanghai, Wang attacked the workers in Wuhan.

George Hicks was secretary of the National Federation of Building Operatives in England. He was on the General Council during the betrayal of the general strike.

17. **The Radical Socialist (or Radical) Party of France,** neither radical nor socialist, was the principal capitalist party of France between World Wars I and II, comparable to the Democratic Party in the United States.

18. **Solomon A. Lozovsky** (1878–1952) was the head of the Red International of Labor Unions (Profintern), responsible for Stalinist trade union policy. He was arrested and shot on Stalin's orders during an anti-Semitic campaign.

19. **Dimitri Manuilsky** (1883–1952) was, along with Trotsky, a member of the independent Marxist organization Mezhrayontzi, which fused with the Bolshevik Party in 1917. In the twenties he supported the Stalin faction, and was secretary of the Communist International from 1931 until its dissolution twelve years later.

20. **Ferdinand Lassalle** (1825–1864) was a major figure in the German working class movement, and founder of the German Workers' Union. His followers joined the early Marxists in founding German Social Democracy.

21. **Harry Pollitt** (1890–1960), a leader of the CP, was elected first secretary of the Minority Movement at its founding in 1924. When Baldwin's police raided the CP headquarters in 1925, Pollitt and **J.T. Murphy,** the editor of **Workers' Weekly,** and ten other principal leaders of the British Communist Party were arrested on charges of sedition.

22. **Arthur Pugh** was chairman of the General Council of the Trades Union Congress during the general strike, and with Citrine and Thomas was one of the negotiators with Baldwin and the Tory government.

Other writings by Trotsky on Britain

Between *Where Is Britain Going?* in 1925 and his death in 1940, Leon Trotsky wrote many articles and letters about Britain in addition to those collected in the present volume. The following is a partial list:

Europe and America: Two Speeches on Imperialism contains "Europe and America," February 15, 1926 (as well as the earlier "Perspectives of World Development," July 28, 1924).

Leon Trotsky on China contains "The Chinese Revolution and the Theses of Comrade Stalin," May 7, 1927, whose sections 41–51 deal with the Anglo-Russian Committee.

The Stalin School of Falsification contains two 1927 speeches that deal with the Anglo-Russian Committee (pp. 167-69 and 199-201) [2009 printing].

Writings of Leon Trotsky (1929) contains "Why I Want to Come to London," June 11, 1929, written shortly after Trotsky had been exiled to Turkey and a new British Labour government had taken office.

Writings of Leon Trotsky (1930–31) contains "Tasks of the Left Opposition in Britain and India: Critical Remarks on an Unsuccessful Thesis," November 7, 1931; "The British Elections and the Communists," November 10, 1931; and "What Is a Revolutionary Situation?" November 17, 1931.

Writings of Leon Trotsky (1932–33) contains "Greetings to *The Red Flag*," May 19, 1933.

Writings of Leon Trotsky (1933–34) contains "Whither the Independent Labour Party?" August 28, 1933; "An Interview by C.A. Smith," August 29, 1933; "How to Influence the ILP," September 3, 1933; "The ILP and the New International," September 4, 1933;

"Principled Considerations on Entry," September 16, 1933; "The Fate of the British Section," September 25, 1933; "The Lever of a Small Group," October 2, 1933; "Cardinal Questions Facing the ILP," January 5, 1934—all written soon after Trotsky's arrival in France from Turkey.

Writings of Leon Trotsky (1935–36) contains "The ILP and the Fourth International: In the Middle of the Road," September 18, 1935, with an addition dated October 20, 1935; "Once Again the ILP," November 1935; "Open Letter to an English Comrade," April 3, 1936; "On Dictators and the Heights of Oslo," April 22, 1936; "Interview by Collins," summer 1936—all written in Norway.

Writings of Leon Trotsky (1937–38) contains "Fenner Brockway, Pritt No. 2," March 6, 1937, and "London Bureau Aids Stalin Frame-ups by Refusal to Join Probe Commission," September 5, 1937—both from Mexico.

Writings of Leon Trotsky (1938–39) contains "The Mexican Oil Expropriations: A Challenge to the British Labour Party," April 23, 1938; and "Mexico and British Imperialism," June 5, 1938—from Mexico.

Writings of Leon Trotsky (1939–40) contains "Will Not Write for the Daily Herald," October 23, 1939—from Mexico.

Index

Act of Union (1707), 68, 401n.
Afghanistan, 51.
Agadir incident, 33, 396n.
All-Union Central Council of Trade Unions, *see* Trade unions, in Soviet Union.
American Federation of Labor (AFL), 262, 281, 411n.
American Relief Administration (ARA), 238, 409n.
Amsterdam International, *see* International Federation of Trade Unions.
Anabaptists, 246, 410n.
Andreyev, Andrei, 345, 361–62, 363, 365–67, 370, 372, 373–74, 375–82, 384, 386, 415n.
Anglicanism, 73, 74, 143.
Anglo-Russian Trade Union Unity Committee, 10–11, 413n; and Chinese revolution, 16, 18, 342, 353, 354, 361, 376; and general strike, 14–17, 326–34, 335–40, 341–60; and Russian Communist Party, 343–60, 361–86; and war danger, 342, 343–44, 352–53, 354, 361, 364–65, 366–67, 379; Left Opposition on, 323–93 passim; as substitute for party, 387; broken, 371, 376–77; meetings of: Paris (July 1926), 326–27, 347, 414n; Berlin (August 1926), 337–38, 347, 414n; Berlin (April 1927), 16, 341–42, 345, 347–48, 350–56, 359, 362, 366, 373–79, 384, 392, 414n.
Arakcheyev, Alexei, 140, 405n.

Arcos raid, 17.
Armed forces (British), 13, 257–62.
Armed self-defense, 204–5.
Asquith, Herbert Henry, 154, 169, 227, 405n.
Atheism, 74, 81, 298.
Australia, 206–7, 232.

Badin, 261.
Baldwin, Stanley, 90, 122, 211, 226, 227, 393, 398n; and Anglo-Russian Committee, 329, 365; and democracy, 115, 154, 162–63; and gradualness, 44–65, 71, 103; jails Communists, 11, 199; and social peace, 66–67, 132–33, 172, 218.
Baltimore Sun, 306.
Barebones Parliament, 149–50, 405n.
Barnes, Julius, 26, 27, 303–5, 395n.
Beaconsfield, *see* Disraeli.
Bebel, August, 177, 406n.
Beer, Max, 32, 138.
Bentham, Jeremy, 279, 411n.
Bevan, Aneurin, 13–14.
Black Friday (April 15, 1921), 33.
Blanqui, Louis, 136, 404n.
Blum, Leon, 255, 410n.
Bolsheviks (Russia), 135, 201, 265, 407n.
Bourgeois democracy, 89, 117–18.
Brailsford, Henry Noel, 23, 208, 214, 228–29, 239–50, 300, 324, 336, 408n; and Communists' trial, 241, 242–43, 273; and pacifism, 253, 257; and religion, 275.
Bramley, Fred, 164–65.

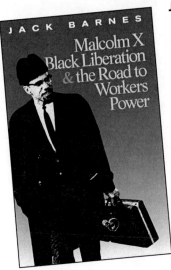

From the dictatorship of capital...

The Communist Manifesto

Karl Marx, Frederick Engels

Founding document of the modern revolutionary workers movement, published in 1848. Why communism is not a set of preconceived principles but the line of march of the working class toward power—a line of march "springing from an existing class struggle, a historical movement going on under our very eyes." $5. Also in Spanish, French, and Arabic.

State and Revolution

V.I. Lenin

"The relation of the socialist proletarian revolution to the state is acquiring not only practical political importance," wrote V.I. Lenin in this booklet just months before the October 1917 Russian Revolution. It also addresses the "most urgent problem of the day: explaining to the masses what they will have to do to free themselves from capitalist tyranny." In *Essential Works of Lenin*. $12.95

Their Trotsky and Ours

Jack Barnes

To lead the working class in a successful revolution, a mass proletarian party is needed whose cadres, well beforehand, have absorbed a world communist program, are proletarian in life and work, derive deep satisfaction from doing politics, and have forged a leadership with an acute sense of what to do next. This book is about building such a party. $16. Also in Spanish and French.

www.pathfinderpress.com

...to the dictatorship of the proletariat

Lenin's Final Fight
Speeches and Writings, 1922–23
V.I. Lenin

In 1922 and 1923, V.I. Lenin, central leader of the world's first socialist revolution, waged what was to be his last political battle. At stake was whether that revolution would remain on the proletarian course that had brought workers and peasants to power in October 1917—and laid the foundations for a truly worldwide revolutionary movement of toilers organizing to emulate the Bolsheviks' example. $20. Also in Spanish.

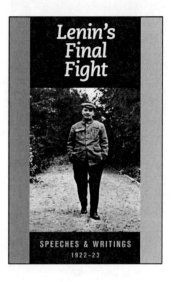

Trade Unions: Their Past, Present, and Future
Karl Marx

Apart from being instruments "required for guerrilla fights between capital and labor," the unions "must now act deliberately as organizing centers of the working class in the broad interest of its complete emancipation," through revolutionary political action. Drafted by Marx for the First International's founding congress in 1866, this resolution appears in *Trade Unions in the Epoch of Imperialist Decay* by Leon Trotsky. $16

The History of the Russian Revolution
Leon Trotsky

The social, economic, and political dynamics of the first socialist revolution as told by one of its central leaders. How, under Lenin's leadership, the Bolshevik Party led the overturn of the monarchist regime of the landlords and capitalists and brought to power a government of the workers and peasants. Unabridged, 3 vols. in one. $38. Also in Russian.

The Cuban Revolution and

Soldier of the Cuban Revolution
From the Cane Fields of Oriente to General
of the Revolutionary Armed Forces
Luis Alfonso Zayas
The author recounts his experiences over five
decades in the revolution. From a teenage
combatant in the clandestine struggle and
1956–58 war that brought down the US-
backed dictatorship, to serving three times as
a leader of the Cuban volunteer forces that
helped Angola defeat an invasion by the army
of white-supremacist South Africa, Zayas tells
how he and other ordinary men and women in
Cuba changed the course of history and, in the
process, transformed themselves as well. $18.
Also in Spanish.

Our History Is Still Being Written
The Story of Three Chinese-Cuban Generals
in the Cuban Revolution
Armando Choy, Gustavo Chui, and Moisés
Sío Wong talk about the historic place of
Chinese immigration to Cuba, as well as more
than five decades of revolutionary action and
internationalism, from Cuba to Angola and
Venezuela today. Through their stories we
see how millions of ordinary men and women
opened the door to socialist revolution in the
Americas, changed the course of history, and
became different human beings in the process.
$20. Also in Spanish and Chinese.

Marianas in Combat
Teté Puebla and the Mariana Grajales Women's Platoon
in Cuba's Revolutionary War 1956–58
Teté Puebla
Brigadier General Teté Puebla joined the struggle to overthrow the US-backed
Batista dictatorship in Cuba in 1956, at age fifteen. This is her story—from
clandestine action in the cities, to officer in the Rebel Army's first all-women's
platoon. The fight to transform the social and economic status of women is
inseparable from Cuba's socialist revolution. $14. Also in Spanish.

World Politics

United States vs. The Cuban Five
A Judicial Cover-Up
Rodolfo Dávalos Fernández

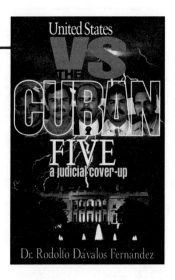

Held in US prisons since 1998, five Cuban revolutionists were framed up for being part of a "Cuban spy network" in Florida. They were keeping tabs for Cuban government on rightist groups with a long record of armed attacks on Cuba from US soil. "From start to finish," says the author, court proceedings were "tainted, corrupt, and vindictive. Every right to 'due process of law' was flouted." $22. Also in Spanish.

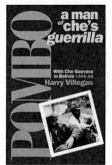

Pombo: A Man of Che's *guerrilla*
With Che Guevara in Bolivia, 1966–68
Harry Villegas

A firsthand account of the 1966–68 revolutionary campaign in Bolivia led by Ernesto Che Guevara. Under the nom de guerre Pombo, Harry Villegas, in his 20s at the time, was a member of Guevara's general staff. Villegas led the small group of combatants who survived the Bolivian army's encirclement and lived to recount this epic chapter in the history of the Americas. $23

Dynamics of the Cuban Revolution
A Marxist Appreciation
Joseph Hansen

How did the Cuban Revolution unfold? Why does it represent an "unbearable challenge" to US imperialism? What political obstacles has it overcome? Written as the revolution advanced from its earliest days. $25

October 1962
The 'Missile' Crisis as Seen from Cuba
Tomás Diez Acosta

In October 1962 Washington pushed the world to the edge of nuclear war. Here the full story of that historic moment is told from the perspective of the Cuban people, whose determination to defend their sovereignty and their socialist revolution blocked US plans for a devastating military assault. $25

www.pathfinderpress.com

The Curve of Capitalist Development

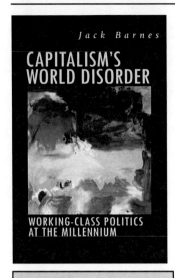

Jack Barnes

CAPITALISM'S WORLD DISORDER

WORKING-CLASS POLITICS AT THE MILLENNIUM

Capitalism's World Disorder

Working-Class Politics at the Millennium

Jack Barnes

The opening of the 21st century, says the author, is marked by a sea change in working-class politics, "defined by the actions of a vanguard resisting indignity and isolation, whose ranks increase with every single worker or farmer who reaches out to others with the hand of solidarity and offers to fight together." $25. Also in Spanish and French.

Imperialism, the Highest Stage of Capitalism

V.I. Lenin

Imperialism increases not only the weight of debt bondage and parasitism in capitalist social relations, writes Lenin, but above all makes the competition of rival capitals—domestic and foreign—more violent and explosive. Amid capitalism's growing world disorder, this 1916 booklet remains a foundation stone of the communist movement's program and activity. $10. Also in Spanish.

Capital

Karl Marx

Marx explains the workings of the capitalist system and how it produces the insoluble contradictions that breed class struggle. He demonstrates the inevitability of the fight for the revolutionary transformation of society into one ruled for the first time by the producing majority: the working class.
Volume 1, $18
Volume 2, $18
Volume 3, $18

PENGUIN CLASSICS
KARL MARX
CAPITAL
VOLUME I

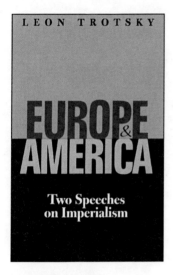

Europe and America

Two Speeches on Imperialism

Leon Trotsky

In two speeches from the mid-1920s, Russian Bolshevik leader Leon Trotsky explains why the emergence of the United States as imperialism's dominant economic and financial power became the decisive factor in international politics following World War I. He describes the sharpening conflicts between Washington and its European rivals and highlights the revolutionary prospects for the workers of the world. $12

The Curve of Capitalist Development

Leon Trotsky

Turning points in the long-term trends of capitalist development, wrote Trotsky in this 1923 article, are a product of factors outside the realm of "economics" as normally understood. Periods of advance, stagnation, and decline, the Bolshevik leader explained, are shaped by major developments in politics and the class struggle such as wars, uprisings, and revolutions. In *New International* no. 10. $16. Also in Spanish, French, and Swedish.

Imperialism's March toward Fascism and War

Jack Barnes

"There will be new Hitlers, new Mussolinis. That is inevitable. What is not inevitable is that they will triumph. The working-class vanguard will organize our class to fight back against the devastating toll we are made to pay for the capitalist crisis. The future of humanity will be decided in the contest between these contending class forces." In *New International* no. 10. $16. Also in Spanish, French, and Swedish.

The History of American Trotskyism, 1928–1938
Report of a Participant
JAMES P. CANNON

Trotskyism is not a new movement, a new doctrine," Cannon says, "but the restoration, the revival of genuine Marxism as it was expounded and practiced in the Russian revolution and in the early days of the Communist International." In twelve talks given in 1942, Cannon recounts a decisive period in efforts to build a proletarian party in the United States. $22. Also in Spanish and French.

Fighting Racism in World War II
From the Pages of the Militant

An account from 1939 to 1945 of struggles against racism and lynch-mob terror in face of patriotic appeals to postpone resistance until after US "victory" in World War II. These struggles—of a piece with anti-imperialist battles the world over—helped lay the basis for the mass Black rights movement in the 1950s and '60s. $25

The First Ten Years of American Communism
JAMES P. CANNON

A founding leader of the communist movement in the US recounts early efforts to build a proletarian party emulating the Bolshevik leadership of the October 1917 revolution in Russia. $22

In Defense of Marxism
Against the Petty-Bourgeois Opposition in the Socialist Workers Party
LEON TROTSKY

Writing in 1939–40, Leon Trotsky replies to those in the revolutionary workers movement beating a retreat from defense of the Soviet Union in face of the looming imperialist assault. Why only a party that fights to bring growing numbers of workers into its ranks and leadership can steer a steady revolutionary course. $25. Also in Spanish.

Class Struggle in the United States

Building a PROLETARIAN PARTY

Teamster Rebellion
FARRELL DOBBS

The first of a four-volume participant's account of how strikes and organizing drives across the Midwest in the 1930s, initiated by leaders of Teamsters Local 574 in Minneapolis, paved the way for industrial unions and a fighting working-class social movement. These battles showed what workers and farmers can achieve when they have the leadership they deserve. Dobbs was a central part of that class-struggle leadership. $19. Also in Spanish, French, and Swedish.

Revolutionary Continuity
Marxist Leadership in the U.S.
FARRELL DOBBS

How successive generations took part in struggles of the US labor movement, seeking to build a leadership that could advance the class interests of workers and small farmers and link up with fellow toilers around the world. Two volumes:

The Early Years, 1848–1917, $20; *Birth of the Communist Movement 1918–1922*, $19.

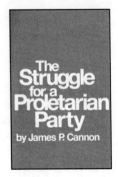

The Struggle for a Proletarian Party
JAMES P. CANNON

The workers of America have power enough to topple the structure of capitalism at home and to lift the whole world with them when they rise," Cannon asserts. On the eve of World War II, a founder of the communist movement in the US and leader of the Communist International in Lenin's time defends the program and party-building norms of Bolshevism. $22

Women's Liberation and Socialism

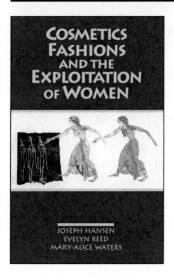

Cosmetics, Fashions, and the Exploitation of Women
Joseph Hansen, Evelyn Reed, Mary-Alice Waters

How big business plays on women's second-class status and social insecurities to market cosmetics and rake in profits. The introduction by Mary-Alice Waters explains how the entry of millions of women into the workforce during and after World War II irreversibly changed US society and laid the basis for a renewed rise of struggles for women's emancipation. $15

Abortion is a Woman's Right!
Pat Grogan, Evelyn Reed

Why abortion rights are central not only to the fight for the full emancipation of women, but to forging a united and fighting labor movement. $6. Also in Spanish.

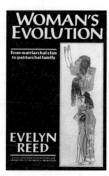

Woman's Evolution
From Matriarchal Clan to Patriarchal Family
Evelyn Reed

Assesses women's leading and still largely unknown contributions to the development of human civilization and refutes the myth that women have always been subordinate to men. "Certain to become a classic text in women's history"—*Publishers Weekly*. $32

New International

A MAGAZINE OF MARXIST POLITICS AND THEORY

NEW INTERNATIONAL NO. 14

REVOLUTION, INTERNATIONALISM, AND SOCIALISM: THE LAST YEAR OF MALCOLM X

Jack Barnes

"To understand Malcolm's last year is to see how, in the imperialist epoch, revolutionary leadership of the highest political capacity, courage, and integrity converges with communism. That truth has even greater weight today as billions around the world, in city and countryside, from China to Brazil, are being hurled into the modern class struggle by the violent expansion of world capitalism."—Jack Barnes

Also includes: "The Clintons' Antilabor Legacy: Roots of the 2008 World Financial Crisis"; "The Stewardship of Nature Also Falls to the Working Class: In Defense of Land and Labor" and "Setting the Record Straight on Fascism and World War II." $14. Also in Spanish, French, and Swedish.

NEW INTERNATIONAL NO. 12

CAPITALISM'S LONG HOT WINTER HAS BEGUN

Jack Barnes

and "Their Transformation and Ours,"
Resolution of the Socialist Workers Party

Today's sharpening interimperialist conflicts are fueled both by the opening stages of what will be decades of economic, financial, and social convulsions and class battles, and by the most far-reaching shift in Washington's military policy and organization since the US buildup toward World War II. Class-struggle-minded working people must face this historic turning point for imperialism, and draw satisfaction from being "in their face" as we chart a revolutionary course to confront it. $16. Also in Spanish, French, and Swedish. *Capitalism's Long Hot Winter Has Begun* is available in Arabic.

WWW.PATHFINDERPRESS.COM

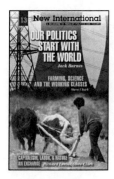

NEW INTERNATIONAL NO. 13
OUR POLITICS START WITH THE WORLD
Jack Barnes

The huge economic and cultural inequalities between imperialist and semicolonial countries, and among classes within almost every country, are produced, reproduced, and accentuated by the workings of capitalism. For vanguard workers to build parties able to lead a successful revolutionary struggle for power in our own countries, says Jack Barnes in the lead article, our activity must be guided by a strategy to close this gap.

Also includes: "Farming, Science, and the Working Classes" *by Steve Clark* and "Capitalism, Labor, and Nature: An Exchange" *by Richard Levins, Steve Clark.* $14. Also in Spanish, French, and Swedish.

NEW INTERNATIONAL NO. 11
U.S. IMPERIALISM HAS LOST THE COLD WAR
Jack Barnes

Contrary to imperialist expectations at the opening of the 1990s in the wake of the collapse of regimes across Eastern Europe and the USSR claiming to be communist, the workers and farmers there have not been crushed. Nor have capitalist social relations been stabilized. The toilers remain an intractable obstacle to imperialism's advance, one the exploiters will have to confront in class battles and war. $16. Also in Spanish, French, Swedish, and Icelandic.

NEW INTERNATIONAL NO. 8
CHE GUEVARA, CUBA, AND THE ROAD TO SOCIALISM
Articles by Ernesto Che Guevara, Carlos Rafael Rodríguez, Carlos Tablada, Mary-Alice Waters, Steve Clark, Jack Barnes

Exchanges from the opening years of the Cuban Revolution and today on the political perspectives defended by Guevara as he helped lead working people to advance the transformation of economic and social relations in Cuba. $10. Also in Spanish.

NEW INTERNATIONAL NO. 7
OPENING GUNS OF WORLD WAR III: WASHINGTON'S ASSAULT ON IRAQ
Jack Barnes

The murderous assault on Iraq in 1990–91 heralded increasingly sharp conflicts among imperialist powers, growing instability of international capitalism, and more wars. *Also includes:* "1945: When U.S. Troops said 'No!'" *by Mary-Alice Waters* and "Lessons from the Iran-Iraq War" *by Samad Sharif.* $14. Also in Spanish, French, and Swedish.

02.06.16

PATHFINDER AROUND THE WORLD

Visit our website for a complete list of titles and to place orders

www.pathfinderpress.com

PATHFINDER DISTRIBUTORS

UNITED STATES
(and Caribbean, Latin America, and East Asia)

Pathfinder Books, 306 W. 37th St., 10th Floor,
New York, NY 10018

CANADA

Pathfinder Books, 7107 St. Denis, Suite 204,
Montreal, QC H2S 2S5

UNITED KINGDOM
(and Europe, Africa, Middle East, and South Asia)

Pathfinder Books, First Floor, 120 Bethnal Green Road
(entrance in Brick Lane), London E2 6DG

AUSTRALIA
(and Southeast Asia and the Pacific)

Pathfinder, Level 1, 3/281-287 Beamish St., Campsie, NSW 2194
Postal address: P.O. Box 164, Campsie, NSW 2194

NEW ZEALAND

Pathfinder, 4/125 Grafton Road, Grafton, Auckland
Postal address: P.O. Box 3025, Auckland 1140